D1133272

EXPLANATION IN SOCIAL SCIENCE

EXPLANATION IN SOCIAL SCIENCE

BY

Robert Brown

WITHDRAWN
UTSA Libraries

ALDINE PUBLISHING COMPANY
CHICAGO

LIBRARY
University of Texas
At San Antonio

Copyright © 1963 by Robert Brown
All rights reserved
First published 1963, reprinted 1964, 1966 by
ALDINE PUBLISHING COMPANY
320 West Adams Street
Chicago, Illinois 60606

Printed in the United States of America

Library of Congress Catalog Card Number 63-13010

LIBRARY
University of Texas
At San Antonio

CONTENTS

ACKNOWLEDGEMENTS

APOLOGETIC disclaimers are often written and seldom read. This is probably as it should be, since excuses addressed to the reader can benefit only their author. The obvious exception arises when, as in the present case, the author takes the opportunity to point out how quickly some important topics have been dismissed. Each reader may compile his own list from this essay, but at the head of my own list stands 'the logical features of scientific laws and theories'. It is some consolation, of course, that the errors I might have fallen into will now be made by someone else. It is more useful, however, to remind the reader that there is now an extensive literature devoted to the philosophical problems raised by scientific laws and theories. Many of these are discussed, for example, in Ernest Nagel's *The Structure of Science*, a book which arrived too late to save me from mistakes that I might otherwise have learned to avoid.

The labour of reading the first draft of this book was undertaken by Mr D. M. Armstrong; drawing his attention to it once again is poor recompense, I am afraid, for his help and advice. Professor P. H. Partridge read an early version of some chapters, and I am grateful for his comments on them. I am deeply indebted to Professor J. C. Harsanyi for much criticism, for the wording of certain passages, and for several examples. Mr F. H. G. Gruen's reading of two chapters brought out their weaknesses, but in thanking him I cannot claim to have fully met his criticism. Professor I. F. Pearce and Drs F. Stacey and E. K. Inall have generously supplied me with examples. I recall the time and effort they have spent on my education with gratitude. But above all, I should like to thank Professor John Passmore. It is on his resources that I have drawn most heavily, and I have done so with no acknowledgement other than this.

For permission to quote I thank the following: from an article by D. Braybrooke in *American Political Science Review*, the Executive Director, The American Political Science Association; from an article by N. R. Hanson in *The Philosophical Review*, the author, and the managing editor; from an article by P. C. Dodwell in *Mind*, the author, and the editor; from an article in *Africa*, the Director of the International African Institute; from an article of mine in *Philosophical Studies*, the editor; from her book *Studies in Applied Anthropology*, the author, L. P. Mair; from his book *The Great Crash, 1929*, the author, J. K. Galbraith; from *Street Corner Society* by W. Whyte, the publisher, the University

ACKNOWLEDGEMENTS

of Chicago Press, copyright 1943 by the University of Chicago; from G. Homans and D. Schneider: *Marriage, Authority and Final Causes*, the publisher, The Free Press; from *Risk, Uncertainty and Profit* by F. Knight, the holders of the copyright, Hart, Schaffner and Marx; from E. E. Evans-Pritchard: *Witchcraft, Oracles and Magic Among the Azande* the author, and the publisher, The Clarendon Press; from E. Krige and J. Krige: *The Realm of a Rain Queen*, the co-author, E. Krige: from J. Barnes: *Politics in a Changing Society*, the author, and the Director of the Rhodes-Livingstone Institute; from his book *Wildcat Strike*, the author, A. W. Gouldner.

I thank Mrs. F. Dadd for reading the proofs of this book.

INTRODUCTION

THERE is a sense in which the question 'What is this book about?' is best answered by an examination of the volume's table of contents. What is not given in the list of chapter headings, however, is an indication why some topics are listed there and why others with an apparently equal claim to recognition are not. The present study has as its aim the discussion of certain questions of philosophical interest as they come to be imbedded in the work of social scientists. It is intended to be an essay which might be of interest to the practising scientist. For most studies in the philosophy of the sciences, natural and social, fall into two distinct groups: those written by philosophers for other philosophers and those produced by scientists for their fellow-scientists. And since many writers on these subjects at least imagine that they have a catholic audience, it is a constant disappointment on both sides that the works submitted are usually unsuccessful in this respect. Yet the reasons for this are obvious.

Consider the case of a demographer who is investigating the social origins of recent immigrants to Australia. He may wish to predict how rapidly the various national groups will be assimilated. If, on the basis of the social adjustment of a sample population, he makes predictions about the behaviour of a future population his inference may be challenged. It may be said that he is merely assuming that the future will be like the past; he is mistaking trends which depend on temporary and obscure conditions for laws based upon known factors. In short, he is misusing a description as an explanation. Now he may be disturbed enough by this criticism to become interested in the general question how social description differs from social explanation. But if he does so he will not receive much help from the writings of social scientists. Their writings tend to consist, on the one hand, of instruction in research techniques, and on the other, of some remarks on induction as viewed by John Stuart Mill. There are, of course, studies which fall into neither of these two categories. Robbin's *Essay on the Nature and Significance of Economic Theory* and Nadel's *The Foundations of Social Anthropology* are familiar examples. They would give little aid to anyone interested in the demographer's question, however. The first does not deal with it, and the second deals only with such related questions as the connection between facts and theory or between observation and interpretation. Thus the demographer might well turn to the writings of philosophers for assistance. There he would find a rich literature on problems of the

1

physical sciences and psychology. In contrast, the literature concerned with social science would, if confined to modern work, hardly fill a small shelf. Kaufmann's *Methodology of the Social Sciences* and Gibson's *The Logic of Social Enquiry* stand almost alone in English as being extended treatments by philosophers of the questions of social science. Even so, the larger portion of the first book is on 'General Methodology' and has no special interest for social scientists. Nor does Kaufmann have much to say about the distinction between description and explanation. This leaves the field to Gibson, to the book by Popper entitled *The Poverty of Historicism*, and to occasional essays by such authors as Ernest Nagel and Carl Hempel in the United States and Morris Ginsberg in England. Under these circumstances the social scientist is likely to fall back upon narrow and eccentric views culled from nineteenth-century sources, or to apply, rather haphazardly, conclusions drawn from modern observers of the methodology of the natural sciences. The other alternative is for the social scientist to read the general discussions which philosophers conduct amongst themselves. But the scientist who is self-taught in philosophy is unlikely to comprehend the import of such discussions. Furthermore, we must assume that our puzzled demographer is impatient to apply the general lesson to his own problem, that of justifying his right to make predictions about the assimilation of immigrants. He will not wish to become so immersed in philosophical disputes that he is unable to carry on his scientific work.

There are philosophers who would argue that any attempt to discuss issues of philosophical interest in the context of the social sciences is misguided. The interesting problems, they would say, arise only in the more developed sciences. Most of the difficulties which trouble social scientists are so elementary that time spent on them by philosophers must be counted as the work of charity. How could anyone take seriously as science an inquiry whose hypotheses are: 'first, that the motivation of political behaviour is effective in direct relation to the number of congruent forces that motivate a person, and second, that the effectiveness of these motivating forces is reduced if there is conflict among them'? Or which issues in the conclusion that: 'We have found that those people who felt themselves strongly identified with one of the major parties, held strongly partisan views on issues which were consistent with those of their party, and were strongly attracted by the personal attributes of their party's candidate expressed preference in nearly every case for the candidate their party put forward. In contrast, among those people for whom none of these factors was active, equal numbers preferred each of the two candidates.'[1] Nor, the critics say, is this example an isolated one. Any journal of social science will supply its share of curiosities: 'The concept of communication extensiveness would seem to be relevant

---

[1] A. Campbell, G. Gurin and W. Miller: *The Voter Decides*, 1954, pp. 182–3.

to an understanding of the community and processes through which it is changed. We may assume that the phenomenon of community life is itself dependent upon rather extensive communication in a local population. As Wirth points out, "If men of diverse experiences and interests are to have ideas and ideals in common they must have the ability to communicate." It may also be assumed that the democratic process requires some extensiveness of contacts among diverse elements of the population.'[1] Nevertheless, it can be shown that the segregation, by philosophers, of the social sciences into a pariah class is based not only on a scanty acquaintance with the better works in these fields, but also on a protective lapse of memory with respect to the earlier follies of philosophers and natural scientists. An obvious example of the kind of fault now said to be peculiar to social scientists was Dalton's refusal to admit either Gay-Lussac's Law or Avogadro's hypothesis. Dalton had to ignore the experimental evidence produced by Gay-Lussac to the effect that compounds of gases are formed in simple ratios. He rejected the evidence merely because it conflicted with his own view that if there is only one compound of two given elements the combination consists of one atom from each element. But this view of Dalton's was merely the result of applying Occam's Razor to a case about which nothing was known. Once Gay-Lussac's evidence became available there was no reason for Dalton to cling to his belief. 'The results of this extraordinary situation may be read with great patience and no little boredom in the struggles of the great chemists of the first half of the nineteenth century to find a consistent system of atomic weights. The history of this branch of chemistry is of interest chiefly as a commentary on the human mind; it is a succession of ingenious and even heroic attempts to find a way out of a situation which, but for prejudice and purblindness, need never have arisen.'[2] Even if this remark were also to apply to the social sciences at present, it simply shows that their situation is not unique in the history of science.

In any case, it is not true that the methodological problems encountered by social scientists are merely an unimportant sub-set of those confronting natural scientists. Consider, for example, the following three cases:

(1) The 'self-fulfilling prophecy', often thought to be of considerable importance in the social sciences, especially in connection with the prediction of social events, is not present in the natural sciences. As Merton put it, 'Predictions of the return of Halley's comet do not influence its orbit. But the rumored insolvency of Millingville's bank did affect the actual outcome. The prophecy of collapse led to its own fulfillment.'[3]

(2) It is only in the social sciences that explanations in terms of purposes,

---

[1] A. Fanelli: 'Extensiveness of Communication Contacts and Perceptions of the Community', *American Sociological Review*, Vol. 21, No. 4, August 1956, p. 440.

[2] W. Wightman: *The Growth of Scientific Ideas*, 1951, pp. 239–40.

[3] R. Merton: *Social Theory and Social Structure*, 1949, p. 181.

motives, intentions, and reasons have any place. True, attempts are often made to explain the behaviour of animals in some of these ways. But while it may be the case that an ape can display intentional behaviour, this must form, at best, an insignificant proportion of its activity. (3) There is a special case of (2) which is of particular importance. Social scientists can assume, as natural scientists cannot, that the behaviour which they study is produced by agents who are fully informed, completely rational, and capable of acting on the basis of their information and rationality. The problem for the investigators then becomes one of estimating or measuring the extent to which the actual behaviour of people in a given situation diverges from that of completely rational agents. The attempt to explain the divergency leads to different methods of explanation from those present in the natural sciences.

There is a difference of another and more curious kind between the natural and social sciences. It is this: few people would now take the view that a science of nature cannot exist, that there are logical considerations which will forever prevent human beings from constructing theories that can be used to explain and predict the course of natural events. On the other hand, there are still people who set out to demonstrate the impossibility of a genuine science of society. Such arguments have a long history. They usually revolve about the notion that since human beings learn from experience the behaviour which they exhibit is neither subject to laws nor predictable; for if, for example, the decisions of a man were predictable, we should no longer be entitled to refer to them as 'decisions'. The arguments against this sort of view are well known, and it is no part of our intention to discuss the problem in its general form. What we shall consider, rather, is whether proponents of a 'natural science of society' are right in believing that they can produce instances of what is supposed to be impossible: scientific explanations and predictions of social behaviour. For if they are right, then the opposing arguments are idle.

The same holds true of the more general assertion that the social sciences, as opposed to the natural sciences, contain no problems of philosophical interest. Here, too, the most convincing answer is the production of countervailing examples, examples from sociology and anthropology, economics, demography, and political science – the most characteristic social sciences.

Now one of the methodological topics with which philosophers have long been engaged is explanation. They have asked and answered a great variety of questions dealing with the problem of what we are doing when we offer an explanation of something. Our task here is to take up this problem in a particular setting, that of the social sciences. Our most general questions, then, will be these: 'How, in the social sciences, is explanation related to observation and description? In what senses of 'explain' do the social sciences provide us with explanations? If there

4

are different methods of explanation how are they related to each other? How are these related to the explanations given by physical scientists? What roles – successful and unsuccessful – do the various methods of explanation play in the social sciences?' We shall begin by examining a set of common complaints about the work of social scientists. The first such complaint is that social scientists, by and large, do not ask the right questions. The second is that the social sciences offer us mere description and not genuine explanation. And the third is that there are no theoretical laws and deductive theories in social science and that, therefore, the resemblance between them and the developed physical sciences is tenuous indeed. It will be worth our while to examine each of these in detail; that, indeed, will be our first theme.

PART ONE

Description, Observation
and Explanation

I

QUESTIONS ABOUT SOCIETY

MANY critics have fastened their attention on the questions
asked by social scientists. The questions have been accused of
ambiguity, theoretical irrelevance and triteness; their authors
of confusion compounded by logomachy and illiteracy, of grandiose
promises and self-evident absurdity. One historian, for example, referred
to sociologists as 'fanatical in their zeal and shameless in their claims',
and summed up his views of sociology by saying: 'Its practitioners are
in the stage of alchemy, not of chemistry. Probably that is why they
proclaim so loudly that they are on the verge of discovering the
philosopher's stone.'[1]

There is no doubt that such charges are sometimes true. Some social
scientists are muddle-headed, some are trying to prove a thesis at all
costs, and some are desperately trying to conceal from themselves –
with the aid of a 'barbarous patois' – that they have nothing to contribute. But sometimes it is their critics who are at fault. Often they
don't like questions because they probe into 'closed' areas. Nor do
critics always ask themselves whether the questions have arisen in a
serious context. And some critics assume that because a question is
common or familiar the answer must be equally so. We can illustrate all
these faults, perhaps, by taking a single case.

Suppose, then, we learn that 'conceptions resulting in illegitimate
births are far more numerous in Finland during the season from April
to September than during other months of the year'.[2] We may wish to
explain this seasonal variation in the rate of illegitimate births for urgent
practical reasons: there may be an unwelcome and fluctuating demand
for maternity facilities; questions may be asked in Parliament about
'summer madness'; placement of infants in foster homes may be
difficult during the period of summer vacation, and the military authorities may object to the increase in spring and summer births because of

---

A. Schlesinger, Jr.: 'The Statistical Soldier', *Partisan Review*, Vol. XVI, No. 8,
August 1949, p. 856.

[2] R. Chambliss: 'Contributions of the Vital Statistics of Finland to the Study of
Factors that Induce Marriage', *American Sociological Review*, Vol. 22, No. 1,
February 1957, p. 47.

the effects upon their call-up system. Yet it may be claimed that the answer is as obvious to any literate European as it is to the scientist who raised the question. For in view of Finland's climate both believe that the opportunities for unmarried persons to secure privacy are greater during the warm months of April to September.[1] And both will be quite ready to advance the generalization that the number of illegitimate conceptions in Finland, as elsewhere in Europe, varies directly with the knowledge about opportunities for privacy.[2] From the truth of these beliefs and that of others too trivial to mention, it logically follows that the number of such conceptions is greater during the months of privacy. We do not, says the plain critic, require the services of a demographer in order to hit upon answers of this kind or, indeed, the questions which provoke them.

Perhaps we do not, but we do need someone to look into the issues at greater length. Is it true, for example, that in Finland privacy for unmarried persons is more easily obtained in warm months than in cold ones? Whether this is so or not will depend upon a host of conditions about which nothing has been said: the use of space in the homes, the social arrangements for unmarried persons, the ways in which land is employed, and the severity of the weather with respect to the hardiness of the Finns. The question can be settled, of course, without an investigation of these factors. We can simply poll an appropriate sample of people, since we are interested not in whether they are making full use of their opportunities but only in the knowledge upon which they act. Assuming that the results of such a poll support the contention about summer privacy, we may still demand evidence for the general statement that illegitimate conceptions in Finland vary directly with the knowledge of the opportunities for privacy. And this evidence may be difficult to obtain – even by the plain critic.

It is clear that the questions asked by social scientists represent many different kinds of problems. Almost any sample will bring out something of their variety. Consider these questions:

(1) What is the average population per dwelling unit in Cairo?

(2) What method shall we use for obtaining a sample of unmarried men who have no permanent residence?

(3) How did the banking houses of Morgan, Drexel, and Bonbright obtain control of the electric utility industry in the United States?

(4) Why can devaluation of currency sometimes worsen the balance of trade?

(5) What are the functions of political moieties among the Berbers?

(6) Why is there some form of incest taboo in all known societies?

(7) What were Eden's intentions in ordering the British troops to occupy the Suez Canal in 1956?

[1] *Loc. cit.*   [2] *Ibid.*

(8) Why in Western Europe do men have their hair cut shorter than do women?

(9) What motives have the Indonesians for claiming Dutch New Guinea?

(10) What grounds are there for calling Japan a 'shame society'?

(11) Suppose an excise tax on a commodity raises its price by the amount of the tax. Can this occur when the supply curve is stable and horizontal, the demand curve is stable, and the conditions competitive?

(12) Are there stages common to the social development of all systems of ethics?

These questions have been chosen in part for their apparent simplicity. Yet it is not likely that critics of the social sciences will find plausible answers to all or indeed any of them in some storehouse of common knowledge. It is not obvious, for example, that the reason why a devaluation of currency can sometimes worsen the balance of trade is as follows: when the exchange rate falls 'This has the effect of making home-produced goods appear cheaper to foreigners and so increasing the volume of exports. If the physical volume of exports increases their home price cannot fall, therefore the value of exports in terms of home currency must increase. . . . Foreign goods are now dearer at home, and while the physical volume of imports purchased out of a given income will decline, total expenditure upon them may increase. Thus a decline in the exchange rate will not necessarily increase the balance of trade. If the value of imports (reckoned in home currency) increases by more than the value of exports, then a fall in the exchange rate will reduce the balance of trade.'[1] It is surely incorrect to say either that this answer is trivially true or that the problem with which it deals is unimportant. A government might mistakenly believe that its trade balance would improve if its currency were devalued, and the consequences of this error might be financially disastrous.

Nevertheless, one objection to the questions on our list may be reasonably made. It is that questions like 'Why is there some form of incest taboo in all known societies?' are ambiguous as they stand. We need a context to show us what kinds of answers are desired. For the questioner may be interested in the history of the custom, or in the motives of those who practise it, or in its psychological sources, or in its social effects. The same form of words will entitle him to any of these types of answers and to other types as well. This ambiguity of interpretation to which interrogatives are liable is especially prominent in the case of 'why' questions. Almost any dictionary will tell us that 'why' can be used indifferently to elicit a variety of information: the reason for a state of affairs, the cause of an occurrence, the motives of a person, or the

---

[1] J. Robinson: 'The Foreign Exchange', in *Readings in the Theory of International Trade*, The American Economic Association, 1949, p. 87.

purpose of his action. Such questions may be taken as requests for a story about what happened in the past; or they may be understood as expressing puzzlement about the usefulness or point of a state of affairs which might easily have been different. Again, the notion that the social institution has been deliberately created may be involved, so that the questioners in asking 'why?' may wish to know the motives or intentions of those responsible for this state of society.

Now it is an important though elementary truth that we sometimes fail to distinguish scientific inquiries from historical questions because of the indiscriminate use of 'why'. But it is also important to realize that an interest in the origin of something need not be simply historical; it may include a desire for a causal or scientific explanation. That is, the questioner may be interested both in the unique details of the story and in some of the generalizations that connect one detail with another. A person who asks how the Philippine practice of hepatoscopy originated is not, as a rule, chiefly concerned to obtain psychological information. He wants to know when and where it began, and whether or not it developed from some different kind of activity. He can learn, if he wishes, that the prediction of the outcome of events by means of rules for examining the livers of sacrificed animals can be traced to the Babylonian priest of 2000 B.C.; that the system spread from Western Asia to Greece and the Etruscans; that the Christian Church eliminated the practice in Europe, only to find it well established later in the islands of Southern Asia. While the story unfolds, however, the listener may become interested in asking another sort of question, namely, 'Why does any person want to know his future?' The answer to this would very commonly be understood to require psychological generalizations and not the production of personal histories. It is these generalizations, after all, which allow us to assume that some of the items in a personal history will fall into a recognizable kind of behaviour.

Critics of the questions dealt with by social scientists often underestimate the size of their target. To assert that the questions asked by anthropologists, sociologists, economists, demographers, and political scientists are unworthy of serious attention is to make a judgment which is so sweeping as to be useless. It is useless because it indicts so many different kinds of inquiry at once. The frivolities of one field are not those of another, nor do the mistakes made within one science necessarily have much to teach people in other sciences. No small set of criticisms is likely to embrace the deficiencies of both Gorer's swaddling hypothesis and Herskovits' study of social organization in Dahomey, of both the Keynsian solution for unemployment and Cressey's explanation of the circumstances under which embezzlement occurs. There is only one criticism that will fit all these studies, though this has to be shown separately for each case. It is simply that each is defective as an answer to its questions. This is in fact the conclusion which confirmed attackers

12

of the social sciences usually draw. The eventual result, then, so far as some of the critics are concerned, is that they are in a state of permanent melancholia – or is it permanent cheerfulness? – with respect to the future of the social sciences. They believe that there are insoluble difficulties presented by the nature of the subject matter, and that social scientists cannot help but disappoint us with the slightness of their conclusions. Questions about society, they argue, differ radically from questions about nature. In chemistry, physics, and biology we can produce explanations by means of laws and theories. In the social sciences we have not done so and cannot do so; for there are reasons, either logical or empirical or both, which forever prevent us from attaining the same kind of knowledge about society as we have about Nature.

There is nothing to be gained by pretending that to refer in this brief way to criticism of the work of social scientists is to fairly present the case against their results. That case, if it can be made at all, can only be constructed from the close scrutiny of a large number of examples. It might be the conclusion of a study such as this, but hardly its introduction. It does, however, suggest in a quite general way the kind of topics with which we shall be dealing; and it suggests, as well, that there is at least the appearance of disagreement on the issue of whether scientific questions about society are possible.

II

SOCIAL DESCRIPTION

LET us take three passages chosen from three studies in the social sciences. Each passage is of a kind which often comes under the criticism of natural scientists. 'This sort of thing may be quite interesting,' they say, 'but is it science? When we learn from the first passage, for example, that a group called "the corner boys" ranked people, individually and in groups, by their success at gambling we have a piece of information which seems to foreshadow a valuable discovery. All too often, however, the foreshadowing occupies the entire study. Instead of explanation we receive a *mere description* of how some people behave in their particular circumstances.'

Now this comment may be harsh and unjustified; or it may simply be harsh. In either case the question is whether the three excerpts which follow are really examples of *mere description* – whatever that may turn out to be. Or is there something about them which would lead us to think of them as 'scientific'? And if so what?

(1) Gambling plays an important role in the lives of Cornerville people. Whatever game the corner boys play, they nearly always bet on the outcome. When there is nothing at stake, the game is not considered a real contest. This does not mean that the financial element is all-important. I have frequently heard men say that the honor of winning was much more important than the money at stake. The corner boys consider playing for money the real test of skill, and unless a man performs well when money is at stake, he is not considered a good competitor. This helps to fix the positions of individuals and groups in relation to one another.[1]

(2) In other situations, where the Administration endeavours to intervene in some matter in which the chief is thought to be dilatory, the Native Authority may shield a man because of the danger of possible repercussions. Thus, for instance, a District Officer on tour found a man living in a village at which he was not registered. He turned the offender over to the Native Court. The offender had a perfectly good defence but his story would have involved reference to incest by an important person and it was therefore undesirable that the District Officer should hear of the matter. Accordingly, the Court

[1] W. Whyte: *Street Corner Society*, 1943, p. 140.

delayed the hearing of the case on some technicality, and after the District Officer had left the area nothing more was done.[1]

(3) This paper will describe what happened when a naval bureau in Washington changed the goals of one of its laboratories on the west coast. The change was, in essence, from applied research to development. If the personnel of the department had behaved as obedient employees, they would simply have changed their behavior to conform to the new policy. But these employees were engineers and scientists who had professional opinions about their work and about the organization. The change in policy produced a sharpening of factions, a power struggle, an extensive reorganization, and the resignation of a number of persons. In this series of changes the actors were mainly the scientists and engineers in top staff and line positions. Each man had a set of beliefs about his professional work, about the organization and its goals, and about the other persons in the organization. The alignment and conflict of persons holding these beliefs produced a number of changes in the organization which had little to do with the purported aims of the policy change.[2]

A person who says that passages like these present us with mere descriptions is mistaken on two separate counts. Firstly, none of the passages is primarily descriptive. Secondly, each passage contains reports and explanations whether or not it contains any description. The critic takes it for granted that scientific work can be exhaustively classified into two parts – description and explanation – whereas a third class, that of reports, is needed as well. Having neglected the difference between reports and descriptions, the critic then finds it easy to mistake the relationship between report and explanation for that between description and explanation. He believes that he is referring to the latter when, in fact, he is referring to the former. The objections which he wrongly directs against 'mere description' apply only to reports.

Consider the relevant senses of 'description' given in the *Oxford English Dictionary*: (1) 'The action of setting forth in words by mentioning recognizable features or characteristic marks; verbal representation or portraiture.' (2) 'A statement which describes, sets forth, or portrays: a graphic or detailed account of a person, thing, scene, etc.' (3) 'The combination of qualities or features that marks out or serves to describe a particular class. Hence, b. A sort, species, kind, or variety, capable of being so described.'

Now compare this with what is usually called 'reporting'. For there are a number of differences between pure reporting and pure describing, even though there are intermediate forms in which they are blended. Merely to report something is to give an account of it or to tell someone what occurred, and it may be that no description will be employed in the telling. 'A small kangaroo and a man walking home from his office

---

[1] J. Barnes: *Politics in a Changing Society*, 1954, p. 137.
[2] P. Brown and C. Shepherd: 'Factionalism and Organizational Change in a Research Laboratory', *Social Problems*, Vol. 3, No. 4, April 1956, p. 235.

collided last evening in Canberra' is not a description, if by 'description' we have in mind only the mentioning of characteristic features. The sentence taken by itself is a report. On the other hand, to describe something is to tell someone what some state of affairs is like. A successful description enables its auditor to recognize what has been described to him, when he will not otherwise be able to do so.[1] A successful report need not do this; though it may if it includes a description.

If to describe is to mention 'recognizable features or characteristic marks', then it may be argued that the first excerpt is a sketchy description of the attitude of Cornerville people toward the playing of certain games for money. But to ask someone to describe his attitude toward gambling games is not merely to ask the person to rank the activity on a scale of his preferences and dislikes – to report how much he likes it. It is, in addition, to request that he portray or set forth in words his emotions, opinions, feelings, and behaviour with respect to gambling games. There are public opinion polls which contain requests like: 'State your attitude to the following proposal: "Great Britain should immediately legalize gambling".' To support the proposal by saying 'I agree' is to report an attitude without describing it, for when an attitude is portrayed or described, as distinct from being merely reported, the result is something like this:

I was distinctly conscious of partially attributing to some defect or stupidity in my own mind, every venture on an issue that proved a failure; that I groped within me for something in me like an anticipation or warning (which, of course, was not to be found) of what the next event was to be, and generally hit upon some vague impulse in my own mind which determined me; that when I succeeded I raked up my gains, with a half impression that I had been a clever fellow, and had made a judicious stake, just as if I had really moved a skilful move at chess; and that when I failed, I thought to myself, 'Ah, I knew all the time I was going wrong in selecting that number, and yet I was fool enough to stick to it', which was, of course, a pure illusion, for all that I did know the chance was even, or much more than even against me. But this illusion followed me throughout. I had a sense of *deserving* success when I succeeded, or of having failed through my own wilfulness, or wrong-headed caprice, when I failed.[2]

A passage like this does more than simply *report* that someone has an attitude. It helps us to account for that attitude because, as we shall argue presently, descriptions in social science are typically employed on behalf of explanations. Reports, on the contrary, are of only minor scientific interest in themselves. They do, of course, have their uses, e.g. they can serve to test hypotheses. Thus the report that when a certain

---

[1] There is a most useful account of describing in the article by K. Baier and S. Toulmin entitled 'On Describing', *Mind*, Vol. LXI, No. 241, January 1952.

[2] Quoted in J. Cohen and M. Hansel: *Risk and Gambling*, 1956, pp. 147–8.

part of the patient's inner ear was removed he temporarily lost his balance might be used to test the hypothesis that the loss of this portion of the inner ear is sufficient for the patient's permanent loss of equilibrium. But divorced from contexts such as this a report has little to offer the scientist.

The second of our examples – that dealing with the shielding of a man by the Native Court – contains a report which is illustrated by a brief description of a case. The report states that sometimes the Native Court protects natives from administrative action if there is a 'danger of possible repercussions'. The description which follows it is of such an incident.

The third example concerns the unintended consequences of a change in policy at a government laboratory. The consequences are listed in summary fashion: 'a sharpening of factions, a power struggle, an extensive reorganization and the resignation of a number of persons.' Clearly, this is not a *description* of what happened, for no details about the power struggle or the resignations are supplied here. Nor does the body of the paper pretend to be more than a general account of the way in which the organization changed and why it did so. There are descriptive passages but there are also many paragraphs which are simply direct answers to straightforward questions.

Thus none of the three examples can be correctly called 'merely descriptive'. We have been arguing that they contain reports as well. But much more important is the fact that they are attempts at explanation, however unsuccessful. In each case the author tries to explain why something happened as it did, or why a set of social events or processes occurred. This feature is quite obvious if we consider the essays from which these excerpts are drawn. For example, *Street Corner Society* is to a considerable extent a study of two subjects: the relationship of the street corner gang to its members, and the relationship of Cornerville people to the larger community of which their slum district is a part. Under the first subject there fall the answers to such questions as 'From what activities do corner gangs develop? Why do they retain their membership so long? How does the corner gang fit into the social organization of Cornerville?' We realize that these questions have related answers when we learn something about the structure of Cornerville society: 'The masses of Cornerville people are little people. They cannot approach the big people directly but must have an intermediary to intercede for them. They gain this intercession by establishing connections with the intermediary, by performing services for him, and thus making him obligated to them. The intermediary performs the same functions for the big man.'[1] The corner gangs, the racketeering groups, the police and political organizations are all elements in this 'hierarchy of personal relations based upon a system of reciprocal obligations'.[2]

[1] Whyte, *op. cit.*, pp. 271–2. [2] *Loc. cit.*

Under the second subject, that of Cornerville's relation to the larger community, are included questions like 'What means of social advancement are open to Cornerville people? Why cannot a Cornerville man be socially successful both in his district and his city?' It turns out that both questions are illuminated by the same piece of information. 'To get ahead, the Cornerville man must move either in the world of business and Republican politics or in the world of Democratic politics and the rackets.... If he advances in the first world ... he is recognized in Cornerville only as an alien to the district. If he advances in the second world, he achieves recognition in Cornerville but becomes a social outcast to respectable people elsewhere.'[1]

On the face of it the answers given to the questions arranged under these two headings are attempts at explanation. So that until arguments are advanced to show that attempts such as these do not yield scientific nor any other kind of explanations, it is reasonable to assume that studies like *Street Corner Society* are not merely descriptive essays.

2

Now anyone who disagreed with the view that none of the three studies under discussion simply reports or describes might wish to argue in this fashion:

I grant you that the book on Cornerville and the essay on factionalism in a laboratory are not chiefly works of reporting and description. But I do not grant this point in the case of the other work, Barnes' *Politics in a Changing Society*. First, if a pure description is a portrait, then an anthropological memoir will be the most likely source of such a description, for anthropologists constantly talk of giving us portraits of the tribes which they study. Secondly, there are the author's own words to consider. At the beginning of the second chapter he writes, 'In our first chapter we outlined some of the more significant events in Ngoni history prior to the arrival of Europeans. In this chapter we shall examine the political system within which these events took place. It is not the task of social analysis to determine why these or any other events occurred. What we shall attempt is a discussion of how they occurred, and what were the principal social relations involved in them.'[2]

The sorts of events to which reference is made in the first chapter are the emergence of larger states 'after about 1775' and the attack on the chief Kasungu by Mwambera in approximately the year 1860. Yet is it not obvious that to discuss how they occurred rather than why they occurred is simply to give a description instead of an explanation? And if this is the 'task of social analysis' then the author's adherence to his own view will produce the kind of unscientific work to which I am objecting. My case is further strengthened by what is said in the postscript about the effects of the political union of Rhodesia and Nyasaland on the Ngoni people. It is there said that federation

[1] *Op. cit.*, p. 273.
[2] Barnes, *op. cit.*, p. 29.

'has been accompanied by a major shift in the balance of power between the Administration, the White settlers and the indigenous African population. I do not know in detail how the Ngoni people have responded to this change . . . I have described relations between the Ngoni and their white neighbors as I saw them during 1946-9, but this description may not necessarily be valid now.'[1] Surely this quotation indicates that social analysis is a taxonomic discipline, at most a prelude to genuine science. No chemist, for example, would be similarly interested in any particular example of a given reagent. If he were testing gastric juice for the presence of free hydrochloric acid by means of Günzberg's Reagent, he would prepare a solution of vanillin and phloroglucinol in alcohol and then evaporate this solution with the test liquid. He would certainly be ready for the appearance of the red margin that indicates free hydrochloric acid is present. As long as he believed that the test had been properly carried out he would have no reason to dwell on the particulars of that occasion; neither on the relevant details such as that 95 per cent alcohol was used, nor on the irrelevant ones such as that 50 per cent of the reagent was used in the evaporation process. In brief, a chemist would not be primarily concerned with *describing* either his apparatus or his results. He would state that he employed Günzberg's Reagent and report on the chemical response. There would be no question of altering a description in order to portray new details, for the only relations in which the chemist would be interested in this case would be those bearing on the test reaction.

The first question at issue in this argument is whether the distinction drawn between how events occur and why events occur is also a distinction between their description and their explanation. Perhaps we need go no farther for the answer than to remind ourselves, once again, that queries of the form 'Why did it happen?' are ambiguous. 'Why did larger states emerge after about 1775?' may be a demand for an origin story. In that case the 'why' question means exactly the same as 'How did larger states come to emerge after about 1775?' One answer serves both questions: for example, 'As a result of military conquest by ambitious kings who transformed the age-sets into national regiments, etc.' It does not matter here whether the answer is called a 'description' or an 'explanation'. Whichever one is chosen will apply equally to both questions. Hence, in this interpretation the two questions cannot be distinguished by means of the different answers they are supposed to elicit. Nor is there any other interpretation which would invariably make the answers to 'how' questions into descriptions and the answers to 'why' questions into explanations. It was pointed out previously that questions about causes can be phrased either in the 'how' form or in the 'why' form. Thus we can ask 'Why was it that there were two sons as legal candidates for Zwangendaba's throne?' or we can ask 'How was it . . . ?' The answers will not differ.

An obvious reply to these claims might be that there are many occasions when 'how?' and 'why?' can precede the same form of words

[1] *Ibid.*, pp. V, VI.

and yet be used to ask quite different questions. 'Why did the Puritans persecute bachelors?' is not the same query as 'How did the Puritans persecute bachelors?' The first may receive an answer in terms of slavish pursuit of Biblical injunctions, of the motives of a set of women, of views about maintaining the numbers of true believers, or of the survival of a useless practice. Whichever answer is given, it will not be an answer to the second question. It will not tell us whether the Puritans taxed bachelors heavily, placed them in stocks, or disenfranchised them. And this distinction between the reasons for an action or the occurrence of an event, on the one hand, and the means by which it was done or the way in which it took place, on the other hand, is what in the present context we refer to by the words 'explanation' and 'description' respectively. Thus the problem at issue is not whether 'how' questions always demand descriptions as their answers. They clearly do not. The problem is whether the author of *Politics in a Changing Society* has faithfully followed his own prescription by attempting to answer some such 'how' questions. He said nothing about descriptions; it was our imaginary critic who did this. The reason, however, why we should not grant that 'the task of social analysis' is merely to determine how events occurred, is that it may not always be possible to discuss how they occurred without at the same time 'explaining' why they occurred. Consider the present instance more closely.

In the second chapter of *Politics in a Changing Society* the author undertakes a discussion of how certain events occurred and 'the principal social relations involved in them'. Is this carried on in the absence of any explanation as to why they occurred? Not at all. Here are half a dozen 'explanatory' passages drawn from as many more scattered throughout the chapter. Each one is a partial answer to the question which precedes it; and the form common to all these questions is 'Why – for what reason – did it occur?' Italics have been added.

Why did the tribe move periodically?

(a) After dwelling in any one area for five years, or so, the tribe moved on, *partly because* the fertility of the soil had been exhausted and partly for other reasons.[1]

Why did raiding occur?

(b) The principal index of power was the number of a man's dependants. Political struggles were essentially not struggles to control wealth but to enjoy the support of followers. The main source of dependants was from raiding, and *hence* the allocation of captives was *crucial* to the working of the social system.[2]

Why did the State split as it did?

(c) . . . If the village of a great wife was annihilated and later a new village was founded for her, this could never replace the original one. Her subordinate

[1] *Ibid.*, p. 30.   [2] *Ibid.*

bands of co-wives had formed their villages by breaking out from her original village, and that had been their headquarters. The new village was founded after they had made their own, and was not their headquarters, even though they still acknowledged that its head was their great co-wife. As we have seen, such a sequence of events occurred at a critical stage of Ngoni history, and *may have influenced* the way in which the State split.[1]

Why was so much reliance placed upon the Army?

(*d*) The Ngoni *depended largely* on the efficiency of their army for the continual inflow of captives on which the strength and continued existence of the State depended.[2]

Why is a generation system of kinship nomenclature used?

(*e*) The present kinship nomenclature, which mainly employs words of Nsenga origin, does not group relatives on a lineage, or segmental, basis but by generation. Presumably the system of nomenclature in use during the early stages of the Ngoni migration was similar to the present Zulu system in which lineage categories are used slightly. Tribes like the Shona and Cewa, from whom many captives were taken, employ systems of nomenclature with great lineage emphasis, but this emphasis is patrilineal among the former and matrilineal among the latter. The difficulty of combining patrilineal and matrilineal categories *may have prompted* the emergence of a generation system of nomenclature.[3]

Why did the State not split more often?

(*f*) The State as a whole was *primarily held together* by its enemies, the external enemies who made it unsafe for small bodies of Ngoni to venture across the no-man's land on their own, and the internal rivals who competed for the Paramount Chief's favour and who bided their time until they could lead off their major segments as independent states. The flexibility of the system allowed men to achieve power within it, and provided a way of balancing the interests of different groups, as well as making possible the few instances of fission that did occur.[4]

It is important to notice that the passages selected are not answers to the question 'How did it occur?' if that question is to be interpreted as a request for information about the means by which something was done or the way in which it took place. If the word 'why' in each question is replaced by the word 'how' the new question is quite irrelevant to the answer given. (*a*), for example, does not tell us how the tribe moved periodically; nor does (*b*) give the answer to 'How did raiding occur?' The same holds for the other passages. Hence if 'the task of the social analyst' is merely to satisfy the question of how an event took place, the author of *Politics in a Changing Society* has exceeded the terms of his self-imposed commission. And, in general, any social analyst will find it impossible to give an extended account of the way in which an event occurred as long as he ignores its causal connections with past and

---

[1] *Ibid.*, p. 36.   [3] *Ibid.*, p. 55.
[2] *Ibid.*, p. 39.   [4] *Ibid.*, p. 62.

future events. But unless he ignores these connections the sharp distinction made previously between 'how' questions and 'why' questions will be lost: an account of how something happened will turn into an account of why it happened as well, and the restrictions placed upon himself by the analyst will no longer matter. If he refers to the motives or intentions responsible for an action, or to the origin of an event, or to some regularity of social behaviour as a necessary condition of an occurrence, he will also be referring to a reason why something happened. In a discussion of human activity it is not easy to avoid doing this, because the story of how an action was performed is so often incomplete without an indication of why it was performed. Thus in the following excerpt the removal of the italicized clause which mentions why the Foreign Office acted as it did, would introduce a serious gap in the account of how the British Government extended its authority. There would be nothing to connect Rhodes' offer to Lugard and the arrival of Johnston. Without such a connection there would be no point in mentioning Rhodes and Lugard, nor, consequently, the fighting at Lake Nyasa. The sentences remaining after this operation would form a very curious story of *how* the British Government enlarged its power in the Lake Nyasa area. The full paragraph with italics added is presented first and then the truncated version:

(*a*) The British Government had been reluctant to extend its commitments in the Lake Nyasa region beyond the appointment of a consul. During 1888–89, however, there was fighting at the north end of Lake Nyasa between Arabs and the African Lakes Company in which Lugard was involved. Rhodes' attention was attracted to the area and he offered Lugard a large subsidy to develop it. *The proof of Rhodes' interest emboldened the Foreign Office*, and on 28 July, 1889 Johnston arrived at the mouth of the Zambezi as the representative of the Foreign Office and of Rhodes and with the task of consolidating the British position in Central Africa.[1]

(*b*) The British Government had been reluctant to extend its commitments in the Lake Nyasa region beyond the appointment of a consul . . . and on 28 July, 1889 Johnston arrived at the mouth of the Zambezi as the representative of the Foreign Office and of Rhodes and with the task of consolidating the British position in Central Africa.

Our conclusions, then, are these: there is often a difference in the kind of information obtainable by the use of 'how' questions and 'why' questions, though the difference does not amount to that between soliciting descriptions and soliciting explanations. For however description is to be distinguished from explanation, each may appear in proper answers to both kinds of questions. *Politics in a Changing Society* is far from merely answering questions of how events occurred. It deals frequently and at length with the problems of why certain events took

[1] *Ibid.*, p. 69.

place. These answers are what would usually be called 'explanations'. Thus not only does the study exceed the limits suggested by the author for the field of social analysis, but it makes plain how impractical and unrewarding the work of social analysis would be if confined within such limits. The question, for example, of how the British Government brought the people of the Lake Nyasa region under its administrative control would have to be answered by an account which began with Johnston's arrival at the Zambezi. The account would go on to tell of the treaties he arranged with various chiefs, the Protectorates he proclaimed, the commercial concessions he helped to establish, and the engagements fought by his troops. At each point in the story it would be possible and reasonable to interject the question 'Why this?', e.g. 'Why did Johnston oppose the Ngoni chief, Mpenzi?' No account could give the answers to all such questions: their number would be indefinitely large since each answer could produce a further question. But an account which satisfied *no* such queries would be a monstrosity, since we should not know which events were responsible for the occurrence of other events. Each statement would be irrelevant to every other in the story. Of course, in practice the obvious relations between occurrences are not made explicit. They are left to the common knowledge of the reader to supply. If we are told that the Puritans successfully discouraged men from remaining single by taxing bachelors very heavily, we do not have to ask 'Why did the tax discourage them?' Rightly or wrongly, we take for granted a causal relationship between an activity which is financially penalized and an avoidance of that activity. This presumptive relationship might be challenged and then the question would have to be answered. To do that would at the same time be to satisfy the question 'How – by what means – did the tax discourage them?' In other words, an account of how something occurred presupposes a background of information about why things of that kind occur; and at any time it will be a reasonable demand that the presuppositions be made explicit. If the demand cannot be met then we have not been told how the event occurred. We have only been told that it did occur – we have been given a report. But we can learn that much from an ordinary factual statement which is an element neither of an explanation nor of a description. Few social analysts, surely, would wish to maintain that their job was simply to report certain types of occurrences, past and present. Hence the task of social analysis must include the answering of 'why' questions as well as 'how' questions. The volume under discussion obviously succeeds in doing this, and so we must say that *Politics in a Changing Society* is not merely descriptive. In coming to see the point of saying this, however, we have also seen that the division of scientific work into description and explanation assumes too much: we need to distinguish the different reasons why an essay may not deserve the title 'merely descriptive', and it is to these distinctions that we must now return.

Our contention has been that any extended account of social behaviour will both contain and presuppose explanations of some portions of that behaviour. The reason we have given is that otherwise there will be no way of indicating the causal connections which hold amongst the events in question. The importance of indicating such connections will be obvious when we recall that accounts of social behaviour are chiefly concerned, as the phrase suggests, with processes and activities. If we are not shown how one part of a social process is causally related to another part, of how one aspect of an activity is causally connected to another, we are given no analysis of either an activity or a process. We certainly are given no description of them. It is easy to think that describing a social class is rather like describing a man's clothes; but it is not. It is more like describing how his clothes are cleaned and pressed and returned to him with a bill. Our paradigm of description is too often something like the sketch provided by Surtees of Mr Stotford's dress: '. . . the fat boy's great stomach came looming along, tightly buttoned into a bright green double-breasted cut-away coat, with a buff vest, yellow leathers, and rose-tinted tops; his short neck being adorned with a bright scarlet sensation tie, secured by a massive blue and gold ring.'[1] This tells us what the clothing looked like; but in the social sciences our interest is usually in how something works. We become interested in the appearance of people or buildings or landscapes only in so far as it is needed for understanding such activities as how political appointments are made, how funds are invested, and agricultural land distributed. Yet if we read Surtees more carefully we find that Mr Stotford's appearance reveals the workings of his character. It is for this reason that his clothes are described. The close alliance of his behaviour and appearance is clearly shown: 'With a radiant smile to each, out then he rolled, wrapper and all, and presently began squeaking for a porter – "Porter! Porter! Porter!" – attracting all eyes to the windows to see such a jolly cockatoo, all green and yellow and red, for the fat boy did not seem to think he could make himself sufficiently conspicuous.'[2] In a work of social science the descriptions of the appearance of things are similarly justified by the connection between appearances and social behaviour.

Here is an example in which a violation of safety rules in a factory is described in terms of the workers' actions and used as an illustration of a quite general point.

One day a main office executive passed through the plant on an inspection tour and noticed a rope leading down into a vat. He looked over the side and

[1] *Mr. Facey Romford's Hounds*, Chapter 44.
[2] *Ibid.*

saw a worker cleaning it out, but there was no one around at the top watching the man and guarding the rope. Immediately the executive looked for the man's foreman, who was not to be seen. After a search, however, he discovered the foreman doing exactly the same thing, cleaning out a vat without having someone watch him. The executive then 'raised hell' with the foreman and took it to higher plant authorities.

In short, the first thing the executive did when he discovered the infraction of vat-cleaning rules, was to look for someone to punish and blame. Instead of calling the man up from the vat, he left him down there. Instead of doing something to forestall an accident, the manifest function of this rule, he exploited the situation as an opportunity to inflict a punishment.

The rules thus channel aggression, providing permissible avenues for its expression and legitimating the utilization of punishments.[1]

Thus, the use of the phrase 'social description' is often quite misleading. It is very rare to find a piece of social research that has in it no reports of arguments and conclusions, interpretations and evaluations. To argue, then, that we commonly receive from social scientists 'a mere description of how some people behave in particular circumstances' is to argue falsely if the words 'mere description' are taken in their dictionary meaning.

The question remains, however, whether there is any reasonable basis for the old complaint recast: that no matter what social description amounts to, it does not represent truly scientific investigation, since its aims and procedures are more akin to those of social history than to those of a social science. 'No one', say these critics, 'can look at the empirical studies made by political scientists, economists, and sociologists without being struck by the remarkable similarity between some of their work and that of political historians, economic historians, and social historians. Even if we group these different kinds of historians into one class for the sake of convenience and call them "social historians", is there any important difference between them and some social scientists? Or is the difference merely that the scientists are professionally ignorant of the history of their subjects whereas the historians prefer to examine documents and museum pieces rather than the behaviour of living people?'

Are we to say, then, that this feature can on some occasions, at least, serve as a criterion for distinguishing economics from economic history, and – by extension – some empirical studies in the social sciences from all empirical work in social history? If so, why do we retain the distinction between that kind of investigation in social science which produces social descriptions and that sort of history which we have called 'social history'? If the historian's interest in past events *cannot* serve as a criterion to divide social description from social history, then why not? And how *is* the distinction to be made?

[1] A. Gouldner: *Patterns of Industrial Bureaucracy*, 1955, pp. 171–2.

III

SOCIAL OBSERVATION

1

LET us try to be as clear as possible about the question at issue, for as yet we do not know whether the problem to which it refers is a genuine one. The question is this: 'Does what we have called "social description" resemble in its aims and procedures a *history* of social life more than it does a *science* of social life?' Some critics wish to argue that it does. Their claim is that the work of social investigators is a form of current history. The investigators themselves, far from being scientists, are merely sophisticated commentators on topical events. They have at their command a large mass of established propositions about the details of their subject matter, and in some senses of 'explain' they can sometimes be said to offer sound and effective explanations. These are not, however, scientific explanations; they are the kinds of explanations given by historians. Even if social descriptions contain reports and explanations as well as descriptions, this does not show that in giving a social description we are also producing a piece of scientific work. We may simply be engaged in historical research.

Now when the field of history is contrasted with the field of science there are two features in which these two studies are commonly said to differ from each other. Both features are thought to be jointly present in historical studies and jointly absent in scientific work. The first characteristic is that of being concerned with human actions performed in the past. The second characteristic is that of being interested in establishing true statements about particular events, processes, and situations, rather than in establishing the soundness of laws, law-like statements and theories.[1] There is no *science*, it is argued, which has as its sole subject-matter the past actions of human beings. This is the province of history. Nor is there any science which takes an interest in particular events for their own sake as history does. The aim of the scientist is always to explain the occurrence of a given event or the presence of a process as the result of the workings of general laws. And it is a further aim of the

[1] See, for example, W. Walsh: *An Introduction to Philosophy of History*, 1951, Chapter 2.

26

scientist to relate and explain these laws, in turn, by means of theories. The scientist tries to exhibit particular occurrences as explicable instances of more general connections. The historian is interested in the occurrences themselves; he wishes to know how they came to be as they are. Where the scientist looks for the similarities among events in order that he may bring them under the scope of some generalization, the historian emphasizes those properties of events which mark off one event from another.

Thus if we compare typical studies made by political historians with those made by political scientists we ought to find that the two sets of studies are distinguishable in the respects in which history differs from science. But – so the argument goes – this is not what we discover. Instead we find that many studies by political scientists, whether of administrative reform in Colombia or of practical politics in the United States, are indistinguishable from historical research. For they meet the two requirements previously laid down; they deal with human actions of the past, though admittedly of the recent past; and they aim at reporting on and describing a set of occurrences (or a situation) in some detail. They do not attempt to view their topics as mere examples of the operation of general laws. Hence, the conclusion to be drawn is that either the two criteria given for historical work are unsatisfactory or that some large part – perhaps all – of what is called 'social science' is really social history.

But can we show that the criteria under discussion admit at least some work in 'social science' into the category of social history? An essay, for example, like Wright's 'Agrarian Syndicalism in Postwar France'[1] is most easily summarised by saying that it (a) sketches the development of a farmers' confederation from its origin to the date at which the article was written, and (b) discusses, in particular, confederation policies with reference to the important parties of French politics. The nearest thing to a law-like generalization in the article is expressed in its first sentence: 'In an age of mass movements and pressure groups, even the most rugged individualists find that organization pays.'[2] The conclusion of the article is: 'The future form of agrarian syndicalism, then, is obscure, but the survival of one or more mass movements to represent the farmers seems certain. Divided though the peasantry may be, there is a new self-consciousness in the French rural districts which is likely to grow in strength, and to manifest itself in some institutional form.'[3] This remark is not likely to be called a 'scientific prediction', for the relationship holding among what are referred to as 'mass movements', 'the new self-consciousness', and 'some institutional form', is left rather vague. Could any of these exist independently of the other? If not, then the

[1] *The American Political Science Review*, Vol. XLVII, No. 2, June 1953.
[2] *Ibid.*, p. 402.
[3] *Ibid.*, p. 416.

certainty of survival of a mass movement would ensure the presence of some institutional form as well as the existence of the new self-consciousness. If, on the other hand, the three elements could exist separately, what then would be the relationship between the certain existence of a mass movement and the likely manifestation of the new self-consciousness? The future form of both would be obscure.

Similarly, it would be eccentric to interpret Wright's essay as an attempt to provide supporting evidence for a social law expressed by his initial sentence ('In an age of mass movements and pressure groups, even the most rugged individualists find that organization pays'). This sentence is probably not intended to assert, as a scientific law would, that in such an age *every* rugged individualist - suitably defined – would in fact discover that his interests lead him to join an organization. The sentence says, in so far as it says anything precise, that in an age in which mass movements and pressure groups are common and powerful, *some* people will join them, even though these people do not in general favour group action.

If an essay consists mainly in a discussion of historical details, with the addition of a few hazy remarks about future developments, is it to be classified as science or as history or as neither? 'Clearly not as science', it may be said; yet as what kind of history? Is it not an unusual historical work that is concerned with what is likely to happen in the future? Still, it seems unreasonable to argue that simply by changing all the present and future tenses in Wright's article into the appropriate past forms we change a piece of political *science* into a piece of historical research. Yet this seems to be all that is required to turn this article into one which fulfills completely the demands made by our criteria. For they are that the work deal chiefly with the details of past human actions, that is, try to establish true statements about particular events of the past and not to test the soundness of laws. But it also seems clear that no matter how detailed an account of past actions is given by an author, we do not for that reason alone judge him to have produced an historical essay. Only if he makes a particular use of his details do we claim that he is interested in history and not in science. It is the aim of the writer, and his success in achieving it, that determines the classification of his work. Freud's interest in the seventeenth-century painter, Christoph Haitzmann, is a scientific one, though the essay in which the painter's case is discussed gives us a large amount of biographical information. What Freud is primarily interested in, however, is showing how 'cases of demoniacal possession correspond to the neuroses of the present day'.[1] He uses Haitzmann's case as an unfamiliar illustration of known psychological processes, and in this way explains what had previously been mysterious – why people make pacts with the Devil. 'This man',

---

[1] 'A Neurosis of Demoniacal Possession in the Seventeenth Century', in *Collected Papers*, 1950, Vol. IV, p. 436.

says Freud, 'sold himself to the Devil, therefore, in order to be freed from a state of depression.'[1]

2

We have claimed – in connection with Freud's interest in biography – that a concern with human actions of the past is not sufficient to qualify a piece of work as historical research. On the other hand, a concern with human actions of the present is not in itself enough to mark a work as falling outside the province of history. Thus in his short book entitled *India*, C. H. Philips, the historian, devotes a chapter, written in 1947, to the partition of India which took place in that year. The chapter begins with the sentence: 'The British Cabinet Mission's proposals of May, 1946, sought to maintain the unity of India.'[2] The chapter goes on to sketch the policies of the Muslim League and Indian Congress, the failure of bi-partisan government, and the success of the British plan for partition. 'It represented', says the author, 'a state of affairs which had come to pass largely through Muslim fear and Hindu despair.[3] Thus the partition of India was in 1947, a current event for which Philips tried to give an historical explanation.

Occasionally, an historian may wish to connect his interest in past actions with his interest in the likely consequence of those actions in the future. The last chapter of Philips' book, for instance, takes up some of the present and future problems of India, especially those created by partition. He writes:

The Indian National Congress, inevitably regarded the separation of Pakistan from India as a major personal defeat, dangerous in that it might encourage the Indian princes, especially the Nizam of Hyderabad who may look to Pakistan for help, to assert their independence; and therefore it finds difficulty in accustoming itself to the Partition; as its leaders in Bengal have declared, 'Congress will work for an undivided Bengal in an undivided India'. For some time to come each of the two new Dominions is likely to gird against the other; each is doubtful whether to remain within the British Commonwealth and in these circumstances the weak, unbalanced economic and strategic situation of Pakistan becomes the more dangerous to the peace of India and the world.[4]

It might be said of this last example that it could equally well have come from the work of a political scientist; and so it could have. The question is, 'What does this show?' It shows that either our first criterion is too restrictive in laying down that history deals only with human actions in the past, or that Philips, and other historians as well, some-

---

[1] *Ibid.*, p. 445.
[2] P. 143.
[3] P. 150.
[4] P. 152.

29

times venture beyond the province of their subject. They predict what is likely to happen in the future on the basis of their knowledge of the past; but, someone may urge, in making such predictions they are not engaged in historical research or the proper business of an historian. There is no doubt that Wright's article on French syndicalism and Philips' final chapter in his book on India must be classified alike. Both deal mostly with the recent past, and both contain some predictions about the likely course of future events. Each undoubtedly meets the demands of the second criterion: that an historical work be concerned to establish true statements about particular events and processes rather than to establish laws and theories. It seems, then, that the two essays do not differ as a piece of scientific work and a piece of historical work are supposed to differ. And a political scientist whose work is indistinguishable from that of an historian cannot set his own work apart by claiming that he is producing 'case studies' which, in distinction to the work of the historian, will be used later as a basis for the construction of law statements. For if this is the intention of any political scientist, then the same use can be made of appropriate historical studies. In each instance the scientific work will consist in the proper employment of these case studies and not in their production.

Work of the kind that we have been considering *is* primarily historical work. It is historical even though it includes a number of statements about what is likely to happen in the future. It is historical work because to a large extent it meets our criteria. Indeed the very way in which the work fails to meet these criteria – by the unauthorized use of a certain kind of prediction – indicates that the writers' interests are historical ones. Consider the paragraph previously quoted from Philips' book. It contains the sentence 'For some time to come each of the two new Dominions is likely to gird against the other'. Philips is not advocating this action nor is he merely speculating about it in the sense of saying, 'Perhaps it will happen, but it is equally likely that it won't.' He is employing the sentence to make a prediction, and this is what is said to strip him of his role as historian.

At first sight it seems odd to claim that historians do not and ought not to make predictions, however much they know about the history of the topic in question. As Walsh puts it, 'A person who knows a good deal about, say, the history of Germany is in some respects at least better equipped to say how Germany is likely to develop in the future than one who is utterly ignorant of that history.'[1] But in what respects is he better equipped? Only in the sense that if some scientific laws about the behaviour of people in societies were available then he would be able to add his detailed information to those laws in such a way as to deduce some statements concerning the future behaviour of the relevant people. Unless the historian is in possession of laws of this kind his predictions

[1] *Op. cit.*, pp. 40–41.

can only be obtained by assuming that present trends will continue in the future. Since a trend is merely a progressive change in a property common to a sequence of events, there is little reason, in the absence of knowledge about its causes, to believe that it will hold beyond the present. There is little reason, for example, to believe that the following trend-statement will continue to hold in the future: 'In the family Equidae there has been a progressive increase in total body size and a correlated increase in snout length since the beginning of the Cenozoic era.' Of course predictions based on observed trends and those based on causal generalizations must not be too sharply separated. The difference is that in the first case we use as evidence only some isolated observations, whereas in the second case we use a body or system of such observations. In both cases, however, our basic evidence consists in observation of regularities. Naturally anybody who suggests, as Philips does, that a social trend will continue, usually has some views about the conditions responsible for the trend. It is highly debatable, though, whether at present any such views can be put in the form of a schema consisting of those scientific generalizations and other statements from whose conjunction the statement of the social trend is logically derivable. Yet, as will be emphasized later, this schema is necessary if a prediction is to be a scientific one. Because both Philips' prediction and Wright's (' . . . the survival of one or more mass movements to represent the farmers seems certain') are simply extensions into the future of present trends, we take this as evidence that the two authors are writing history and not science. The reason why we interpret their statements as supported only by a reference to trends is that nothing of *theoretical* interest turns upon the truth or falsity of the predictions, and this is typical of non-scientific predictions. A scientist uses predictions as a method of testing some of the statements from which his prediction-statement is deducible. Thus a physiologist might say 'If these crystals are scopolamine they will dilate the pupils of my eyes'. In saying this he knows that he may be mistaken on two major points: one, in believing that all scopolamine dilates all human pupils under the given conditions; or two, in believing that the crystals at hand are scopolamine. By determining the effects of these crystals on his eyes the physiologist has partially tested his two beliefs. But what would the predictions about India and the farmers' movement be used to test?

Suppose after the date at which Philips' prediction was made (1946–47) India and Pakistan had not 'girded against each other'. What statement other than that used to make the prediction would have been falsified? The answer, for a variety of reasons, might well be 'We don't know' or even 'None'. The error could always be blamed on some unforeseen and perhaps unforeseeable factor: Nehru managing to change the policy of the National Congress in exchange for American financial aid, or the Soviet Union guaranteeing the safety of the Muslims in India. This kind of explanation would be particularly easy to produce, since we have no clear notion of what factors were foreseen and taken into account when the prediction was made. Because we do not know the generalizations and factual statements from which the prediction is supposed to be derived, we do not know how to separate unforeseen factors from known ones. Hence we cannot determine exactly which statements, if any, have in fact been tested.

It might be thought that an historical account which did not contain generalizations would give the required support to the prediction. If so, there would then be no reason to disqualify the prediction under discussion for being based only upon a trend. It would be based as well upon statements like ' . . . the sturdy warrior Sikhs, four million strong in the heart of the Punjab, detest the thought of, and will resist the fact of, their own inclusion wholesale or in part, within Pakistan'.[1] Yet how could statements such as these, even if a number of them were taken together by themselves, support the prediction? They could be evidence for the prediction only if they were causal antecedents, immediate or remote, of the predicted event; otherwise they would have no part in the production of the event. Granted this, however, we should have to say that a causal statement like 'The resistance of the Sikhs will produce tension between the Indians and Pakistanis' could not be known to be true unless the truth of a set of generalizations was assumed: for instance that if two populations are competing for a scarce resource the competition will become keener whenever the prospect of an immediate advantage in the struggle becomes apparent to both sides; or that two populations already distrustful of each other will become more so by competition for a resource each believes to be both vital to it and scarce. It does not matter, of course, whether these particular generalizations are trivial and even unsound. What is important is that statements of this general type are required. Without them we should have no good reason for predicting that the resistance of the Sikhs would cause tension. We must have some beliefs about the kinds of actions which cause tension, and we must believe that Sikh resistance belongs to one of these kinds. Without such a background of beliefs based upon some people's experience, we should have no way of telling what effects might follow from Sikh resistance, and our prediction would be completely arbitrary guesswork.

Our conclusion, then, is that an historian is not in a sound position to make predictions. The reason, as we have seen, is simple. He cannot use prediction as a method of correcting his information; and if he cannot do that then there is no point in his making predictions, since he will never know whether they are the result of knowledge or luck, or, as in fact they are, a mixture of both. Most historians do not make predictions. When they do, and the essays of Wright and Philips are examples here,

[1] Philips, *op. cit.*, p. 152.

their predictions must either be inadequately supported or must be based on scientific knowledge. When the first alternative is true the historian has misapplied his knowledge of history. When the second alternative is true the historian has left the field of history for that of science.

The articles of Wright and Philips are, for the most part, essays in current history with brief excursions into non-historical work. Hence the present argument has not shown our criterion to be faulty. The criterion implied that the academic field of history did not deal with human actions of the future, and this is the view which our argument has led us to uphold. The academic field of history deals with human actions of the past and through those actions with the present. In taking the two essays under discussion to fall within this field we are, of course, saying that the work of which Wright's essay is representative also falls within the province of history. That is, we are claiming that a substantial portion of the work produced by people called 'social scientists' is not really scientific; it is historical. We admit, then, the justice of the criticism that the work of some social investigators is really current history. But the question 'What other sorts of investigation are there in the social sciences?' remains to be examined. And upon the answer to this query will depend the answer to the question with which we are chiefly concerned: 'Does social description resemble a history of social life more than it does a science of social life?'

3

Now many people who argue that the social sciences are not really scientific have more in mind than the belief that social scientists often write out-and-out history under the name of science. They believe, in addition, that there is a class of work whose status is ambiguous, for it seems to lie somewhere between outright history and downright science. Characteristically, this work is marked by the use of the timeless present tense, and the writings of some anthropologists provide good examples of the type. In these examples it is often impossible for the reader to date the events and situations being discussed even if he knows the date of the field work. Thus in Eggan's volume entitled *Social Organization of the Western Pueblos*, the chapter on the pueblo of Hano is based upon two important sources dated 1914–15 and 1920–21 respectively, and upon field work which began in 1932. The volume itself was published in 1950. The pueblo has been, says the author, in 'a situation ideal for acculturation'.[1] Hence it is difficult to know of what period a statement like the following is supposed to be true: 'From the data available, however, it is clear that the Hano kinship system, while retaining its Tewa terminology, is structurally very similar to the Hopi and quite different in most respects from the Eastern Tewa organization.'[2] It may be that the answer is:

[1] P. 140.   [2] P. 141.

'1914, the date of the quoted source, naturally.' What, then, of 1950? or 1850? If the reply is 'We don't have that information', our point is made; for the statement seems to be applicable to a rather indefinite past, present, and future, and this fact is indicated by the employment of the timeless present tense.

Eggan's essay is not primarily concerned, as is Wright's essay, with the dated development of specific processes and with the associated sequences of events. The origin, development, and end of the Hano kinship system remain unknown. Yet the two essays have an important feature in common. Both are unconcerned with the establishment and testing of scientific laws and theories. There are, if anything, fewer attempts at generalization in Eggan's essay than there are in the essay by Wright. Thus the kind of work illustrated by the article on Hano pueblo fulfils only the second criterion of 'history'. It does not fulfil the first criterion – that history deal only with human actions of the past, or with present actions through their antecedents – because it treats the past, present, and future indifferently by means of the timeless present tense. What the first criterion implies is that an historical account must clearly state the times at which the actions and events under discussion have occurred in the past. The dates at which things happen are taken by the professional historian to be of the first importance in explaining why they happen. If no attention is paid to dating, then no interest is taken in historical explanation. Any author, then, who makes constant use of the timeless present tense is displaying his lack of interest in the writing of history proper.

But how are we to classify the sort of work which is represented by Eggan's chapter? It seems to fall outside the provinces of both history and science. There is, however, an analogue to this situation in the natural sciences. The border zone between the history of natural events and the sciences of natural events is occupied by the study known as 'natural history'. There is a similar zone between the studies concerned with human history and the studies we call the 'social sciences'. Since the phrase 'social history' has already been pre-empted by historians, we shall refer to the social border-land by an awkward phrase: 'the natural history of society.'

In general, the natural historian is concerned with reporting and describing rather than with theoretical explanation. He identifies, classifies, and describes, what he observes. His chief interest is in finding out what has occurred, not in providing a scientific explanation of why it has occurred. The regularities which he observes take the verbal form 'All (or most) known As are also Bs'. In other words the generalizations which he contributes are records of observation. They give no good grounds for expecting future cases of A to belong to the class of Bs except that all or most known cases of A are in fact cases of B as well. The perfect bird-watcher, then, is the perfect natural historian. He

34

watches the arrival of the first kookaburra of the year with the same keenness as he watches the last one depart; he maps the nesting sites of the district magpies, notes colour variation in galahs and records the various cries of the rosella. It is all welcome information, though it is more easily organized in terms of topics than in terms of problems, especially theoretical problems. The bird-watcher's ideal is to observe the behaviour of birds in a state of nature, and so he does not place the birds in controlled conditions, testing them in ways which would not otherwise be possible. Hence the bird-watcher may observe the homing habits of pigeons, but if he is only a watcher he will not be able to produce a scientific theory to account for this ability of pigeons. For by definition he lacks the biological knowledge which would allow him to connect the behaviour of birds with the behaviour, structure, and functioning of other kinds of animals. His interest is not in fitting his observations and conclusions to a set of biological laws. That is the job of the scientist. The bird-watcher merely supplies a journal whose entries may be arranged to tell various kinds of stories: the life cycle of the willy wagtail, for example, or the observations made during a particular season on the lyre bird.

Now the social analogue of the bird-watcher is the social observer. The social observer has the same pre-occupation with observing, reporting, classifying, and describing; he has the same diminished interest in conducting experiments, and in producing laws and theories which fit into a body of scientific knowledge. The natural historian of human society resembles the social scientist in that, unlike the historian he has no particular concern with actions of the past as distinct from those of the present. Neither has he any special concern with problems of dating or questions of tracing social developments. On the other hand, the natural historian of human society resembles the ordinary historian in that both try to establish 'true statements about particular events, processes, and situations'. The social observer is satisfied if he can show that a particular custom exists to a specified degree in a given society or that a particular cause operates. He leaves it to the social scientist or to the historian to explain either why the custom and the cause are present at all or why they are present in the specified degree. Thus it is not correct to say that natural historians are not interested in causal explanations. They are; what does not interest them are *general* explanations, ones which account for all cases of a certain type, rather than merely this case or that case. The social observer gives explanations of this sort: 'Leaders of the development faction had achieved their status only recently. Their rapid rise was due to a combination of ability, ambition, adaptability, loyalty to the organization and support of the new organizational goals.'[1] Knowing this answer may not help us to know the answer to a

[1] Brown and Shepherd: *op. cit.*, p. 238.

question about the rise of some other faction. The investigator who wishes to solve scientific problems must also be prepared to consider the question 'What are the necessary and sufficient conditions for the rise of factions of type A?'

4

It does not follow from these remarks about natural history that the three kinds of work which we have distinguished – that of science, natural history, and history – must always be performed by three different kinds of professional workers. Very often they are performed by the same person on different occasions. In some cases the three types of interest are displayed successively within a single article. Many of the longer studies by social scientists consist of a mixture of all three types of work. Nevertheless, there are instances of pure natural history, as there are instances of pure history and pure science. Ethnographic studies, for example, usually confine themselves to the natural history of the society in question. Typical studies are: Burrows and Spiros' ethnography of Ifaluk in the Caroline Islands,[1] Hu's essay (1948) on *The Common Descent Group in China and Its Functions*, Wagley's Memoir of 1949 entitled *The Social and Religious Life of a Guatemala Village*. It is true, perhaps, that the purer forms of social observation can be found in greater abundance in the writings of some anthropologists than in the work of other social scientists. Demographers, for example, are almost always concerned with the past composition of a population as well as with its future growth, stability, or decline. Much work in demography deals with the dated changes in such factors as family size, sex composition, reproduction rates, and fertility differentials. It is exceedingly difficult, therefore, to distinguish those sections of a demographic report which trace the development of a population from those sections which give an account of its present status. For the operation of factors in the past is constantly compared with their present operation, so that the result is a demographic history of a particular group of people. A quotation from a volume published in 1957, G. W. Robert's *The Population of Jamaica*, will illustrate this point.

Except for the year 1881, when birth registration was probably defective, the gross reproduction rates for Jamaica between 1844 and 1921 show very little variation. During these years there is no evidence of any upward or downward movement, the rates being within the range 2·5 to 2·7 throughout. This confirms the picture yielded by the birth-rates; fertility between 1844 and 1921 has remained unchanged. Between 1921 and 1946, however, a sharp fall has been witnessed, the gross reproduction rate for both sexes declining from 2·64 to 2·08, that is by 21%.[2]

An Atoll Culture, 1957.
[2] Pp. 278–9.

Within the fields of economics and political science there can be found rather lengthy examples of pure natural history, but they are not numerous and form no great proportion of modern work. In ruling out both theoretical discussions and historical inquires we remove a large portion of the two fields. And by eliminating from the remainder all questions of policy, planning, and recommendation, we almost reduce our examples to occasional articles and subsidiary sections of longer studies whose main purpose is of a different sort. Nevertheless, a monograph published in 1928 by the National Industrial Conference Board of New York comes as close to meeting our specifications as seems practical. The contents of the monograph are accurately referred to by its title: *The Cost of Living in Twelve Industrial Cities*. The results of a survey conducted 'in twelve representative American industrial cities between August and October, 1927' are given in some detail. Food prices, housing costs, clothing prices, fuel and light costs are itemized and compared for the various cities. The chief conclusion is that the difference in living costs between the most and least expensive of the cities was relatively small, a difference of 13 per cent. No substantive question other than that of 'How much does it cost?' is allowed to intrude. This closely resembles the bird-watcher's question: 'How much food does an English robin eat per day?'

Political scientists, like economists, are not often content to produce unadulterated natural history. The branch of political science in which it appears most commonly is that of local government. Thus the authors of an essay on *The Government of Victoria* (1958) begin by classifying the functions of the State; they then go on to discuss the cabinet, the departments and the statutory bodies. Under these headings they discuss such topics as the division of functions; statutes administered by each department; departmental expenditures; and terms of office. But most studies of local government include chapters on historical development and policy questions. H. L. Brittain's volume, *Local Government in Canada* (1951) is a case in point. It contains in addition to sections on history and policy, a detailed account of many features of local government: the control of municipalities by legislation, boards, and commissions; a classification of city corporations into six types; a description of the kinds of revenue available, and so forth. The interests of the author are given in his foreword. One of his aims, he says, is 'to supply a factual basis for further studies in the field of local affairs'.[1] This is a typical goal of the natural historian: to observe what goes on around him and to give the benefits of his experience to other workers with similar interests. The kind of experience in question is that presupposed by the recommendation that 'matching grants should be avoided as they are apt to encourage expenditure'.[2] An economist or sociologist might

[1] P. V.
[2] P. 146.

37

well be interested in testing the hypothesis that under certain conditions the offer of matching grants will encourage municipal expenditure. The natural historian of a society is content to record the observation that in his experience such grants do tend to stimulate expenditure. Thus it can be said that as the physical sciences developed from the generalizations of common sense, so the social sciences develop in part from the generalizations of social observers.

Wildcat Strike (1955) by A. W. Gouldner clearly exhibits this relationship between social science and social observation. For the author begins by summarizing his intentions:

The following account seeks to realize several objectives. Our most general intention is to present the facts of the case and to describe in some detail the events that occurred. This is especially needful since there are few descriptions of wildcat strikes written from a sociologist's viewpoint ... therefore it will become necessary to ask, just what is a 'wildcat strike', and how does it differ from other types of strikes? Such conceptual clarification is a second objective of this study, and is a necessary preliminary to the explanation of what happened.
We shall want to know how this strike came about: Did the parties expect it? Did they want it? What did they do to prevent it? How did the belief systems and social relations of workers and management enter into the events that occurred? ...
The final objective, however, is not simply the explanation of this one strike but, instead, the development of hypotheses and conceptual tools which can illuminate other similar processes. In short, it is possible that the careful examination of this one case may provide occasions to test and develop instruments of more general application to industrial sociology and to a theory of group tensions.[1]

In fact, this study cannot be divided into three distinct parts. The first objective – presenting the facts – and the second objective – conceptual clarification – are closely bound together in a number of chapters. But the third objective – the development of hypotheses with general application – occupies the final two chapters on its own. The author himself provides an accurate report of the way in which he proceeds from the task of social observation in the earlier chapters to that of social science in the later chapters.

A wildcat strike is a distinctive type of a social tension. Yet, in analysing this strike, we were compelled, as any social scientist would be, to employ certain general assumptions concerning the manner in which human beings behave under tension. Many of these assumptions are applicable to the study of almost any kind of social tension. What will be done here, then, is to make these broad, latent assumptions manifest, and to codify them. In this form, they will be more readily susceptible both to critical inspection and to cumulative development.[2]

[1] Pp. 11–2.
[2] P. 124.

38

The question with which the section on social description closed and with which this section opened can now be answered in this way. The phrase 'social description' is not only misleading, since the work to which it is applied is often not descriptive work; it is also ambiguous. Sometimes the phrase is used to refer to ordinary historical investigation carried on by social scientists. It is true, therefore, that some studies made by political scientists and some made by political historians are methodologically indistinguishable in that members of both groups have engaged in the same kind of historical investigation. The same holds true of certain work by economists and economic historians, of sociologists and social historians. Yet if the phrase 'social description' were applied only to historical studies it would not be ambiguous. However, we have indicated that the phrase is also used to refer to the sort of investigation known as 'natural history' or 'social observation', investigation which is neither fully fledged history nor theoretical science. For it differs from the field of history in having no special concern with the past, and resembles it in concentrating entirely upon particular 'events, processes, and situations'. In this respect natural history differs from theoretical science. Thus the social observer is primarily interested in existing societies and in current problems. There are undoubtedly persons who are called 'social scientists' but whose interest is chiefly in social observations. They come very close indeed to sharing the interests of social historians. Nevertheless there is a practical as well as a theoretical difference between them. An historian usually spends his working hours in libraries and museums; a social observer must spend at least some time observing the activities of social groups and perhaps participating in them. This is a practical difference which aligns the actions of the social observer more closely with those of the empirical scientist than with those of the practising historian.

Our original question was based upon a misconception. For it asked whether social description resembled in its aims and procedures a history of social life more than it did a science of social life. And this question was a preamble to the claim that social investigators are more akin to historians than to scientists because no scientific explanations are offered by social investigators. They are, it was said, merely historians of recent events. This last claim we have already shown to be false. The further view that social investigators do not supply us with scientific explanations often rests upon the belief that the phrases 'social science' and 'natural history of society' are synonymous – that social scientists produce nothing but works of social observation. We have been trying to show that social scientists do in fact produce such works as well as essays in history. Nothing that has been said can show, however, that social scientists do not also give us studies which put forward scientific explanations. Indeed, the contrary has been both suggested and assumed. The case for this view will be stated in succeeding chapters.

39

IV

SOCIAL EXPLANATION

ONE of the questions which we have been considering is this: 'What distinguishes social science from social observation?' We have already touched upon the answer in comparing social science with history. If what we have said is correct, social observers are typically interested in establishing statements about particular events and the operation of particular causes. On the other hand, social scientists proper attempt to do more than this; they try to establish sound generalizations about classes of events. In brief, an important difference between social observation and social science lies in the kind of conclusion they hope to establish. Thus the full answer to any question about the relation of these two fields to each other must include some scrutiny of the methods by which these conclusions are reached. And to examine the methods is also to examine the structure of the arguments that support the conclusions. The advancing of such arguments is called 'giving an explanation'.

Now the notion of explanation is at the centre of almost all controversies about the success or failure of the social sciences. For they are commonly attacked on the ground that they do not give us knowledge of laws and theories as do the physical sciences. From this deficiency the conclusion is often drawn that knowledge of laws and theories is not obtainable about the social behaviour of human beings – that explanations of human conduct cannot be offered in terms of laws but must take some other form. Correspondingly, the social sciences are sometimes defended by arguing that in fact they do parallel the physical sciences in their explanatory methods, and sometimes on the quite opposite ground, that they do not and ought not to resemble them in this way, since they have their own, distinctive, methods of explanation. A combination of logical and factual reasons is ordinarily advanced in support of both these positions, and in discussing the reasons we have to distinguish clearly between the two types. This task is not made easier by the failure of many writers to separate their descriptions of how social scientists do in fact behave from their recommendations about how they ought to behave. Too often the prescriptions are put forward as if they

40

were an account of the procedure actually followed by all genuine social scientists.

If we are to avoid exhuming controversies which died of inanition, we must pay some attention to the difference between description and explanation as that difference functions in everyday life. Neglect of the distinction between everyday descriptions and everyday explanations has been reflected in confused views about scientific descriptions and scientific explanations. These confusions, in turn, have made it difficult to sketch the relationships holding between social observation and social science.

The verb 'explain' is such a general term that in the sense of 'making matters plain or intelligible' it is often used as an inclusive synonym for a number of more specific terms. A Christian minister may be said to explain a chapter in the Bible; alternatively, he may be said to *clarify* or *elucidate* its obscurities by the way in which he *expounds* the dogma and brings out the meaning of the passages with his sympathetic *interpretation*. In clarifying a point, expounding a view, interpreting a character, he is often, according to common speech, giving an explanation. And when two lovers adjust their differences this may be the result of one having managed to 'explain away' what troubled the other. Explaining away, then, is the removing of an impediment, an impediment either to someone's relationships with other people or to his intellectual understanding. All explanations are attempts to explain away impediments of some kind. They are efforts to deprive puzzles, mysteries, and blockages of their force, and hence, existence.

The methods by which we explain may be classified in many ways. For our purposes it will be sufficient to take account of nine common methods; that is, we shall classify the methods into nine types, basing the classification upon the different kinds of information used in the course of the explanation. Of these various methods only seven bear directly upon the work of social scientists. The other two methods have no special claim to our attention, but they should be noted because of their general employment throughout all the sciences as well as in daily speech. The first of these two methods is that of making one's meaning clear and plain to other people as well as to oneself. The request 'Explain yourself!' often means no more than 'Speak plainly!' But while some impediments to communication can be explained away by plainer speech, others cannot. In these cases, 'Explain yourself!' must be taken as a request for definitions, details, or illustrations, or for elaboration of the argument. But it is obvious that this means of explaining contributes nothing to the methods in which we are presently interested. The explanations of social behaviour supplied to us by social scientists are distinct from subsequent efforts to clarify those explanations. What scientists wish to explain is the behaviour of human beings; the improvement of communication between writer and reader is a rather different problem, a fact for which the writings of some social scientists provide abundant evidence.

The second of the two methods is that of explaining a logical derivation or a logical proof. A beginner in logic might say: 'Explain to me why the truth of "Jones was not in command of his mount" follows from the truth of: (1) If the horse was going backwards or if it was on the right-hand side of the track, then Jones was responsible for the collision. (2) If the horse was not on the right-hand side of the track, then Jones was not in command of his mount. (3) Jones was not responsible for the collision.' The explanation would consist in showing how the conclusion is deducible from the three premises by reference either to valid forms of inference or to valid statement-forms. When the student had understood how each statement in the derivation forms a link in the chain of implications that ties the conclusion to the premises, he would have understood the explanation. To explain correctly and effectively in such a case is to produce the logical steps leading from premises to conclusion and to have the student understand them. The explanation of a mathematical proof, in this method, simply consists in supplying an effective mathematical demonstration. This method of 'explanation', like the previous one, is not a method with which social scientists, more than other scientists, have a special concern. All scientists make use of logical derivations and some make use of mathematical proofs. Their main energies, however, are directed not toward logical and mathematical techniques but toward the results obtainable by such techniques. Two of their important interests are: finding the truth-value of certain premises from which conclusions known previously may be derived, and discovering whether given premises lead to *true* conclusions. It is the content of the premises and conclusions that occupies their attention in these cases, and not the machinery of derivation.

The remaining seven methods of explanation are by no means independent of each other. They will be considered in detail later, and some of the relationships amongst them will then be examined. But to begin with we shall distinguish six of them in the ordinary manner without considering whether any of them is reducible to one or more of the remainder. The seventh we shall reserve for later attention. The six methods of explanation are these: (1) Genetic, (2) Intentions, (3) Dispositions, (4) Reasons, (5) Functions, (6) Empirical Generalizations. Each will be discussed in turn in the order here given.

(1) *Genetic*

Explanations of this type give a description or an outline of a temporal sequence of events. When this temporal sequence is thought of as supplying an answer to a puzzle-question about the origin or development of an event we say that the account forms an historical explanation. 'Why in Western Europe do men have their hair cut shorter than do women?' and 'Why is it that so many English legal terms are of French derivation?' are questions to which genetic explanations may typically be given as answers.

(2) *Intentions*

We constantly refer to our intentions in our explanations of our own actions, and we very frequently wish to know what a person's intentions are or were in performing an action. When we give the intention of an agent's action we presuppose that the action was done by design. We exhibit his action as a means towards a goal – his aim or purpose. If we say 'Bruce lowered his rifle just then, because he intended to empty the magazine' we are saying that his action was a means to a particular purpose – emptying the magazine. This information will only serve as an explanation, of course, if there is something odd, strange, curious, or puzzling about the action. Only then will learning what Bruce's goal was *explain* why he lowered his rifle at just that moment.

(3) *Dispositions*

We can explain many of the things which people do and say by reference to the tendencies or dispositions that they have. The puzzlement behind the question 'Why does he insist upon going out into the pouring rain today?' may be removed, by the answer 'Because being avaricious, he can't wait to collect his debts.' The explanation consists in exhibiting, however sketchily, the particular example as an instance of a behaviour tendency – or disposition – in the person. Avariciousness can take many forms, one of which is an eagerness to obtain money. The fact that a person's haste to collect a debt is an instance of one of his personality traits accounts for his action, since it is the sort of behaviour which he exhibits when the appropriate conditions arise.

(4) *Reasons*

'The reason why I refused to speak to my wife yesterday was that she invited her sister to stay with us over the holidays and neglected to tell me. I was furious with her and I decided to teach her a lesson.' His wife's action is taken by the husband as his own reason for deliberately not speaking to her. Learning what his reason was would provide us with an explanation of his silence if we were puzzled by it. The husband has taken his belief about his wife's neglect as a sufficient reason for attempting to punish her. When we learn that he takes this particular belief to be such a reason we have accounted for his action.

43

(5) *Functions*

There are two different kinds of questions which can be answered by function explanations. The first takes the form 'To what goal is it a means?' Thus to ask 'What is the function of that second arm on the turn-table of your gramophone?' and to receive the answer 'It holds a pad for removing dust and static from the records' is to ask for and be told the purpose of the dust arm. Under the appropriate circumstances, it is to receive an explanation in terms of the particular end to which a given means is directed. The second kind of question is represented by 'What is the function of the custom of throwing rice at weddings?' Here we are asking how the custom fits into the set of practices which make up the marriage ceremony – how the custom operates so as to help maintain a system. No agents or their goals are involved.

(6) *Empirical Generalizations*

One simple example of an explanation in terms of a law is this: suppose we wish to explain why the pupils of Ruth's eyes are dilated this morning. Then we might argue that she put scopolamine crystals in her eyes this morning, that all scopolamine causes rapid dilation of the eye pupil, hence, that Ruth's pupils are dilated. The statement about scopolamine causing dilation is taken as a law. It is used as one of the premises of an argument in which the fact to be explained is derived as the conclusion. The explanation of Ruth's condition is given by interpreting it as an instance of the operation of a law

PART TWO

Methods of Explanation

V

GENETIC

1

MOST work in the social sciences, like most work in history and in the natural sciences, is not directly concerned with the furnishing of explanations. It may well be true, as is so often said, that the tasks of any empirical science are to explain, to predict, and to apply. But in any such field these tasks are embedded in a workload that may be referred to as identification, classification, description; and measuring and reporting as well. These activities intersect, of course. We may be able to identify the practice of cross cousin marriage by the description that we have given of it, though identifying the practice is different from describing it. Nor is it true, as is sometimes said, that 'classification and description are really the same process'.[1] The view supporting this belief has been put as follows: 'To describe a given animal as carnivorous is to classify it as a carnivore; to classify it as a reptile is to describe it as reptilian. To describe any object as having a certain property is to classify it as a member of the class of objects having that property.[2]

Now it follows from what has already been said (in Part One, Chapter I) about the nature of describing, that classifying a given animal may be, and often is, simply a way of avoiding the onerous task of describing it. If we wish to refer to the horse named Phar Lap, then to classify the animal of that name as a member of the genus Equus caballus is certainly not to mention the characteristic marks of Phar Lap. A description of him would include the features which distinguished him from other horses: his appearance, his temperament, his abilities. But if the auditor did not know what a horse was, a certain amount of classificatory information would be needed as well. It might have to be said that a horse is a large, solid hoofed quadruped of the family Equidae, etc. This information would not be a description of Phar Lap, but it would be a *description* of Equus caballus if it allowed the auditor to distinguish horses from such other Equidae as Equus

[1] I. Copi: *Introduction to Logic*, 1954, p. 427.
[2] *Ibid.*

47

asinus and Equus zebra. If the information were not sufficient for this it would be merely a *classification* of Equus caballus as a member of the genus Equus. It would also be a description of the Equidae, for this same information would enable the genera to be distinguished from related genera. Thus, in classifying an object by mentioning the defining features of the class to which it belongs, we are also describing the class; but we are not describing the object. In short, we describe something in order that its distinctiveness may be recognized. We place it in a class in order that its similarities to certain other objects may be recognized. We need not be describing an object every time we attribute a property to that object. We may merely be classifying it – though we may also be describing the class to which it belongs.

The bearing of these distinctions on our present topic – genetic explanations – is this. When we correctly argue that explaining is different from such other activities as describing and classifying we may be tempted to reach an incorrect conclusion: the conclusion that a *description* of historical origins cannot serve as an explanatory answer. In consequence, we may take description and explanation to be distinguished by the absence and presence, respectively, of answers to 'why' questions. We may then deny that any but 'why' questions can receive explanatory answers.

But this denial is obviously mistaken. It is easy to produce examples in which both 'why' and 'how' questions correctly receive the same explanatory answer. 'Why did larger states emerge after about 1775?' and 'How did larger states come to emerge after about 1775?' are cases in point. Thus the difference between an explanatory account of historical origin or development and a non-explanatory one cannot be simply the difference between giving an answer to 'why' questions and giving an answer to 'how' questions. Moreover, an explanatory answer can be appropriately offered, in certain contexts, to a question like 'How did the Nazis kill such a large number of people in concentration camps when so few armed guards were used?' And here the replacement of 'how' by 'why' produces a different question, one to which a quite distinct answer will be needed.

The same considerations which tell against the claim of a privileged position for 'why' questions tell also against the broader claim that 'a description of origins or a narrative of development cannot serve as an explanatory answer'. If such an answer is sometimes given to a 'how' question, then there is no reason why it cannot sometimes be given to a 'why' question. However, that answers to questions of both kinds can serve as explanations can best be shown by an examination of some examples drawn from the social sciences.

There is a distinction to be made between two sorts of examples. One sort consists of answers to questions explicitly set by the scientist. Another sort consists of information which can be used as an explanatory answer to some question, even though it is not used in that way by the scientist who supplies the information. Consider the following passage as a genetic-explanatory answer of the latter kind. The passage is part of an essay entitled 'The Growth of Economic Individualism in African Society'.[1]

... there is one other important aspect of the separation of economic privilege from social obligation which needs to be considered. Such a separation – or else the mere disregard of traditional claims on superior wealth as soon as more attractive uses for it appear – seems to be almost universal among primitive peoples when they are brought into contact with European trade and initiated into the use of money. In the Ganda, its peculiar form is due to a deliberate act of administrative intervention – the allocation to the chiefs in freehold tenure of the land over which they exercised authority at the time of the Uganda Agreement. This measure, by fixing the existing distribution in perpetuity rendered the chiefs' economic position independent of any of the services which they formerly rendered to the king, such as the administration of justice or the organization of public works.

Next these chiefs ceased even to be expected to render such services. They were persuaded to retire from office and be replaced by younger, educated men, or when they died their official position was filled by a stranger, while their land passed to their heirs. Thus the landlord had no longer to render any return to superior authority for his privileged position – apart from a very low tax. In his relation with his inferiors – who now became tenants paying rent – a certain standard of leniency was imposed by the fact that there was plenty of land available, and they could leave him if they were dissatisfied. Some of the first generation of landlords kept up the old paternal relationship with their tenants. But when cotton was introduced, many of them made such heavy exactions on the yield of the peasants' crops that their dues had eventually to be limited by law, and none of this came back in any form to the tenants. It was devoted entirely to the personal uses of the landlord, who bought a motor car, sent his children to school, built a two-storied house in the capital, or perhaps visited Europe. One founded a native newspaper. Now, though the standard of exaction is fixed, the number of landlords who insist on their full rights is increasing, and the ingenuity which they show in interpreting the law in their favour is considerable. Many of them do not live on their land, but in the capital, and it is only through the collection of rent that they come into even indirect contact with their tenants. There is no longer any question of the peasants looking to them for personal assistance, and the moral obligation on the landlord to devote some of his returns to the improvement of the land itself which is recognized by European tradition is quite undreamt of. The peasant's ambition now is not to become a chief, but to buy his own piece of land and be independent of the landlord's claims.

Neither in this passage nor in the essay from which it is taken does the author explicitly state a question to which the passage supplies an explanatory answer. But it is easy enough to state a number of such questions: (1) 'How did Ganda change so quickly from a society in

[1] L. Mair: *Studies in Applied Anthropology*, 1957, pp. 29–30.

which the wealthy were obliged to perform certain social tasks to a society in which the wealthy ignored these obligations? (2) How – considering his previous power – could the king have lost economic control over the chiefs while they retained their's over the peasants? (3) Why have the peasants – traditionally bound to their chiefs by many ties of mutual obligation – ceased to look to them for help?'

The answer to the first question is this: the origin of the sudden change is 'a deliberate act of administrative intervention – the allocation by the chiefs in freehold tenure of the land over which they exercised authority at the time of the Uganda agreement. This measure, by fixing the existing distribution in perpetuity, rendered the chiefs' economic position independent of any of the services which they formerly rendered to the king. . . .' The chiefs ceased to give these services since their wealth and authority no longer depended upon them.

The same answer with some additions from the original passage will serve as a reply to the second question about the king's loss of economic power. The additions are necessary to answer the other part of the question, i.e. 'Why did the chiefs retain their economic power over the peasants?' Both the first and the second questions begin with the word 'how'. The third question differs in that it begins with the word 'why'. But its answer can be found in the same passage. The peasants ceased to look to their chiefs for help because (a) the chiefs no longer provided such services as 'the administration of justice or the organization of public works', (b) the chiefs moved away from the areas in which their peasants lived, (c) the peasants became the hard-pressed tenants of their landlord chiefs. Obviously the first two 'how' questions are replaceable without change of meaning by 'why' questions. 'How did Ganda change so quickly . . .' becomes 'Why did Ganda change so quickly. . . .' The same answer will do for both. And the phrasing 'How could the king have lost his economic control . . .' can mean the same in some contexts as 'Why should the king. . . .'

The three explanatory answers with which we are concerned have much of the imprecision and incompleteness of an everyday explanation. They do not contain explicit generalizations which are known to be true. When we look, for instance, at the answer given to the question 'Why have the peasants ceased to look to their chiefs for help?' it is plain that a number of generalizations are presupposed. These are such psychological or sociological statements as: the disappearance of services rendered by a superordinate group (the chiefs) lessens the demands made for further aid by a subordinate group (the peasants); the demand for aid lessens with the decrease in face-to-face relationships; and the demand decreases as the superordinate group increases its economic exactions. Each of these is crudely stated, each requires testing. But without something like them we are left with gaps in our account. Unless, for example, we know that the imposition of economic

50

hardships upon a group of people somehow modifies their requests for help directed to the oppressing group, we have no reason for concluding that the peasants ceased to request aid because their potential helpers were identical with their actual oppressors. If the subordinate group were composed of very dull people they might not realize that their mis-directed appeals had no chance of success. But they did realize this, and their response is what is asserted by means of our rough generalization. The importance of implicit generalization of this crude type for explana-tions given in terms of historical origins and development is well known. The fact that such generalizations are presupposed in these, as in every-day explanations, is an argument for granting the answers in which they occur the title of 'genuine explanations'.

2

When we come to examine the category which we have labelled 'genetic explanations' we find that it includes three types of cases: those explanations which refer only to origins; those which refer to both origins and development; and those which refer only to development. All three types of explanation are said to 'give the history' of an event or a process or a state of affairs. But it is sometimes important to dis-tinguish amongst the three different cases. Plainly, what counts as the historical origin of an event in one context may be taken as a stage of historical development in another context. This is easily illustrated.

Suppose the question to be: 'How did the great drop in prices on the New York Stock Exchange, 29 October 1929, originate?' A brief answer might take the form: It originated in a bankers' meeting of the previous afternoon:

... the statements released after the meeting made clear what had been dis-cussed for the two hours. It was no part of the bankers' purpose, the statement said, to maintain any particular level of prices or to protect anyone's profit. Rather the aim was to have an orderly market, one in which offers would be met by bids at some price ...

Like many lesser men, Mr Lamont and his colleagues had suddenly found themselves overcommitted on a falling market. The time had come to go short on promises. Support, organized or otherwise, could not contend with the overwhelming, pathological desire to sell. The meeting had considered how to liquidate the commitment to support the market without adding to the public perturbation.

... Now prices were to be allowed to fall. The speculator's only comfort, henceforth, was that his ruin would be accomplished in an orderly and becoming manner.[1]

This answer might be satisfactory to anyone concerned with the question: 'What was the last effective action that could have been taken

[1] J. Galbraith: *The Great Crash, 1929*, 1955, p. 115.

by investment bankers to prevent the imminent fall in stock prices on 29 October?' The origin of that drop in prices, it might be claimed, lay in the decision of the meeting, because that decision was the precipitating cause of the price fall. A different decision might have prevented the fall in prices on 29 October, though it might well not have prevented a drop on succeeding days. This answer, however, would certainly not be satisfactory to someone who was interested in the origin of the fall in prices on 29 October because he was also interested in the price drop of 24 October – the first day of the panic of 1929. He would want to know what happened between those two dates, and what took place immediately prior to 24 October. The exact nature of his problem would determine how far back into the past beyond this point he would wish to extend his inquiries. But in any event, the origin of the drop in prices on 29 October, as far as he was concerned, would not be the decision taken in the meeting of the 28th. The meeting would simply be a point in a more extensive series of events. If the interests of the investigator were sufficiently extensive he would be led from a concern with explanation in terms of historical origin and development to a concern with other methods of explanation. In that case he might interpret the question 'How did the stock market crash of 1929 originate?' as an inquiry into the *causes* of the Great Depression. He might then begin as Galbraith does: 'The task of answering can be simplified somewhat by dividing the problem into two parts. First, there is the question of why economic activity turned down in 1929. Second, there is the vastly more important question of why, having started down, on this unhappy occasion, it went down and down and down and remained low for a full decade.'[1]

When a social scientist deals, as in the present example, with a series of questions which can be arranged in an order of increasing generality, the same event or situation may be explained by various methods used successively. In our example the price fall of 29 October is explained in terms of (*a*) the bankers' intention (to let prices fall) and (*b*) their reason for intending to do this (they believed they were 'overcommitted on a falling market'). We have already stated that the explanation offered for the price fall can be classified as one of historical origin. Thus three of the methods of explanation we distinguished are employed within the compass of a few paragraphs. The natural question, then, is whether these methods of explanation are related, and if so, in what ways they are connected to each other and to the rest of the methods.

Now it is clear that the method of genetic explanation may take the origin of any given state of affairs to lie in events, or processes, or situations which differ greatly in kind. Amongst these kinds are people's intentions and purposes, their dispositions, and their reasons. The first and last cases have already been illustrated by reference to an explana-

[1] *Op. cit.*, p. 179.

tion of the fall in prices on 29 October 1929. The second case can be illustrated by means of the same example slightly enlarged; we could well locate the origin of the price-fall in a disposition possessed by the bankers, namely, the disposition to protect their own financial interests first and foremost. This disposition, it could be claimed, was the origin of the drop in stock prices on that day.

On many occasions an explanation in terms of origin is combined with an account of historical development from the time of origin to some chosen date or period. Sometimes, however, the method of historical explanation merely provides an account of some historical development without taking up any question of origin. For example, 'grants of exclusive privilege to the British East India Company with respect to the China trade and to the South Sea Company with respect to the west coast of the Americas', provide, it is alleged, the explanation for the gradual "elimination" of British enterprise from the North Pacific by the New Englanders. That elimination, it is maintained, testifies to the stultifying effects of special privilege – the neglect of opportunity deriving from lack of initiative, excessive overhead costs, and the exclusion of more enterprising firms from business opportunity.'[1] In a case of this kind no problem of historical origin arises. The grants of exclusive privilege are claimed to have had certain causal effects upon the *development* of the British fur trade, but no claim is made as to the historical *origin* of the British decline. It might be that supporters of the explanation would wish to argue that the decline had its origin in the grants of privilege. However, they might equally well wish to claim that the origin had an earlier date, perhaps associated with previous British trading in the area. The fact that either claim could be made with equal propriety indicates that an explanation in terms of historical development can be distinct from an explanation in terms of historical origin.

In the same way as a person's intention, disposition, or reason, may be identified as the historical origin of some state of affairs, so these three factors may be identified as causal conditions of the historical development through which something has passed. From early 1928 to late 1929 values on the New York Stock Exchange rose very rapidly. In part this was the result of speculative manipulation. In trying to explain how or why certain prices rose during this period we naturally turn to the market operations of individual speculators, and, thence, to their reasons, dispositions, and intentions. 'A financial columnist of the *Daily News*, who signed himself "The Trader", received some $19,000 in 1929 and early 1930 from a free-lance operator named John J. Levenson. "The Trader" repeatedly spoke well of stocks in which Mr Levenson was interested. Mr Levenson later insisted, however, that this

[1] G. Elliott: 'Frontiers and Forms of Enterprise: The Case of the North Pacific, 1785–1825', *The Canadian Journal of Economics and Political Science*, Vol. 24, No. 2, May 1958, p. 253.

was a coincidence and that the payment reflected his more or less habitual generosity.'[1] Whatever Mr Levenson's motive was, the effect of The Trader's remarks may well have been to increase the value of the stocks held by his benefactor. An explanation of this rise in their value could certainly include, then, an account of the intentions, reasons, or dispositions of the two men. And though the origin of the rise might be located elsewhere, the effects of Mr Levenson's operations upon the rise might still prove to be causally important.

The question which naturally follows is this: 'Can functions and laws bear the same relation to genetic explanations as do the three factors just mentioned?' Obviously, the answer in the case of laws must be a negative one. In asking for the historical origin of something and for the causal conditions of its development, we are asking for dated occurrences or processes. A statement of law, on the other hand, refers only to uniform connections between particular types of events and properties, irrespective of the date of any given occurrence or instance which belongs to one of the types. The uniform connection itself has no *absolute* date and so can be neither an origin nor a causal condition of development. This is not to deny that statements of dynamic laws may contain dated variables, that, for example, a country's expenditure in one year may be a function of its income for the previous year. But the dates associated with these variables are *relative* dates, not absolute dates. Thus if expenditure at time t refers to year t (where t may take any value), then income at $t-1$ will refer to year $t-1$. It is the manifestations of laws – the results of their operation – which can be correctly called 'historical origins or causal conditions' of events, processes, and situations. The death of Lenin from arterio-sclerosis in 1924 was a manifestation of what might be called 'biological laws'. His death could be said to be the origin, or at least an important condition, of the open political struggle between Trotsky and Stalin.

The case of functions is somewhat different, though the answer to our question is again a negative one. We have said that to give the function of something like a custom is, in the sense relevant here, to state the effects of the custom upon the maintenance of the system to which the custom belongs. Thus, to explain the social function of gift exchange at Christmas is to report on the *effects* which the custom has upon the social relationships of the participants. But in asking for an explanation of Christmas gifts in terms of historical origin and development, we are asking for the historical *causes* of the custom, for the past events which explain how or why it arose when it did. An explanation of the function – causal effects – of gift exchange cannot, then, serve as a statement of the historical origin and development – the causes – of this custom. If we demand an account of its historical causes we cannot be properly served by an account of its effects, past or present.

[1] Galbraith: *op. cit.*, p. 78.

3

If it is true, as it seems to be, that in giving a genetic explanation we may at the same time be giving an explanation by reference to intentions or dispositions or reasons, then obviously our six methods of explanation are not mutually exclusive. Our classification of methods would seem to be based upon at least two different sets of criteria, and perhaps upon more. Now a moment's review of the six methods will make it plain that genetic explanations are to be contrasted with explanations in terms of laws. The former explain by appealing to specific events and to particular stages of processes. These are occurrences and processes which can be dated; they include, as we have said, the intentions and purposes, the dispositions, and the reasons for acting, possessed by any given person at a particular time or throughout some limited period of time. Law explanations, in contrast, appeal to uniform associations between kinds of events and properties. These relationships between kinds and types are not subject to dating, though instances of the relationships are. If there are laws about the relations holding, for example, between people's intentions and their actions, or between their dispositions and their reasons for their actions, then a law explanation may incorporate these generalizations. But in giving such an explanation we should be doing something different from what we do in explaining merely by a reference to someone's intention, disposition, or reason. An explanation of the latter sort does not actually cite a law statement or generalization. It cites non-universal statements. Thus suppose that there is a law statement represented by the formula 'Whenever p, then q'. Then the expression 'p holds here' may be used in tacit conjunction with the law statement to explain why 'q' holds here. Or we may give a more explicit account by stating that this particular case of 'p' holding is also one of 'q' holding. It makes no practical difference which statement we give since the auditor will receive the same information from the two accounts, and they can be used on the same sorts of occasions. The two answers are alike in implicitly appealing to the truth of 'Whenever p, then q' without explicitly asserting this formula. They do not explicitly assert a generalization because a generalization cannot state the historical origin of anything: for example, the struggle between Stalin and Trotsky, though the remark 'Trotsky did so-and-so because Stalin did such-and-such' will be false if certain relevant generalizations are not true. To give an explanation in terms of historical origin and development is to assert a statement of subsumption – of initial conditions. To give a law explanation, on the other hand, is to state the generalization in question and the initial conditions as well – if that is needed to bring the case in hand within the scope of the generalization.

Our conclusion, therefore, is quite ordinary. It is that a genetic explanation provides statements which are neither universal nor

statistical generalizations. On the contrary, they are statements reporting or describing specific events, processes, and situations which are
either dated or datable. Such statements, if incorporated into the arguments upon whose soundness their usefulness as explanatory statements
depends, would be called 'statements of initial conditions'. They may be
provided by simple assertion ('p holds here'), or by conjoint assertion of
'p holds here' and the statement to be explained ('q holds here').

These various points can be illustrated and expanded by means of our
stock market example. Suppose our question to be once again, 'How
did the great drop in prices on the New York Stock Exchange, 29
October 1929, originate?' One answer was: 'Mr Lamont and his
colleagues intended to preserve their own financial security and that of
their institutions, and for that reason intended to let market prices fall.'
Assume that we hold a generalization to the effect that whenever a set
of known financiers with specific resources and intentions publicly
remove their support from a falling market its prices fall precipitously
('Whenever p, then q'). If we believe such a group to have removed its
support from the market of 29 October 1929 ('p holds here'), then we
may phrase our answer to the question 'Why does q hold here?' in any
of four ways. We may reply, 'A set of financiers ... removed their
support on 29 October 1929', an expression corresponding to 'p holds
here'. Or we may reply, 'A set of financiers ... removed their support
on 29 October 1929 and prices fell precipitously.' This corresponds to
'p holds here and q holds here'.

The third way of putting our answer is to give the generalization
'Whenever a set of financiers ... then prices fall precipitously.' Given
a knowledge of the original question, the information that a set of
financiers did in fact remove their support from the market on 29
October 1929 could easily be gathered from the answer. It is only the
fourth way of putting the answer, however, which *explicitly* indicates
that there is a connection between the price fall and the financiers'
intentions. This is the statement 'The great drop in prices on the New
York Stock Exchange, 29 October 1929, occurred because a set of
financiers ... publicly removed their support from the market.' We call
this kind of reply an 'open explanatory statement' because it explicitly
relates the desired answer to the question asked. The other answers
merely supply various pieces of information from which such an explicit
answer may be constructed.

If we now reconsider our classification of explanation methods into
six types, we shall see that at least two different criteria have been
employed in the scheme. One criterion classifies explanations according
to whether or not they contain a generalization; if they do, they are
classified as Law Explanations in our scheme; if they do not, they are
classified as Genetic Explanations. The other criterion separates
explanations by the differences in what impel social agents to act as they

do. These are the differences between behaviour explainable in terms of reasons, that explainable by means of intentions, and that referable to dispositions. At the moment we are not concerned with the question of how function-explanations fit into this scheme; nor are we concerned with those relations amongst reasons, intentions, and dispositions, which permit us to say of all of them that they 'impel social agents to act as they do'. These topics will be taken up later. At present we have only to decide whether the fact that our scheme of classification is based upon two distinct criteria affects its usefulness. Surely the answer is that its utility remains unaffected. It is simply a list, and like most lists its value lies in its being complete. What we are chiefly concerned to avoid in such a list are errors of omission. Unless our scheme of classification omits some method we have no reason now to complain of the scheme. For the relationships amongst the six methods of explanation recognized by it will form an important topic of discussion in succeeding chapters.

VI

INTENTIONS

1

THE importance of intention-explanations in daily life does not seem open to serious doubt. We explain why Ruth kicked her husband's foot under the dinner table by saying that her 'intention' – or 'desire' or 'wish' – was to have him be quiet; that Fernanda loosened the runner because she intended to bring the craft's head nearer the wind; that the government will increase its food subsidies because it intends to keep the prices of foods at pre-war levels. Yet curiously enough, the words 'intended', 'intention', and 'intentional', occur most infrequently in the explanations provided by social scientists. The words are not merely absent; they are conspicuously absent. Instead, even in contexts where intention-explanations would seem to be appropriate, people are referred to as 'having no desire to do' what they did, or as 'planning to achieve' their objectives without the use of higher tariffs, or as 'aiming at an increase in the gold reserves'. It is almost as though the employment of the word 'intention' were being avoided. Perhaps this is because explanations in terms of purposes and intentions are not useful in the social sciences. Or perhaps it is only that there are reasons for preferring other expressions to 'intention'. To settle this question we must begin by examining the actual practice of social scientists.

Consider, first, the following passages in which the words 'intended' or 'intentions' actually appear but not in explanatory contexts.

(a) While exploring all possibilities from round-table conferences to wages boards, it was clear that Latham in fact intended to set up a new arbitration court to determine national issues such as wages, hours, and child endowment and to act as a co-ordinating agency.[1]

(b) In New South Wales, the intentions of the Bavin-Buttenshaw-Nationalist Country Party coalition were vague. As early as 1923, Bavin had made it clear that he thought industrial regulation was a state matter and that Federal

[1] A. Wildavsky: 'The 1926 Referendum' in *Studies in Australian Politics*, 1958, p. 64.

arbitration had 'been an almost unmitigated disaster to Australia ever since it came into being'.[1]

(c) The Senate, as we have seen, was intended to be primarily the embodiment of the federal principle in the Constitution. It was hoped that it would 'conciliate the spirit of independence in the several states by giving each, however small, equal representation with every other, however large, in one branch of the national government'.[2]

It does, moreover, in an eminent degree, fulfil the intention of its founders by providing a 'body of men whose greater experience, longer term of membership, and comparative independence of popular election' makes them 'an element of stability in the government of the nation, enabling it to maintain its character in the eyes of foreign States, and to preserve a continuity of policy at home and abroad'.[3]

(d) Budgeting for a surplus is intended to prevent aggregate money income from expanding.[4] The argument is that a budget surplus leads 'to money that would otherwise have been expended being absorbed into idle government balances or being used to enable the Government to pay off indebtedness to the banks, so that again expenditure by it and the public together would be reduced to the extent of the surplus. Aggregate money income would, therefore, fall correspondingly.'[5]

A feature shared by all four of these examples is this: each of them could be used as an explicit answer to a request for an explanation, but none of them was in fact so used. The first example, concerning Latham's intention, is taken from a description of the debate over Bruce's proposal to extend the powers of the Commonwealth Parliament. Latham's intention is reported as a piece of information about the Government's plans if it won a referendum. It is not employed as an answer to a question like 'Why did Latham say what he did during the campaign for the referendum?'

The second example is part of an answer to the question 'What were the Government's plans on arbitration?' This question was not one that required an explanatory answer; what was asked for was information about the future, since Bavin refused to make his intentions explicit. In the present example the problem is not that of revealing the purpose of certain baffling actions. It is simply that of learning what purpose will be pursued. The difference between the two problems lies in the difference between the two questions being asked. The question which demands an explanatory answer is 'What *can* his intention be in doing that?' The question which requires an information answer is: 'What is his intention?' The same answer will satisfy both questions, though in

[1] D. Carboch: 'The Fall of the Bruce-Page Government' in *Studies in Australian Politics*, p. 193.
[2] J. Marriott: *Second Chambers*, 1910, pp. 106–7.
[3] *Ibid.*
[4] A. Pigou: *Essays in Economics*, 1952, p. 146.
[5] *Ibid.*, pp. 139–40.

the one case it provides an explanation, and in the other case it does not.

There is a different distinction to be made in the case of the third example. For one query to which the passage would be an explanatory answer is 'What could the intention of the framers of the American Constitution possibly have been in organizing the Senate as they did ?' The question that the passage is thought by its author to answer, in part, is quite different. It is: 'How far has the federal Second Chamber of the United States answered the expectations and fulfilled the intentions of the framers of the Constitution ?'[1] This question does not even require that the intentions of the framers be given in the answer, though in fact this information is supplied by the quoted passage.

The fourth example is taken from an essay whose author does not attempt to employ it to answer any question about purposes or intentions. On the contrary, the author is not concerned with why government officials sometimes budget for a surplus. He says, 'when money wage rates are pushed up', budgeting for a surplus cannot prevent the expansion of aggregate money income 'unless either employment is diminished or the proportion of aggregate money (and real) income accruing to wage-earners is increased'.[2] The government is thus faced with three unpalatable choices in its struggle against an increase in the aggregate money income (inflation): the preventing of money wage rates from rising; the creation of unemployment; the reducing of the money incomes of non-wage-earners. In showing us these results the author supplies the answer to the question 'What are the *unintended* consequences of budgeting for a surplus ?'

What do these examples illustrate then ? If they are accepted as a casual but not misleading sample of the ways in which the words 'intended' and 'intention' are employed by social scientists, the examples illustrate the difficulty of finding cases of explanation put in terms of explicit intentions or purposes. The examples also suggest why this should be so.

Consider the circumstances under which intention-explanations are commonly given. Someone asks a question about an action whose purpose is unknown to him. Or he asks what action another person is planning to take or wishes to bring about. In each of these cases the questioner asks his question because he is ignorant of the connection between a known action and an unknown goal. That is, an intention-explanation is given as the answer to a question about a particular sort of goal-directed behaviour, a question which arises from the questioner's puzzlement as to the purpose or goal of an action, past, present, or future.

When a social scientist produces his report, the situation is rather different. He attempts to give a finished account of what happened: how

[1] Marriott: *op. cit.*, p. 106.
[2] Pigou: *op. cit.*, p. 146.

the agents and actors behaved, how their actions led or did not lead to their goals. Their behaviour is reported as the social scientist views it after he knows what intentions were present in the past or are present now. Since an intention-explanation is required only in the absence of information about a goal, the completed study is not likely to make use of such explanations. They will be present only if the author recapitulates his original puzzlement; and the chief reason for doing this will be stylistic rather than scientific. The report will then be written like a detective story in which all the clues are fairly given and the solution withheld till the last page.

This whole procedure of reversing the order of discovery for the purposes of exposition is aided by the resources of our language. In many cases the verbal phrases we use presuppose that the actions are intentional. We cannot pay our respects unintentionally; nor can we take aim at a target, cultivate a plant, cook a meal, or build a garage, without any intention to do so.[1] Once we give an account of an action by means of such a phrase there is no longer any room for an intention-explanation. All that remains is the explanation of slips and mistakes – unintended results. Thus a detailed account can remove the need for explanations couched in terms of explicit purposes. And this substitution of the former for the latter is what in fact takes place.

In the work of social scientists most of the references to the intentions of people do not take the form of explanations. They arise in somewhat different contexts. One situation is that in which the intentions of the subject are known to the author and he wishes merely to state what they are, e.g. 'Latham in fact intended to set up a new arbitration court. . . .' Another situation in which a reference to intentions may be useful arises when an author tries to compare a person's achievements with his intentions. The disparity between the two may itself require explanation, but this will not be what we have been calling an 'intention-explanation'. On the contrary, it will be an explanation to account for the fact that an intention-explanation does not work in the case at hand. 'Budgeting for a surplus is intended to prevent aggregate money income from expanding', but under certain conditions this intention will not be realized. The question to be answered, then, is 'Why is the intention not achieved?' rather than 'What is the intention?'

All these considerations lead us to say that *explicit* intention-explanations do not play an important part in the social sciences. It should be remembered, however, that in making this claim we are not asserting either of two further claims: (*a*) that in the social sciences the concept of intention is unimportant, and (*b*) that important explanations in terms of intentions cannot be extracted from the writings of social scientists. What we are emphasizing is that the situation in which intentions and purposes are given as *explanatory answers* seldom arises.

[1] See G. Anscombe: *Intention*, 1957, p. 84.

It is not that the literature of social science is filled with circumlocutions for the terms 'intended', 'intention', and 'intentional'. It is rather that each of these three terms fails to find employment for the same reason. When we are told what the agent did we usually assume that he did what he intended to do. If he did not, then we call for an explanation of why he did not do what he intended to do or of why in doing this he did not achieve his objective. If he was successful – as we ordinarily assume – then we simultaneously know what his intention was, that he intended to do what he did, and, of course, that his action was intentional. Thus the questions 'What was his intention?' – 'What was his action intended to do?' – 'Was it an intentional action?' become redundant.

Since to describe or narrate or report what people did is quite commonly to refer to their goals, the writings of social scientists are filled with accounts of goal-intended behaviour, but these accounts do not often contain the terms 'intention' and 'intended'. All that the social scientists need to do is to make clear the nature of the ends toward which certain actions are directed.

The meagreness of the salaries paid to their employees by the socialist party and the trade unions is not due solely to that employer's arrogance and arbitrariness from which the working class is by no means exempt when it becomes an employer. Where the younger organizations are concerned, the trouble may arise simply from lack of means. Moreover, in paying at a low rate there is a practical end in view, the desire being that the employees should serve for love of the cause, and not with an eye to the material advantage attaching to their office. It was hoped that in this way the idealism of the leaders would be artificially fostered, and that it would be possible to prevent them from raising themselves above the social level of their proletarian comrades.[1]

Of this example it cannot be correctly said that the phrases 'the desire being' and 'it was hoped' are synonymous here with 'the intention being' or 'it was intended', and that the author's choice is merely based upon a preference of style. For we can have an intention, or intend to do something – such as foster the idealism of proletarian leaders – without desiring it, having our heart in it, or hoping for its success. We can even hope and pray that we won't try and yet believe, at bottom, that we will. This, too, is intending. Parallel to the cases of hope and desire, we may intend to do something without planning to do it – planning, that is, in the sense of making a plan. We may intend to have the alarm clock repaired tomorrow without making any arrangements for doing so or giving the matter any thought; we simply intend somehow, at some time during the day, to take it to some shop. So that unless we know that an author or speaker will be satisfied with such substitutions as 'intend' for 'plan' we have no license to make them.

After having said this much about the unimportance of explicit

[1] R. Michels: *Political Parties*, 1949, pp. 124–5.

intention-*explanations* in the social sciences, we are still faced with the fact that in one way or another the notions of purpose, goal, and intention, bulk very large in any scientific work concerned with the group behaviour of human beings. Obviously, what is important here is not whether an agent's intentions are *explicitly* mentioned in the explanation of his behaviour. What matters is whether the explanation assumes that his intentions operated so as to produce his behaviour. This assumption is much more common than explicit mention, and is one which is often combined with other assumptions about the agent's abilities and motives to form the complicated set of hypotheses called 'the model of rational behaviour'. Social scientists often speak of using this model to explain something. In such explanations, reliance upon intentions as a factor plays only a part. Nevertheless, if we wish to learn how the notion of intention enters into the accounts given by social scientists of human behaviour, then we must pay attention to both implicit and explicit explanations of a simpler sort, ones that make use of intentions alone. We have, in brief, to answer two questions: (1) What are we referring to when we explain the action of an individual or a group by means of an intention? (2) What is the relationship of this kind of explanation to other kinds?

2

There are two separate queries we may ask about intentions when we demand an explanation. One has the form 'Did he – or they – do it intentionally or unintentionally?' The other query takes the form 'What was his – or their – intention in doing what was in fact done?' The question 'intentional or unintentional?' arises within the social sciences only in rather special circumstances. A large proportion of the activities carried on in any society are intentional ones. They are not done by accident or by mistake, and they are not done involuntarily. It does not follow, of course, that if actions are excluded from the class of un-intentional ones, they are therefore intentional. There are many activities, such as a tendency to over-eat, which are neither intentional nor unintentional. A great host of daily activities, nevertheless, are intentional: withdrawing money from a bank, making bark cloth, calling on the doctor, are usually carried out intentionally. Because this is so, we ask the question 'intentional?' only when we have some reason for doubting whether the action was done wittingly. If our doubt is confirmed we understand only why this particular piece of behaviour is different from what we should have expected it to be. We learn no more than that it was due to a miscalculation, or was the result of an accident, or was somehow beyond the control of the agent, e.g. he did not know what he was doing. Into which of these groups it fits we do not know. Nor do we know anything directly about the agent's intention, if he had one. Thus a government might pursue a deflationary policy in such a way that the numbers of unemployed rose sharply. If we learned that the increase in unemployment was an unintended consequence of its policy – the relevant details of the policy remaining unspecified – then we should not find out either why unemployment rose or what the government's intention was in pursuing its policy.

By itself, then, the answer to the query 'intentional or unintentional?' is of limited interest. It is only when we mention an explicit purpose or intention that we offer anything like an explanation of why an event took place.

The question then is: 'What kind of information are we supplying when we give the intention or purpose with which someone acted?' The ordinary view is that intentional behaviour is a species of goal-seeking behaviour. Is this correct? And if so, how are we to characterize the species?

Clearly, the questions 'What was his intention?' and 'What was his intention in performing that action?' must be distinguished. Not all intentions result in actions. If we are trying to explain a piece of behaviour, as in the social sciences, then the second question is one that we can usefully ask. If, on the other hand, we are interested in explaining the absence of some expected piece of behaviour, we can ask the first question, and perhaps account for the missing action in terms of a frustrated intention or a change of mind. When we explain the absence of an action by means of an agent's unrealized goal we are referring to a belief, a belief held by the agent about his own future action; namely, that he will try to perform the action in question. If it turns out that he did not really believe that he would attempt it then he certainly did not intend to do it. He cannot intend to perform an action which he himself does not believe that he will attempt to do. A person cannot have an aim which he never under any circumstances tries to achieve. In short, it cannot be *his* aim unless he believes that he will try, when possible, to take the steps which seem to him necessary for realizing it.[1] Otherwise, it is a mere wish or hope or desire. It may have been 'clear that Latham in fact intended to set up a new arbitration court' but his intention remained unfulfilled. If we were to refer to it as explaining why Bruce said what he did during the debate in the 1926 Referendum, we should be referring to a belief of Latham's about what he would try to do with respect to an arbitration court if the government won the referendum. If Latham had held no such belief then he would have had no such intention. In indicating that he held this intention, either he or someone else would have misled the public. Thus the question 'What was Latham's intention?' asked after the referendum, amounts to asking

[1] This point is made by S. Hampshire and H. Hart in 'Decision, Intention and Certainty' in *Mind*, Vol. LXVII, No. 265, January 1958, p. 11.

'What did Latham believe that he would try to do? What goal did he believe himself to have?'

Goal-directed behaviour comprises a very large category. It consists in all behaviour which occurs either as a means to some further goal or for its own sake. That an agent snaps his fingers because he enjoys producing a sudden noise by finger-snapping is both intentional and goal-directed, though it is not a means to any further end. Of course there is much behaviour that is not goal-directed even in this broad sense. Some involuntary, inadvertent, casual, random, automatic, and uncontrolled behaviour is not goal-directed. Some dreams and slips of the tongue, some cries of pain, a fault of performance in the exhibition of a skill, as in a fall from a circus trapeze – all these are neither 'done for their own sake' nor as a means to some further goal.

Yet while all intentional behaviour is goal-directed, the converse clearly does not hold. Instinctive behaviour such as the sucking movements displayed by infants is goal-directed without being intentional. Even adults are unconscious of at least some of the goals toward which their behaviour is directed. Of course it should be added that simple unawareness of an act is not sufficient to establish lack of intention. Many people are unaware while doing so that they brush their teeth with a vertical motion. Some of them, if asked, would answer that it is, nevertheless, an intentional motion because it is the one which they were originally taught, and are now satisfied to achieve. The fact that it is not under constant surveillance or that the process can be gone through without the performer being aware of it is neither here nor there. If he cannot tell or show us what he was trying to accomplish – if at no stage is he aware of the goal toward which his behaviour is directed – then, and only then, is his behaviour goal-directed but unintentional. In other words, the agent's unawareness of any given action does not prevent it from being an intentional one, any more than his awareness of the action makes it intentional.

Intentional *behaviour*, it has been argued, is a species of goal-seeking behaviour. It is a species characterized by the following features: (1) the agent must have known what his goal (or aim or purpose) was; (2) the agent must have believed in a connection between his goal and some action he took to be a means of arriving at it. The agent must have known or believed these things in the sense that he could display his knowledge and beliefs, either verbally or by other behaviour. (3) In satisfying the first condition a person must also have believed that he would try to achieve his purpose when possible.

Thus the kind of information which we supply in stating that an act performed by some human agent was an intentional one is rather complex. Knowledge of this sort can be genuinely explanatory when the question which it answers arises from a background of a certain kind. The questioner must be familiar with the fact that people are able to knowingly pursue their ends. He must know that they can and will adopt those means which seem appropriate to them. His demand for an explanation must take place in this setting, so that what he wishes to find out will be merely how a given act fits into a means-to-end pattern, a pattern with which he is well acquainted. If what he wishes to know is not the intention of an act, but *why* the agent had that particular intention or goal, he will be asking for a different method of explanation. Or if it comes as a shock to him that people often display intentional behaviour, then being told the intention of an action will not be an explanation of it for him. The explanatory force of learning the agent's intention depends upon the auditor's familiarity with intentional behaviour; the explanation must solve a puzzle, and in order for the puzzle to exist there must be a 'previous stock of knowledge and beliefs' with which the perplexing event is at variance. It is this stock which we must keep in mind when we ask the question 'Do intention-explanations really explain?'

3

Intention statements can be singular as in 'If the Canadian Parliament adopts both the principle of Crown nomination and the federal principle, it will do so with the intention of functioning efficiently.' They can be general as in 'If all the parliaments in the western hemisphere adopt . . .' or universal as in 'If any parliament ever adopts. . . .' They can provide us either with the necessary conditions of an action or with its sufficient conditions, or with both of these, or with neither. In some countries if the central bank raises its discount rate to member banks with the intention of checking their loans to small borrowers, this intentional action is a sufficient condition for a decrease in the volume of such loans. Under certain economic systems it is both a necessary and sufficient condition of increased investment in a given industry that the members of a planning board have intended that this should happen. But examples like 'Nupe men intend that childless wives shall work' and 'The twirling of her handbag by the London prostitute is intended to be an announcement of her sexual availability', can easily be interpreted as failing to provide us with either necessary or sufficient conditions. The London prostitute may twirl her handbag from habit even when she is engaged, so that it may not be a sufficient condition of her availability; and she may be available even when her handbag is motionless, so that its twirling cannot be a necessary condition. Ordinarily, these statements would be taken, as would most intention statements, to supply neither sufficient nor necessary conditions, but only to give one of a set of conditions which would be jointly sufficient.

It has already been argued that a singular intention or purpose statement of the form 'He did A because he intended to achieve B' entails that the agent believed in a connection between his action and his goal. The converse does not hold, of course, because even with such a belief – and desire for the goal as well – the agent may still not be able to bring himself to act.

The situation in the case of universal intention statements is similar in both respects. 'Whenever agents of such-and-such type perform acts of kind A, they intend to achieve results of kind B' entails 'Whenever agents of such-and-such type perform acts of kind A with the intention of achieving results of kind B, they believe that A is a means to B.' This latter statement-form is tautologically true, for its denial would be self-contradictory. The first form of statement is entailed by the second, but not by any form of statement which is non-intentional, that is, by any form of statement which does *not* ascribe to a relevant agent the following features: (*a*) knowledge of his goal, (*b*) knowledge of the connection between his goal and the means employed, (*c*) the belief that the agent himself would attempt to achieve his goal when possible. A law statement about human beings, for example, that does not mention their beliefs or knowledge concerning their intended actions can hardly entail by itself a law statement that does. There is nothing odd about this, however. What would be odd would be the failure to recognize that statements of the form 'Whenever the Xs of such-and-such type do A they intend to achieve B' are law statements which relate the actions of agents to their purposes.

Now suppose we try to give an intention-explanation of the rule in some societies that a man may not deflorate his own wife. We have to say something like 'The agent believes that the prohibition will preserve him from her revenge', which is Abraham's suggestion,[1] or 'Someone in the society once had the belief and the rule developed from his belief'. In some way it became entrenched as a custom now followed by men who do not have the belief or who have some other belief about the reasons for the rule. But obviously, not all the men following the custom need possess any belief connected with it. Nor need the custom have originated as the result of any belief of this kind. The custom may have been borrowed from other groups, or developed because of some priest's lust, or as a neighbourly gesture, or for many other reasons. The discovery of its origin is an historical problem, although the discovery of the custom's effects and causes is also a scientific one. Of the alternatives available for the attempt to give an intention-explanation it may be that none is satisfactory. For this reason intention-explanations of customs or customary behaviour are often transformed into function explanations, and thence into law explanations.

Nevertheless, intention-explanations are used in the social sciences, as elsewhere, to explain the behaviour of individuals, classes or groups.

[1] K. Abraham: 'Manifestations of the Female Castration Complex' in *Selected Papers*, 1942, pp. 339–40.

To explain why the Labour Government in Britain passed the Steel Nationalization Bill of 1950, we may point out that the Government's supporters in Parliament believed in a connection between their action and the desired nationalization of the steel industry. We may be able to say correctly that if any M.P. voted for the Bill it was because he wanted to have the steel industry nationalized. Or again, we may not be able to make this claim, for some M.P.s may have been forced by party policy into supporting the Bill against their own wishes. Still, the difficulties of intention-explanations in such cases are at a minimum. Anyone who knowingly votes for a Bill and believes that its passage depends, in part, upon his favourable vote, intends the Bill to pass. He may not believe that the measure will attain its objective; he may not even want it to or intend that it shall, but these are different problems and should be distinguished from that of whether the M.P. intends the Bill to pass.

The difficulties of intention-explanations are increased when they are employed in connection with such complicated groups as nations. To explain the actions instituted by national governments in terms of intentions is usually an inadequate way of referring to the goals of various officials. Quite often no public information is available as to whose intentions are the relevant ones. And since the actions are undertaken in the name of the country, we say, either for convenience or out of ignorance, that nations have intentions, while admitting that only individuals, strictly speaking, can have them. Hence, explanation of group and class behaviour by means of group intentions is often vague, and thus misleading. 'One of the intentions behind the founding of the British Home Guard was to frighten the Americans into releasing more dollars for British defence' does not tell us whose intention is at issue. The statement does not even tell us which Americans and how many of them are to be frightened. Sometimes such information is supplied by the context and sometimes it is not.

Of course there are occasions when we can correctly speak of all the members of a group as having the same purpose. The members of a lynching mob may all have the same purpose or intention, and so may those of a concert audience. In each case we may explain the presence of the people by referring to their intention, e.g. listening to music or watching someone being killed. There need be nothing vague about the intentions of all the members of each group; but we cannot know this merely by being told, for example, that the group as a whole intended to listen to music.

The relation between intention statements and function (causal effect) statements is that of logical independence. Consider the two statements, 'The primary function of alcohol is the reduction of anxiety' and 'Most people who habitually drink alcoholic beverages do so with the intention of reducing their feelings of anxiety'. The truth of the one statement does not entail the truth of the other. This holds of intention and function statements generally, so that care must be taken in producing intention-explanations on the basis of function-explanations or vice versa. Many alcohol drinkers do not believe in a connection between their drinking and the goal attributed to them, that is, the reduction of their anxiety, even when, in fact, their feelings of anxiety are reduced by drinking. Nor does it follow from the fact that alcohol reduces anxiety that anyone ever drinks with this intention. Conversely, the fact that some people may drink with this intention does not ensure that alcohol ever reduces anxiety, though their intentional drinking may be based upon the false belief that it does.

4

It can now be seen how explanation *schemas* of intention statements can be constructed and what part they play in the social sciences. Suppose we have the schema:

(1) 'If any member of a society which has features A, B, and C, gives a potlatch, then he does it with the intention of establishing his rank.'

(2) 'X, a Tlingit Indian, is a member of such a society and has given a potlatch.'

(3) 'X's intention in giving a potlatch was to establish his rank.'

There is nothing the matter with a schema of this kind; in fact, many anthropologists and sociologists are engaged in trying to formulate and test universal statements of the kind illustrated by (1). But the usefulness of the schema is limited. Earlier in this chapter it was argued that universal intention statements such as (1) cannot be entailed by non-intention statements alone. This seems clear enough in the case of 'If any Northwest Coast Indian gives a potlatch ceremony, then it is with the intention of establishing his rank'. What statement of the non-intention sort could entail it? Certainly not a statement like 'If any Northwest Coast Indian gives a potlatch, then he establishes his rank'. For, as we know, this does not entail the statement about the agent's belief which is entailed by the intention statement. Even in conjunction with other statements this non-intention statement cannot perform the task. For assume as a further statement that the agent believes his potlatch to be the only sufficient means of establishing his rank. The intention statement will yet not be entailed unless the phrase 'gives a potlatch' means 'gives a potlatch intending to establish his rank'. If it does not, then we have no guarantee that the potlatch is given with the required intention.

There is another point to be emphasized here. One intention statement by itself cannot entail another such statement when the goals or purposes mentioned in them are different. The reason for this is both simple and familiar. A statement like 'He intended climbing to the top of that building from the ground' contains the clause 'climbing to the top of that building from the ground', and in many statements this clause would entail the clause 'being higher than before'. Thus the statement 'He climbed to the top of that building' would usually be taken to entail 'He was higher than before'. In the case of the intention statement, however, it does not follow from the agent's intending the first goal that he intended the second. He may be ignorant of the entailment between them, although this is hardly possible in the present example. We have claimed that it is a necessary condition for an intention statement that the agent believe in the means-end connection between his action and his goal. But he may be unaware of what this belief entails. He may have as his intended goal something whose description entails another description about a different state of affairs. Yet he may have only the first as his aim. This is the distinction between believing something and being committed by logic to believing something. It parallels that between knowing something and being committed to maintaining something which logically follows from what we know. For it is painfully easy to believe or know something while being ignorant of what else we are thereby committed to believing or maintaining to be true.

In summary, then, these properties of intention statements are: (1) the statements which they entail by themselves are limited to belief statements about goals and to statements of belief and knowledge about the means to these goals, (2) intention statements cannot be logically derived from non-intention statements alone, (3) one intention statement by itself can entail another only when they both mention or refer to the same goal. The results of these properties are that explanation schemas are almost restricted in their employment to situations in which a universal intention statement entails a less general one, that is, to examples like 'If any member of a society which has features A, B, and C, gives a potlatch . . .' and 'X is such a person', then 'X's intention was . . .'. What are called 'intention-explanations' in the social sciences are either intention statements, or schemas of this simple type. The limitations on their use are obvious. To explain, by their means, is to state what the agent is knowingly trying to do or to obtain. Sometimes we may be able to infer what this is from knowing that all agents of a certain kind in certain circumstances have such-and-such intended goals. However, if we ask why this *class* of agents has these particular goals, e.g. potlatch givers intending to establish their social rank, we shall have to reply by referring to one or both of two kinds of statements: (*a*) statements, either general or universal, identifying possessors of one sort of intended goal with possessors of another and further sort of goal to which the first is a means, e.g. 'All people who intend to establish their social rank by means of potlatch ceremonies also intend to use their acquired rank as a means to obtaining political power', (*b*) statements, either general or universal, referring to the desires, wants, dispositions, and relevant behaviour of certain groups of certain classes of agents, e.g. 'In contemporary America many adult men who intend to acquire as much wealth as they possibly can, do so because as children they had to compete with their fathers for the love of their mothers'. Statements of this kind are then expanded into explanations in terms of needs, drives, and inclinations. As explanations they may incorporate such notions as 'the goals of the organism' and 'drives toward tensionless states', but the ends referred to are not *intended* goals; the organism does not knowingly try to achieve them. For this reason, while these statements explain intentional behaviour they are not themselves intention statements or explanations; they relate the latter to a wider range of the organism's behaviour.

The limits on the usefulness of intention-explanations are also made clear when we ask what the evidence is for a given intention statement. What, for example, is the evidence that the present political leaders of the Soviet Union intend to keep Germany politically divided? That they have increased the fortifications on the frontier, have integrated the trade of Eastern Germany with that of Eastern Europe, have placed in power leaders who are opposed to the political views of most West Germans, that it is their announced intention to set up rocket stations along the border, etc. Now some of these statements will be about intentions, as the last one is, but some of them will not. And in any case, if we continue to ask the question 'What is the evidence for this?' of every intention statement, we shall soon be thrown back upon reports of occurrences, and these reports will not consist in statements about intended goals. They will consist in statements like 'By accident a secret Soviet dispatch came into the possession of the British authorities in West Germany' or 'The French Foreign Minister has taken an intense dislike to the American representative'. Not only does the truth of intention statements depend, in this sense, upon the truth of occurrence and observation statements, it depends, also, upon the truth of those law-like statements which are used as evidence, either in direct support of the intention statement, or indirectly by their support of the observation statements. For example, if part of the evidence for the claim that the French Foreign Minister dislikes the American representative is that the Minister has refused to return a purely social call, then this piece of evidence may be supported by an appeal to a law-like statement of the type 'People in ordinary diplomatic negotiations do not neglect diplomatic courtesies except for compelling personal reasons'.

These restrictions on the use of both intention statements and intention-explanations are severe. An obvious conclusion to be drawn from their existence is that intention-explanations are narrow in their scope of application, however commonly they can be extracted from the writings of social scientists. But this view might seem to lead to one of two curious results: either that a widely held belief about the important part played by these explanations in the social sciences is mistaken, or that the explanations of social scientists are more restricted in type than we have so far supposed them to be. Thus it has been said that 'explanations in social science consist largely in giving the reasons for actions by showing the end towards which they are consciously directed', e.g. taking a wife, increasing the population. The same author has gone on to say 'The social scientist is also particularly concerned with making generalizations about the unintended consequences of such rational actions – e.g. if people aim at raising the level of education in a community, the suicide rate also goes up'.[1] If these two statements are to be interpreted as claiming that the social scientist is chiefly interested in explanations of these two sorts, then this view, taken together with our previous conclusion about the narrow scope of application possessed by one of these types of explanation, would entail that social explanations leave off where many people think that they should begin. The alternative claim is that explanations in social science consist in more than these two types, and that intention-explanations, whether implicit or explicit, do not have the crucial role ascribed to them.

Now it seems clear that it is the latter claim which is correct. Intention-explanations have a place in social science, but it is not true to say that they are the largest part of explanations in the social sciences. The bulk of explanations in social science do not make use of conscious goals. This is quickly seen when we recall some of our previous examples: the European custom of men wearing their hair short; the consumption of alcoholic beverages; the increase of illegitimate conceptions in Finland during the summer months; the differences in 'social participation' scores amongst the residents of various cities; the reduction of the balance of trade by a fall in the exchange rate; the presence of incest taboo in all known societies; the use by the Ngoni of a generation system of kinship nomenclature. Of none of these can it be said that its explanation has been, or in the future is likely to be, put in terms of conscious goals. 'European men', a sociologist would say, 'do not wear their hair short because they have some goal in mind; they need not even aim to conform to custom. They have short hair because in their societies all men have short hair and because no alternative is ever presented.' In other words, actions are not largely explained in the social sciences 'by showing the end towards which they are consciously directed'. This view is plausible only of the single actions of individual persons. Once we consider the actions of groups it becomes much less plausible for reasons already touched upon, e.g. there is the difficulty of showing that *all* members of a group consciously had the aim in question or had some other aim which led them to the action, or had any aim at

---

[1] Both quotations and the examples are from R. Peters' essay 'Motives and Motivation', *Philosophy*, Vol. XXXI, No. 117, April 1956, pp. 126–7.

all. Furthermore, in the social sciences, as in other sciences, individual actions – those of a given person – are usually interesting only as members of a class of actions. It is the class of actions which is to be explained, not merely the actions of one of the class members. Questions take the form 'Why did the Dyaks practise head-hunting?' or 'Why are the British called "pommies" in Australia?' This has the result of making intention or goal explanations considerably less useful than some other kinds, and certainly less applicable than when only individuals are concerned.

We can also remind ourselves that much explanation in social science does not explain *actions*. It deals with differences between classes of actions, or with increases in the members of a class of actions, or with rates of increase and comparative rates. Social scientists ask 'Why has the consumption of heroin risen in the United States during the last decade, when it has not in Britain?' or 'Why did economic activity in the United States remain low for the decade 1929–39?' Questions like these, as well as those like 'Why do illegitimate conceptions increase during the Finnish summer?' and 'Why do "social participation" scores differ amongst the residents of various cities?' are cases in point. The answers to them are not usually given in terms of changed intentions or of different goals. They may be, of course. When they are, it is a matter of pressing importance to answer the questions 'Why did their intentions or goals change? What changes in the social environment are causally correlated with the change of goals?' This interest in the causal relationship between *changes* in two sets of factors is quite different from an interest in explaining the relation between two sets of actions by means of the consciously goal-seeking behaviour which they illustrate. An explanation may tell us why a group of people have certain intentions (destruction of the gaol in which a prisoner is held), but this does not make the explanation one of the intention sort. Similarly, an explanatory account of why changes in one set of intentions effect changes in another set need not be – and ordinarily is not – an intention explanation.

It is true that the social scientist is 'particularly concerned with making generalizations about the unintended consequences of such rational actions' as raising the educational level, e.g. an increase in the suicide rate. But in explaining this increase by its connection with an increase in the educational level we are not explaining it by reference to intentions. Even if the rise in the level of education were not intentional, the connection with the suicide rate might exist. For the explanation would take either of two forms: a generalization to the effect that whenever the educational level was intentionally increased the suicide rate went up; or that whenever the educational level was unintentionally raised, the suicide rate increased. In neither of these cases would the event or class of events to be explained be part of an intentional means-to-end series. At best the rise in education, whether intentional or not, would be causally correlated with a rise in the suicide rate. We should not be explaining the latter rise by saying that it was an agent's goal or that it was an agent's means to a goal.

The place of intention-explanations in the social sciences is a modest one, even though our social life is composed to a large extent of intentional activities. It is often of interest to the social investigator to learn what the intentions of a person or group of persons are, but this is frequently a matter of acquiring information and not of receiving an explanation. In those instances where an explanation is required, the questions 'What are they trying to do?' or 'What was their intention in doing that?' are usually preludes to other questions like 'Why do the people of Group A have *that* goal whereas the people of Group B have *this* goal?' In seeking the answers to such questions, the investigator is led beyond the scope of intention-explanations. That is, in being forced to explain the presence of different goals in different societies, the investigator is also forced to resort to different methods of explanation. The ways in which these transitions take place will become apparent as we continue with our discussion of the different methods.

VII

DISPOSITIONS

1

WE have been arguing that intention-explanations play no very great part in the social sciences, however important the role of such explanations is in daily life or history or fiction. Now it may be feared that this conclusion will make it impossible for us to do justice to the way in which an appeal to dispositions is relied upon in the explanation of human actions. For it is a popular view that human beings in societies are rule-conforming creatures, and that the standard explanation of a piece of social behaviour is not only to show what the agent's intention was but to indicate, as well, how his goal and the means to it were determined by his disposition to conform to the conventions of his society. It may be thought, therefore, that if it is true that social scientists do not employ intention-explanations, it will also be true that they do not employ disposition-explanations. These, it may be said, are just different forms of what is really the same form of explanation. Thus Richard Peters writes:

The paradigm case of a human action is when something is done in order to bring about an end. So the usual way of explaining an action is to describe it as an action of a certain sort by indicating the end which Jones had in mind. . . . If we ask why Jones walked across the road, the obvious answer will be something like 'to buy tobacco'. Instead of saying this we could say 'because he wanted some tobacco'. This is, logically speaking, another way of giving the same sort of answer; for the answer 'to buy some tobacco' is only an explanation because we assume in Jones some sort of directive disposition – a general tendency to obtain and use tobacco.[1]

Clearly, there are a number of debatable points here. It is difficult, first of all, to know what weight to give to the assertion that the paradigm case of a human action is doing something in order to bring about an end. There is a very large class of human actions of which this is true But there are other sorts of human actions as well: unintentional actions,

---

[1] *The Concept of Motivation*, 1958, p. 4.

such as offending someone unwittingly, habitual actions like sleeping only on the left side, automatic actions like turning the car wheels in the wrong direction in a skid, expressive actions such as scowling or gesturing in conversation, and goal-directed actions which are not intentional, e.g. guilt projection. And unless actions done for their own sake (skipping on the green) are to be classified as goal-directed – a view not held by Peters – then these actions, too, must be added to the long list of those human actions for which his paradigm case is no paradigm. If, of course, 'actions' is *simply defined* as 'goal-directed acts', then all the cases we have mentioned are automatically excluded. But thus to define it would be incompatible with speaking of 'the paradigm case of a human action'.

Secondly, to say that Jones walked across the road in order to buy some tobacco may or may not be to say that he did it because he *wanted* some tobacco. He may *hate* tobacco and not have wanted to buy it. He may have bought it, nevertheless, because he believed that he ought to take some to his elderly father. Hence, it does not follow that 'the answer "to buy some tobacco" is only an explanation because we assume in Jones some sort of directive disposition – a general tendency to obtain and use tobacco'. The answer is an explanation – when it is – merely because it states the goal to which crossing the street was a means. If Jones had never smoked or chewed tobacco the answer might still provide an explanation. If stating a goal never supplied an explanation unless the behaviour in question was an exercise of a general tendency, then tendencies could never be acquired and we could not give an explanation by referring to goals which were sought only once by a particular person. Since tendencies are learned and people do seek some goals (an ocean voyage, for example) only once in a lifetime, it is not a necessary condition of an intention–explanation that the intention be the exercise of a disposition.

Thirdly, it is not correct to say, as Peters does immediately following the passage just quoted, that 'to buy tobacco' is 'an explanation not simply because Jones envisaged walking across the street as a means to getting the tobacco but because it really is a means to getting it'.[1] An intention-explanation does not require that the agent be correct in his choice of means to an end. It only requires that he believe them to be feasible. Jones's beliefs are what count here because they determine his choice of means. If his beliefs are mistaken and he chooses unsuitable means to a goal, as snake dancers do in their efforts to produce rain, even so, his actions, like those of the snake dancers, are still explained by showing what they were aiming at.

The view which we have been criticizing attempts to make a close connection between intention-explanations, on the one hand, and dis-

[1] *Ibid.*

positions on the other. The view consists, in part, of three claims which we have denied: (1) that the paradigm case of a human action is doing something in order to bring about an end; and thus that the usual way of explaining an action is to indicate the agent's intended goal, (2) that giving the agent's intended goal serves to explain only because his goal seeking is an exercise of a directive disposition, (3) that the means used by the agent must be effective if the intention-explanation which explains their presence is to be successful. If these claims are mistaken, however, what *is* the relationship between explaining by means of intentions and explaining by means of dispositions?

Now we must not confuse dispositions with capabilities. A disposition is a tendency to behave in certain ways. Some people tend to avoid high places, small rooms, dishonest business operations, concerts, and dentists They tend to seek out buxom women, gambling houses, jazz records, and trout streams. Their tendencies may be instinctive or habitual, obsessive or the result of acting upon principle. However we classify tendencies, an explanation in terms of a tendency or disposition works by subsuming the behaviour in question under the tendency. What we can explain by the use of a disposition-explanation are these: a particular act (Mary refusing to go to the dentist today); a particular kind of act (Mary always refusing to go to the dentist); a particular set of acts (John examining his fishing tackle, buying new waders, telephoning a friend, in order to go fishing tomorrow); and a tendency of a certain kind (John always performing these acts before his fishing trips). That is, we can explain both particular acts and particular tendencies. Both can be brought within the scope of a disposition-explanation; not only are specific acts taken to be instances of a disposition, but a tendency to perform a number of actions of a particular sort may itself be taken as an instance of a more complex disposition. The answer to the question 'Why did Mary refuse to go to the dentist today?' may be 'She tends to avoid placing herself in the care of medical men'. If someone then asks 'Why does she tend to avoid that?' the reply may still be given in the form: 'She tends to avoid placing herself in a position subordinate to any male authority figure.' Either answer, of course, can serve to answer the original question – 'Why did Mary refuse to go to the dentist today?' – but only the second answer can be appropriate for answering both questions, one concerning a particular action and the other a particular tendency.

Dispositions (or tendencies) are one kind of dispositional property. The other kind is capabilities. In people these take the form of abilities, skills, and competencies. Many people are able to read Chinese newspapers, write out medical prescriptions, drive tractors, and win consistently at poker. Having these abilities they may or may not exercise them during any given period of time. The commonest evidence for the existence of the ability is its exercise at some time, but there are people who have abilities of which they themselves are ignorant, and many people never display those abilities which tests reveal them to have. An obvious difference, then, between a tendency and a capability is that a person can possess the latter while having no tendency to display it. Some people who can easily solve mathematical puzzles have no tendency to spend time on them. In knowing that someone has a tendency to behave in a certain manner we know that he has the ability to behave in that way. For if he constantly tries to do something and does not succeed, he has a tendency to try to do it, but not a tendency to do it. In contrast, if we know that a person has a particular ability we still do not know whether or not he has a tendency to exercise it.

When we use a disposition-explanation to account for people's behaviour we are explicitly referring to their tendencies and implicitly referring to their related abilities. 'Mary tends to avoid placing herself in the care of medical men' may be a disposition-explanation of why she avoided going to the dentist or has refused to go tomorrow. But we cannot use an ability-explanation in the same way. We cannot explain why she avoided going yesterday by supplying only the information that she has the ability to avoid placing herself in the care of medical men. This information will be explanatory only if taken together with certain assumptions, such as that Mary tends to avoid placing herself in these situations. To make this assumption will be to introduce the tendency statement that makes the presence of the ability statement unnecessary. And, in general, any assumption that is made will have to explain why, having the ability, Mary exercised it. The assumption can, of course, simply be that people having the ability in question will exercise it. In all cases, however, the result will be that the ability statement is either dispensable or fills the role of a statement which brings the instance at hand within the scope of the assumption. This is quite different from the task performed by a disposition statement when it is used as an explanation.

We have already noticed that intentional actions need not be the exercises of dispositions. To this we can now add that many exercises of dispositions are not intentional actions. Unlearned reflexive responses, many habitual acts, neurotic symptoms: these are only a few instances of non-intentional behaviour which is nevertheless an exercise of a disposition. Some dispositional actions are intentional, of course. A department head who tends to avoid delegating his authority may do so intentionally, just as a conservative government which tends through the years to pursue a 'tight money' policy does it intentionally. It follows that some intentional actions are also disposition exercises. Therefore, some actions may be given either an intention-explanation or a disposition-explanation. Suppose we ask the question 'Why did the men at Oraibi pueblo perform that dance today?' The answer may be given in terms of their goal – 'To have the rains come soon.' Or it may be given

78

in terms of a tendency: 'They tend to perform that dance whenever their goal is to have the rains come soon.' What is the relevant difference between these two answers? Clearly, that the tendency statement provides us not only with the same information about the goal as does the intention statement, but, in addition, with the information that goal seeking by these means today is a member of a series of similar events. Knowing that today's dance is a display of this tendency we also know the present goal. The use of the words 'they tend' presupposes that today's dance is not the first of this series or at least of this type of series, and that it is not expected that today's dance will be the last one ever given.

Yet this example should not lead us to believe that *all* actions which may be explained either as intentional or as dispositional may also be accounted for in such a way that knowing a tendency answer we must also know the appropriate answer in terms of intentions. Some tendency answers do not tell us which of several goals is the relevant one. The statement 'They tend to perform that dance whenever their chief goal is to have the gods help them soon' does not tell us what may well be true – that the chief goal of the dancers today was to have the gods *send rain soon*. In knowing that a rather general tendency is present we may not know which specific goal is being sought in any given exercise of that tendency. It is only when the disposition statement is specific enough to eliminate the possibility of alternative goals that it can give the same information about the same goal that the intention statement gives. The effect of this is to reduce the number of occasions when the former kind of explanation can substitute for the latter, substitute in the sense that knowing the one we thereby know the other.

The connections, then, between intention and disposition-explanations are not far reaching. Only some intentional actions are also displays of tendencies, and of these tendencies only those specific enough to have but one kind of instance can eliminate the need for ever giving both sorts of explanation of a particular action. The class of intentional actions merely overlaps that of disposition exercises. The corresponding methods of explanation bear the same overlapping relation. But whereas from some disposition-explanations we can derive intention-explanations, the converse does not hold. A man can have as his intention the producing of a certain tendency, e.g. the disposition in his dog to come when called. The man's training activity cannot be explained, nevertheless, as a display of his dog's disposition to come when called. From a knowledge of the man's intention (when it is given as an explanation of his actions), we do not thereby have knowledge of some tendency of which his goal seeking is an exercise. The two methods are partially independent even, as we shall see, in the case of dispositional motives and intentions, however closely related motive-explanations and intention-explanations are often correctly thought to be.

2

Dispositions may be classified into a number of types, the classification being a rough and ready one based upon the complexity and sophistication of the behaviour displayed. Unlearned reflexes like the infant 'startle response' to loud sounds are the simplest of these types, and also the least useful in explaining the social acts of human beings. For social behaviour is learned in societies. The liking which many Italians show for 'social noise', and the dislike for it shown by many Englishmen, cannot be adequately explained by an appeal to a difference in the startle responses of Italian and English babies, since there is no such difference. Explanation in terms of unlearned reflexes or innate tendencies or instincts falls outside the work of the social scientist. Human beings might have been so constituted that much of their social activity was as instinctive as that of the termites, and under those conditions the present distinctions between the social and biological sciences would not have their present importance. But as long as social activity does not consist of unlearned patterns of responses, the need to use the latter to explain the former will be slight indeed.

A second type of disposition is habit and habitual action. The range of human behaviour which can become habitual is very great. Head scratching can be a habit and so can generosity; daydreaming may be habitual as well as punctuality. Habits are stereotyped ways of behaving – dispositions to act or think in fixed fashions – but they may or may not be goal-directed. A woman who has developed the habit of fingering the strands of her hair may be unconscious of doing so, and her action may have no goal. It may simply be a sign of her nervous tension; but, equally, it may have an unconcious goal.

A habitual *act* cannot be either deliberate or premeditated. For a deliberate (or premeditated) act is one that an agent chooses to perform. If he does not understand at the time that he has alternatives before him from which he can choose the act cannot be deliberate. An act done from habit, on the other hand, is not one whose performance presents the agent with alternatives. True, he may be able on any given occasion to stop before taking a cigarette and ask himself whether he really wishes to smoke it. And provided that he does not always decide in favour of smoking – so that the ritual of asking does not merely become part of the habit – we should say that he chose to smoke on that occasion. But then he would not have smoked merely from habit. He would be interrupting his habit and perhaps replacing it with another habit, that of considering each time whether or not he wished to smoke. Habitual acts are just those which relieve us of the need to choose. Even while performing them we may be well aware that we have not chosen to do them; we simply find ourselves displaying them.

Now it is sometimes protested that to interpret such an action as counting change as a habitual one is not to explain it. And this complaint may be generalized: it may be said that in accounting for a particular act by asserting that it is an instance of a tendency or disposition we are not really explaining the act. We are merely relating it to other acts of the same kind; they are all equally mysterious. The tendency itself requires explanation as much as its instance does, and neither of them can be explained by means of subsumption under a disposition.

This protest is not well founded. It gains much of its initial plausibility from neglect of the circumstances under which an answer in terms of a habit-tendency can serve as an explanation. Suppose that Bob carefully counts the money placed in his hand by a friend who is giving him a loan. The friend is inclined to take offence at this, but being puzzled as well, decides to ask Bob's sister why he carefully counted the six five-pound notes. She tells him that Bob used to work as a bank teller and that he has the habit of counting all the money received by him. This 'explanation' removes both the puzzlement and the offence. It removes them because there were a number of possible reasons why Bob counted the money, one of these being that he somehow distrusted the friend who was doing him a favour. Since in their social group it is not customary to show suspicion of the favours of a friend, the oddity of Bob's act is dispelled when his friend learns that the act was not performed from suspicion, that it was not done from choice at all. It was merely habitual, a kind of mechanical routine not appropriate to the situation. He also learns that Bob did not count the notes for any queerer reason: he was not suddenly developing neurotic symptoms and he was not merely displaying a muscular disorder. Of course the explanation supplied may prove not to be a good reason. Someone may be able to show that his case is different from the ordinary ones of habit persistence and that his act is to be explained as a compulsive one. Then it is the habit which is a neurotic symptom, not merely the act in question, for a compulsion consists in a tendency to perform apparently senseless acts. Hence, a psychological explanation would not ordinarily compete with the habit-explanation of this act. To say that the act is not explained by this latter means is to make one or both of two claims: that the act is odd and not properly explicable as the exercise of an ordinary habit; that the habit is odd and itself needs explaining. But, obviously, neither of these claims (nor both of them together) shows that a habit-explanation is not a genuine one. They merely show that a habit-explanation is not always adequate. They do not show that it is never so. Much the same can be said of the more general objection that no tendency-explanation really explains. This will become apparent as we discuss the other sorts of tendencies to which we appeal in explanations.

When we now ask, as we must, what sort of role in the explanations offered by social scientists is played by references to habits, our answer will have to begin with a distinction between habit and custom. Quite often customs are called 'social habits,' but this phrase is as likely to mislead a listener as to enlighten him. We sometimes speak of the customs of one person: 'It is', we say, 'his custom to go horseback riding each day before breakfast.' A custom of this kind is a habit socially displayed. When the thought or act is a private one we replace the word 'custom' with the word 'habit'. More important is the fact that social scientists do not commonly speak of the habits of a community, but of its customs. They do so because there are significant differences between the habits of an individual person and the customs of a group. A social custom cannot be deliberately established by a person. Nor can he change or extinguish it unless other people do what he wishes them to do. But a man can decide to form the habit of smoking a cigar after dinner and establish it successfully. He can also change his habits or even drop some of them. And however difficult this may be, his success does not depend upon other people doing what he is doing. A social custom is maintained by the threat of group disapproval when it is violated, whereas a private habit such as tooth brushing or day dreaming is not. Again, customs are recognized by the members of a group to apply to certain classes of people: it is men who are supposed to go hunting and women who are to cultivate the gardens, cross cousins who are to marry, and certain in-laws who are to avoid each other. The practice of a habit, on the other hand, is open to anyone who is able to perform it: anyone with a voice can learn to clear his throat after each utterance, and anyone with a normal sense of balance can learn to stand on one leg as the Dinkas do. Finally, some customs are performed as habits by some people, while other customs are not. Many men habitually follow the custom of stepping aside for women at doorways, though few men follow the custom of getting married as a habit. Examples such as these make it clear that since customs may or may not be followed as a matter of habit, it is not correct to say that customs are merely social habits, anymore than it is to claim that habits are only private customs.

Once we distinguish habits from customs, the question with which we are concerned – 'What role do habit-explanations play in the social sciences?' becomes much simpler to answer. For the answer is that they do very little work for social scientists; and it is easy to understand why this is so. One reason is that explanations in terms of habits are used largely to account for particular acts rather than particular habit-tendencies. If we ask 'Why is that Dinka woman standing on one leg in what looks to be an uncomfortable position?' we can be told that since the position is an habitual one amongst the Dinka, it is undoubtedly a habit of hers. If we then reply, 'Granted that many women have this habit, why does *this* one happen to have it?' we shall usually be taken as requesting not a habit-explanation but an historical account of the habit's origin and development in the life of this particular woman. Or instead of this we may reply, 'Yes, but why do so many people here have this habit?' A possible (though not plausible) reply is a habit-explanation of a more general kind: 'Because they have the habit of imitating the stances of the crane which is their sacred bird, and this is one of its stances.' Thus a habit can be explained by means of reference to another habit of which it is an instance in the same way that other sorts of tendencies can be explained as instances of more general ones. In the present case the chain of habit-explanations would probably extend no further. The next 'why' question – 'Why do they habitually imitate the stances of their sacred bird?' might be answered by 'They believe in imitative magic – that by assuming the crane's stances they will be endowed with some of its other and more desirable features as well.' To a social scientist at work it is this last reply which is the most interesting of the set. An anthropologist who is interested in habits at all, as distinct from customs, is usually interested in them because they are common to a sizeable proportion of the members of a social group. He is likely to believe that a widely distributed habit may be the result of a social factor which is important in itself or which is associated with important factors. He may be concerned with explaining, for example, why the Dinka have the habit of standing on one foot; that is, with explaining habit-tendencies. But he is not concerned with explaining particular acts in terms of their agent's habits. Similarly, the demographer who wishes to know why on a particular island the rate of infant mortality fell sharply in a certain decade may well look to the introduction of new social habits as part of a possible explanation. Yet his account will be framed in terms of a causal relation between the conditions represented by the new habits and the decline in the rate of infant mortality.

Speaking generally, no social scientist who proposes to deal with the behaviour of collections of people or of classes of people will find much use for habit-explanations, even those of other habits. His first question is 'Why do these people have these habits? – whereas other people do not.' Of course a political scientist may be interested in a person's habits because they are representative of the habits of some group whose behaviour – habits included – is influenced by the non-habitual acts of their political leaders. Under these circumstances the political scientist will be investigating how the habits of a group are modified by political action. Any explanation of such changes, however, will not be one of the sort that we have been calling a 'habit explanation.'

3

Motives form a third kind of disposition as against unlearned reflexes and habits. There are three different classes of motives. We can call these 'intention motives', 'impulse motives', and 'dispositional motives'. Only the last of these properly falls within the scope of this chapter, but it might well be more confusing to distribute each to its appropriate section than to treat them together. Innumerable muddles have developed from the common failure to distinguish them, and it is perhaps useful here to emphasize their differences by contrasting them with each other.

'Intention-motives' is simply another name for intentions or goals or ends. It is this sense of the word 'motive' which is employed, for example, when it is said that 'To ask for his motive . . . is only to ask for the end which explains his behaviour. . . . We just want to know the goal which explains the sequence of his acts and the various moves he is making.'[1] Nothing more need be said about this kind of motive beyond what has previously been said of intentions. In this sense of the word a motive is a goal and not a disposition. As we have already seen, it need not even be the exercise of a 'directive disposition' like ambition, greed, or jealousy. Of course it sometimes is. Then in asking for someone's motive we have to be clear whether we are asking for information about a disposition or about a display of it. 'What was her motive in marrying her boss?' can be answered by 'Her motive was ambition' or by 'Her motive was to obtain a better job than that of a typist'. If we obtain the first answer, and it is correct, we know what her dispositional motive was without knowing what her specific goals, if any, were. If we obtain the second answer, however, we may know what her goal or intention was without knowing of which disposition, if any, it was the exercise. In other words, we may have to be told that an attempt to obtain a particular goal is the exercise of a particular disposition. This being so, it is important not to run together these two different kinds of motive-explanations merely because some goal seeking is also a display of directive dispositions.

'Impulse motives' are of this sort: 'He gave the bicycle to his sister because he wanted to please her. His action sprang from a generous impulse which was never repeated.' To say this is not merely to claim, of course, that something named 'generous impulse' *caused* the person to give a bicycle to his sister. It is also to summarize the manner in which it was given and to refer in a general way to the class of goals pursued. We can contrast an act done in a generous fashion with one performed grudgingly; and what we mean by using these words is that the actor displays a certain attitude. He has a set of beliefs, feelings, and desires which are expressed in his action. If they were absent we could not properly refer to the act as a generous one. Someone who silently handed over a bicycle to a stranger and then disappeared would present us with a mystery and not with a model of generosity. For the desire on the part of the agent to do something agreeable for the recipient in a more than ordinary degree is a necessary condition of his action being correctly called a 'generous' one; but it is not a necessary condition for making a gift.

When all this has been said, however, it may be replied: 'Granting for the moment that the ascription of an impulse motive refers to a manner

[1] Peters: *ibid.*, pp. 33–4.

as well as to a cause, what of the assertion that it also refers to the class of goals pursued? What kind of goals does a man generous on impulse pursue?' The answer, surely, is that he pursues the same kind as the man who is habitually generous: namely, those in which his freedom from petty calculation and his desire to do more than the required minimum are displayed in attempting to benefit someone else. One goal of the man who on a generous impulse cancels the debts of a personal enemy may be to alter the relationship between them for the better. The agent assumes that his enemy will benefit by the action, and this is another – and the more immediate – of his aims. Hence, in ascribing a generous impulse to the agent in this case we are saying both that he acted in a manner free from petty calculation and adherence to the letter of the law, and that he pursued a goal of a certain kind: the benefit of someone else. Unless the manner and the goal are of this sort the action cannot be a generous one.

Similarly, the assignment to any agent of an impulse motive tells us, if the assignment is correct, something of the manner in which a certain sort of goal is pursued. If we know only that an unspecified act was committed from a jealous impulse we know the *kinds* of beliefs, feelings, and desires that possessed the agent: that he believed that something he wanted was in danger of being lost to him, that he found this distressing, desired to avoid the loss, and acted in a manner which expressed his fear and desire. We also know the sort of end being sought: the prevention of loss of the desired things. If we know that a specified act – an assault on Jones – was committed from a jealous impulse, then we know very little more about the *manner* than in the previous instance. And even if we learn, in addition, what the agent's specific goal was, the prevention of the loss of his wife's affections, we still do not know much about the specific beliefs, feelings, and the desires the agent held. In both cases we have been given an explanation of why the agent assaulted Jones without knowing specifically what the agent's beliefs, feelings, and desires were, and in the one case without even knowing what his specific goal was. Thus it is sometimes possible to have an explanation in terms of an impulse motive in the absence of anything that we have so far called an 'intention-explanation'. This is only to say, of course, that the motive-explanations which we are now considering can on occasion refer merely to a *type* of goal, e.g. the prevention of the loss of something desired. Clearly, no intention-explanation is present when we know only that the assault on Jones was committed by a person with a jealous impulse. The person's goal in this case was the prevention of the loss of his wife's affections; it was not *simply* the prevention of the loss of something desired, though it was certainly that. In providing the goal-explanation we have to provide the specific goal of the agent and not merely the type of goal at which his behaviour was aimed. For if we state only the *kind* of goal pursued we do not state what the agent believed that he was trying to accomplish. He did not believe that any result falling within the general category would be acceptable to him, but that only one result would be – his possession of his wife's affections.

Now the importance in the social sciences of explanations phrased in terms of impulse motives is no greater than those phrased in terms of habits, though some of the reasons are different in the two cases. Impulse motives usually account for the behaviour of individual agents. The behaviour, by definition, is unexpected, unusual, and unrepeated. It differs from what the agent ordinarily does in similar situations, or at least from what his previous behaviour has led his acquaintances to believe that he would do. Of course, such acts need not be confined to individual persons. A group of people sometimes acts in concert from an impulse motive. All the people in the audience of a Buddhist monk might simultaneously, in an outbreak of religious generosity, be moved to give all their possessions to the poor. In this event, however, as in the commoner cases of impulse motives, the social scientist would not be much interested in learning – as an *explanation* of that behaviour–that the motive was generosity. The social scientist's question when he is confronted with the unexpected acts of people is not 'What was his or their (impulse) motive?' but – more likely – 'What was the background of social conventions that make the act an unexpected one?' Or 'Under what social conditions will such impulsive acts appear?' Or 'What sanctions, if any, does the group apply when a person or set of persons acts in this way? How is such behaviour received?' In brief, an anthropologist or sociologist would take up the question parallel to that in the case of habits, namely, 'Why do these people display these motives – whereas other people do not?' In neither case is the investigator concerned with particular acts explained in terms of habits or impulse motives. The presence of the motive, like the presence of the habit, is what requires explanation – a social explanation.

The third kind of motive that we have distinguished is dispositional motive. This kind, like the other two kinds of motive, embodies the notion of goal seeking or the pursuit of an end. It embodies much else, however. This can be made clear if we consider the answers given in terms of each kind of motive to the question 'Why did he give her the diamond ring?'

(*a*) 'In order to please her.' An answer like this gives an intention motive, we have said, because 'to please her' will serve equally well to answer the question 'With what intention did he give her the diamond ring?' In both cases the reply merely gives the end to which the action in question is a means.

(*b*) 'In an impulse of generosity.' In knowing that the agent intended an action already performed we know that he knew what his goal was, that he believed that the action which he took was a means to his goal, and that he also believed that he was trying to achieve his goal. The knowledge that the agent acted from an impulse of generosity includes this information but something more as well. It is that the agent was in a certain emotional state. He would not have acted from an impulse of generosity or jealousy or vindictiveness if he *felt* no generosity or jealousy, or did not feel vindictive. If he merely acted from rational calculation – assaulted Jones merely because the retention of his own wife's affections was financially valuable to him, and did not dislike Jones nor like his own wife – we should not think him a jealous man. Similarly, an experienced politician who pursues a campaign of character assassination against his political opponent need not be vindictive, though he does many things that a vindictive man would also do. At the end of the campaign he may resume friendly relations with his rival, and give every indication that he never felt any personal animosity toward him. Whatever his motives were they did not include impulses of vindictiveness.

It is by the strength of his emotion that we estimate the degree to which a person is acting from a given impulse or dispositional motive. The extreme cases of jealousy are those in which the jealous person becomes furious or rages or hallucinates, the mildest cases those in which the agent is slightly apprehensive. But none of these states can be genuinely present without the person being emotionally disturbed. If no such agitation occurs – e.g. no anxiety, no worry, no fear – then an explanation in terms of an impulse motive or a dispositional motive is not applicable, though one in terms of an intention motive may be.

Now it can be argued that an explanation in terms of an impulse motive also supplies us with the reason why the agent pursues his goal. For example, it has been said that 'Jealousy indicates not merely some wish to harm or take down a peg, but the reason for that wish as well: to be jealous is to wish someone ill, or to wish that someone has not got something *because* he has something you have not and would like to have. Thus where jealousy is used as a motive it refers to some sort of purposive behaviour, but the use of the word does more than merely indicate the purpose of the behaviour, it indicates the reason why one has that purpose.'[1] The force of this example is somewhat weakened by a failure to distinguish between jealousy and envy: to be jealous is not necessarily 'to wish someone ill, or to wish that someone has not got something *because* he has something you have not and would like to have'. It sometimes means 'strong effort to keep what one has', as in the phrase 'a woman jealous of her honour'. To envy is to covet what belongs to another person; to be jealous is to wish to keep from losing what is thought of as belonging to oneself. Though the example refers to envy more than it does to jealousy, the chief point remains to be considered. Is there a class of motive words which indicate both the goal of

[1] N. Sutherland: 'Motives as Explanations', *Mind*, Vol. LXVIII, No. 270, April 1959, p. 152.

the behaviour and the agent's reason for pursuing that goal? The answer, clearly, is 'Yes in a trivial sense'. The reason for a person's envy can always be given as 'Because he has what you also want', or more briefly, 'Because you want it'. Then to envy someone is to want what he has *because* you want what he has, or to want him not to have it *because* you do not have it. In this case, however, it is difficult to see any explanatory force in saying that the *goal* of the behaviour (obtaining what someone else possesses) has as its *reason* wanting what someone else possesses. The reason seems empty, because, as we saw earlier, there is an important sense of 'want' in which the intended goal of someone's actions can be something that he intends but does not want to achieve, i.e. does not like. Hence, an envious agent may 'want' to obtain what someone else possesses without liking what he wants. All that we learn is that the goal is sought because the agent wants it, where 'wants' can mean either 'has a liking for' or 'pursues without liking'. True, a number of possibilities are ruled out by giving 'He wants it' as a reason. The goal is not pursued under duress or in a drugged state or by accident. And if such obvious exclusions are taken seriously, then motive words like 'jealousy', 'envy', 'revenge', 'generosity', and 'greed', do indicate both the goal of behaviour and the reason for its pursuit.

(*c*) In terms of a dispositional motive, the answer to the question 'Why did he give her the diamond ring?' might be 'Because he is a generous man'. When 'generous' is used to reflect a dispositional motive in an explanation it tells us everything that the attribution of an impulse motive tells us with only one difference: the motive named is a recurrent feature of the agent's character. It is to explain his act by indicating the goal to which it is a means, and, further, to classify the goal as belonging to a set commonly and knowingly pursued by the agent. Thus in ascribing a particular dispositional motive to a person we assert of his act that it had these features: (1) it was directed toward certain kinds of goals, (2) it was accompanied by a characteristic emotional state as a necessary condition, (3) it was an expression of a dispositional trait. If the motive is a conscious one we can substitute in condition (1) the words 'it was intentional'; if the motive is unconscious we cannot, for though the goal was pursued the agent did not do it knowingly. The phrase 'goal-directed' satisfactorily refers to both kinds of motives, and leaves undecided the question whether a given explanation in terms of a dispositional motive incorporates a reference to intentional behaviour. Even when such an explanation does, it should be recalled that the motive-explanation will not incorporate an intention-explanation. It will not do so because in supplying a dispositional motive we are merely indicating the type of goal pursued and not the specific goal sought by the agent.

Often a motive word is used in explanation when it is not possible, in the absence of additional information, to say whether the explanation refers to an impulse or to a disposition. 'She left him from – avarice, greed, pride, jealousy . . .' does not make this distinction. But both kinds of motive-explanation, and that in terms of intention motives as well, exclude the possibility of certain other types being applied. If any one of the three sorts of motive can be ascribed to an act, then it cannot be explained as being done simply from reflex or habit. There are several reasons for this, but one which is common to all three senses of 'motive' concerns the way in which goals are pursued. We have said that some habits are goal-directed, that is, are initiated in order to bring about some end, as brushing the teeth is usually done in order to keep them clean. Since habits are stereotyped tendencies, however, they are not goal-*seeking* tendencies. Behaviour done from motives alters with changed conditions; habitual and reflexive behaviour does not. Tooth brushing may continue even when it is no longer needed or sufficient to keep the teeth clean, and even when their owner knows this. Motive behaviour, on the other hand, takes changed conditions into account while seeking an unchanged goal. A man whose motive for cheating his acquaintances, stealing his wife's kitchen money, and refusing small pleasures to his children is greed, is a man who displays under a variety of circumstances the pursuit of the same sort of goal. He varies his means to obtain the same end, and thus actively seeks his goal. This is at the other extreme from reflexive and habitual behaviour, for such behaviour recurs unaltered and does not vary with changes in the conditions that lead to the goal. And, of course, any conscious motive refers to intentional behaviour, whereas by definition any given exercise of a reflex or habit cannot. Hence, while reflexes and habits are tendencies, and dispositional motives incorporate tendencies, an explanation of an act in terms of one excludes the use of the others to explain the same act.

Explanations given in terms of dispositional motives are personality characterizations whereas those given in terms of impulse motives are not: a woman does not have to be a generous woman in order to be overcome by a generous impulse. But both sorts of motive explanations have a similarly limited part to play in the social sciences. Much the same considerations which applied, as we saw, in the case of impulse motives apply also in the case of dispositional motives. They account for individual acts and usually for acts performed by individual people. Unless these motives can be related to social processes or situations in such a way as to help answer questions like 'Why do such instances of these motives appear here in this group and not in that group (where other conditions are so similar)?' there is not much point in a social scientist being concerned with a motive explanation. If he is interested in the workings and causes and effects of certain social patterns, e.g. sorcery, vassalage, primogeniture, money markets, hire purchase, immigration settlement, he is not aided by *simply* learning the motives of individual participants. It is the additional information that the person's motives are representative of a group, or that they are not, which is interesting. Similarly, it can be the suspected connection of someone's motive with a structural feature of the society, with a custom, or with an institution, that makes the motive of interest. Behaviour explained by means of dispositional motives is behaviour which is thought to be unexplainable in terms of social conventions alone. If a visitor is given the food bowl before anyone else *merely* because it is customary to do so then there is no sensible answer to the question 'What is their motive for doing this?' The act is not the result of an intention, impulse, or disposition motive on their part. It is the result of social training alone. This is what the social scientist deals with; he takes up questions of motive only in so far as they bear upon such questions, and this bearing is peripheral at best.

It follows from what has been said that people can have motives for departing from social conventions but that adherence to them does not usually raise the question: 'What motive had he for doing what he was expected to do, for doing what anyone in his position would be expected to do?' Both sorts of motives are similar in this respect: the goal-seeking acts to which they refer may or may not be socially acceptable means in any given society of achieving the goal. A generous man may steal in order to obtain gifts for his friends, and an ambitious man may be ruthless in his efforts to make room for himself at the top of his profession. Of course some motive words have a pejorative force, and with respect to these ('vanity', 'jealousy', 'masochism') we cannot say that the people to whom they are applicable use socially acceptable means in their pursuit of unacceptable ends. A woman who is charming to her rival simply in order to stimulate her own masochism cannot be said, in a society that disapproves of masochism, to use unexceptional means to a bad end. It is the disposition or impulse which is judged bad, and any means that lead to – are adopted in order to achieve – a bad goal are themselves judged to be bad. The distinction between acceptable and unacceptable means can only be made if the goal is not itself thought to be unacceptable. The attribution of some motives, then, the non-pejorative ones like patriotism, ambition, and generosity, leaves open the question whether the acts performed in pursuit of the goals are socially acceptable. The assignment of motives to an act differs in this way from an explanation of it in terms of custom or expected behaviour. The latter explanation rules out the possibility that the act is socially unacceptable, and therefore the possibility that the act needs to be justified. The former explanation does neither of these things. This is one reason why in certain contexts to ask the question 'What was his motive?' is to suggest that the agent's act *may* require justification, that the phrase 'Explain your action' may be appropriate where this phrase is used as an exhortation to the agent to both explain and justify his deed.

Nevertheless, it is not correct to claim that 'we only ask about a man's motives when we wish, in some way, to hold his conduct up for assessment', and that 'The word is used typically in moral or legal discourse where actions have to be *justified* and not simply explained.'[1] It is not correct because we often ask about a person's motives when only the problem of explanation is at issue. Thus we can ask 'What was his motive for giving up his legal practice just as he was becoming successful?' or 'What motive could ever lead her to take the veil?' or 'What motive would impel John to leave that cryptic message in his will?' In none of these cases need there be any question of justification. It is the oddity of the action – the mystery of its purpose – which is under question here, not whether it is defensible. And it cannot truthfully be claimed that the examples given demand answers which employ only one sense (or perhaps two senses) of the term 'motive'; hence, that there remains at least one sense of the term in which a motive question requires a justificatory answer. For which sense could this be? All three of our examples can be given an answer which refers to an intention motive or to an impulse motive or to a dispositional motive. For example, we can say (1) 'John left that cryptic message because he intended to disinherit his wife' or (2) 'John left that cryptic message because he was overcome by an impulse of generosity' or (3) 'John left that cryptic message because he was a generous man.' There is no reason to believe that any of these answers must justify rather than merely explain John's action. The three answers give different pieces of information, and since a motive question taken out of context does not indicate which sort of answer is desired, we cannot say that one is preferable to the other. Yet unless we wish to assert that all explanation of human actions is also a justification of them, we cannot claim that any one of the three answers given is a moral assessment of his conduct or must in some way lead to such an assessment.

We have spoken at some length about the features that distinguish the three kinds of motives from each other, but what they have in common is no less important. All three explain, when they are used to do so, by indicating the agent's purpose, end, or goal. Statements about each sort of motive can be the basis for predictions about the agent, though each sort authorizes a different kind of prediction. Knowing that Annette has the fixed intention of owning a particular country property, that Alex, usually an easy-going man, is now in a fit of jealousy concerning his wife, that Emma is a vindictive woman, we can make certain predictions about each, always supposing that we know something of their own grasp of their position: both of the situation in which they are placed and of the likely results of their acts. Of Annette we can make such predictions as 'If you try to sell her a city house for permanent residence she will refuse' or 'She will not receive sympathetically your criticisms of country life.' Of Alex we can reasonably predict that he will

[1] Peters: *op. cit.*, p. 29.

resent even the most innocent advances toward his wife, that he will be quick to criticize her behaviour toward other men, and that he will become emotionally disturbed if she ignores his suspicions. Emma, we should predict, will try to injure the person who passes her over for the promotion that she greatly wants, will be furious if she believes that she has been slighted, and will brood on the wrongs done to her, real or imaginary. Her case differs from Annette's in that Emma's behaviour embraces a much wider range of activities – for Emma can have many fixed intentions throughout her jealous life – and in containing a disposition to become emotionally aroused. She differs from Alex in that his fit may pass, whereas her disposition to become jealous is a relatively permanent feature of her character. If someone argues that none of these three people has the motive attributed to him or to her, then we can produce such verified predictions in support of the attribution. Of course we can also make predictions on the basis of the agent's act being thwarted. We can predict, for example, that if Annette is unsuccessful in purchasing the property she wants at an auction, she will try to obtain it in some other fashion. If this prediction is fulfilled we have additional evidence for the correctness of our view of her intention. It is the fact that we can draw testable predictions from all three kinds of motive explanations as we can from those in terms of habits, that allows us to assert that each is a genuine form of explanation.

4

There is an entirely different way of classifying dispositional behaviour from the one which we have been considering. It is the division of behaviour into the tendency or disposition to conform to rules, on the one hand, and the disposition to violate them, on the other. It is easy to draw up a list of different sorts of rules: by-laws, regulations, self-imposed rules, laws, game rules, moral rules, and rules of thumb. The list could be greatly extended, but the only sorts of rules in which we are interested here are those referred to by social scientists in their explanations. The usual short answer to the question 'What sort are those?' is 'social conventions', and though everyone realizes how little information is given by this reply, not everyone appreciates why this should be true.

Earlier in this chapter it was pointed out that disposition–explanations can be used to account for particular dispositions as well as for particular actions or particular kinds of actions. We can explain why Mary K. failed to increase her production of watch dials yesterday in the painting room of the factory, even though she suffered financially as a result, by appealing to the tendency statement 'Mary K. tends to follow the practice of not breaking the piece-rate.' The answer to the question 'Why does Mary K. not wish to be – or be thought of as – a "job spoiler" ?' may or may not be stated in terms of dispositions. If it is, then a possible way of putting it is 'Because she has a strong tendency to pursue the goals of the group, and these include stabilizing the piece-rate at a level which permits the slowest worker to earn a certain wage'. This is not the full extent to which the disposition reply can be taken, for we can go on to say, 'And she tends to pursue the goals of the factory group because she tends to avoid their sanctions and desire their approval.' At this point the tendency-explanation would commonly be replaced by some other sort: 'She was trained to respond to group goals and rules in this way' or 'Experience has taught her that she can more easily obtain other things that she wants by behaving in this way.' But, of course, the same procedure as this may be followed in accounting for a tendency possessed by the *group* of women in the paint room, the tendency, for example, to stabilize the output in close relation to the piece-rate. This tendency may be subsumed under the more general tendency of the group to ensure that each of its members is paid at least a certain wage.

It is not only small groups of people whose behaviour is open to explanation in terms of tendencies or dispositions. Business corporations or government departments may have their activities explained as the disposition to deliberately pursue certain ends by particular means. Thus a given change in the organization of the sales department of a company may be explained as an effort by its executives to achieve lower costs and greater sales; and the pursuit of this goal may be explained in terms of their disposition to achieve a long range goal to which this one is thought to be a means, namely, the production of goods at the lowest cost and with the greatest profit. We must distinguish three different kinds of tendency-explanations, however. One is the tendency-explanation that explains merely by mentioning the end toward which an act or tendency is directed. A second kind is that which mentions the rules to which an act or tendency conforms without mentioning a goal. The third kind refers to both the rules and the end. Examples illustrating the first sort have already been given. The other two are easily identified. Suppose we ask 'Why does that man always carry a furled umbrella and wear a bowler to his office ?' We can reply 'Because he is a clerk in the city and they tend to have that costume.' Or we may ask 'Why did that group of women move from their huts when the epidemic killed all their husbands ?' The retort 'In this tribe people tend to move from huts in which their relatives have died' refers, as does the previous answer, to social conventions but not to any goals of the agents. On the other hand, some tendency-explanations refer to both. Thus the last example can be appropriately expanded to: 'In this tribe people tend to move from huts in which their relatives have died in order to avoid the spirits of the dead.' Statements of this type supply the rules which are followed by the agents in order to achieve the stated ends. It is not always clear from the use of such statements, of course, whether or not the agent knows that he is doing this. But in either case there is the disposition to conform to rules, and this is absent in the type of disposition which we earlier called 'dispositional motives'.

Now it is obvious that explanations in terms of people's tendencies to conform to rules have an important place in some of the social sciences. We should first make clear, however, that the phrase 'dispositional statement' has two different sorts of use. In one sort of use a dispositional statement is opposed to a general statement or to a universal statement. Thus to say that adult Frenchmen tend, or are disposed, to display their interest in attractive women, is not to say that *all* of them are so disposed. In the other sort of use a dispositional statement is opposed to an occurrence statement. In saying that adult Frenchmen tend to conform to social rules concerning their behaviour toward attractive women, we are not claiming that Frenchmen are in a constant state of displaying these conventions, but merely that they display them when a suitable occasion arises. It is not always possible to determine which use is in question. But when we speak of a tendency to conform to *social rules* we are usually referring to both uses; for we are usually claiming both that the agents do not always conform on every suitable occasion, and that suitable occasions do not occur all the time. However, if there were a group of people who always conformed to a particular social rule on every appropriate occasion, our interest in them, while especially keen because of the effectiveness of their training, would still be based upon the fact that they conformed to rules. It is this feature which is of chief importance to us at the moment.

When explanations of social behaviour are discussed, it is sometimes assumed that any sort of recurrent and widespread behaviour in a society must be explained either as an instance of rule-conforming or of rule-violating. But if we think of all group behaviour as being regulated by a system of familiar goals and conventions we overlook much behaviour that is not. Some regularities of social behaviour are neither prescribed nor proscribed: in a given group the incidence of cigarette smoking may be much higher amongst women than amongst men, or the bonds of affection between sisters may be stronger than those between brothers, or large land owners may show a lower rate of return than small holders. If we wish to explain these differences we may not be able to do so by referring to cultural norms which are being followed. At best we may be able to produce explanations in terms of these differences being the unanticipated consequences of conformity to social rules, rules that have no other connection with the behaviour to be explained. Even if we take the case of proscribed acts, such as drug addiction or sexual promiscuity, it is not usually possible to explain them as instances of rule following, although sometimes, it is true, criminal acts can be explained as the pursuit of goals and the following of rules which have developed in subgroups of a society. Nevertheless, not all proscribed social tendencies can be explained in this way, e.g. the tendency for a given society to produce more female than male alcoholics. Naturally, we can so extend our criteria for explanations in terms of rule-following that we can incorporate all such cases. We can, that is, explain them as the side effects or remote consequences of rule-following behaviour and not as instances of it. Yet in making this extension we should obviously not be confining ourselves to an account in terms of rule conformity. We should have to assert some sort of connection between the pursuit of rules and the side effects. This connection itself would have to be explained in some manner other than that of rule pursuit, and the intent of the original explanation would be lost. For it was to explain that something was done because the agents followed certain conventions, not because, for example, there was a causal connection between their following those conventions and some other events.

The social science which most clearly has a use for rule-explanations is social anthropology. Most clearly, because a large part of the work of anthropologists consists in reporting, observing, describing, and accounting for, the behaviour of people in non-European societies. The anthropologist has as one of his interests the discovery of how the people of such societies have organized themselves to accomplish various tasks and to achieve various goals. Thus an anthropologist might ask why a certain man, 'Batamedi, for instance, every year ploughs the field of his wife's grandmother'? The answer in the case of the Lovedu, a Bantu tribe of South Africa, is that 'in spite of the fact that bride-price is more or less fixed within certain limits, it is always said "bride-price never ends", for a bridegroom can never refuse to help his wife's relatives. He may not even suggest that they are demanding too much, for this would be a breach of good manners reparable only by the handing over of a pardon goat. His only policy is to remain respectful, promise to "look for" what they require, then later to send a message that he has been unsuccessful. . . .'[1] If we next ask the question 'Why can't a bridegroom refuse to help his wife's relatives?' the reply is put in terms of preserving certain arrangements: 'The importance of relatives-in-law lies in the fact that there is conceived to be a lasting bond between the two families for generations to come, since where a man has married there his son will find a wife. . . . Moreover, a man's relatives-in-law become to his children the mother's side of the family, which plays so important a part in their lives. . . .'[2] The further question 'Why is the mother's side of the family so important?' has a very complicated answer which can only be touched upon here. Its interest for us is in the way that rather general queries of the form 'Why is that set of conventions important?' are commonly dealt with by social anthropologists. So we learn that 'There

[1] E. Krige and J. Krige: *The Realm of a Rain-Queen*, 1943, p. 79.
[2] *Ibid.*, p. 78.

is structural tension between the group which gives the brides and the group which gives the cattle; but one notices in ordinary life not so much the tension as the elaborate measures for maintaining good relations. . . There is ample reason for this emphasis because the whole social structure and, through it, the whole tribal system and the strongest bonds with the queen, depend upon the proper functioning of these groups. And these are again a part of, and supported by, the bilateral kin, who, with the cattle, the one relying on the other, constitute the ultimate basis of the social structure.'[1] This kind of explanation is not one phrased in terms of goals and conventions; it refers to the functioning of a system to which the observance of social rules and the seeking of goals makes a contribution. We shall take up such explanations later, but the point to be made here is that they, like law explanations, can be the answers to questions about the presence of social conventions and goals. In other words, an anthropologist, while making much use of the notion of rule-following, need not and does not confine his explanations to explanations of that kind.

The same holds true in the other social sciences. A sociologist might explain why a man rather than a woman had been chosen to fill a particular post in a municipal authority by saying that the employers followed the convention which required that executive power be limited to men. But he might explain the presence of certain cliques by pointing out that they represented two parties who supported conflicting rules: one requiring that all posts be filled on the basis of knowledge and competence, the other requiring that seniority and sex be taken as the criteria. The struggle for supremacy could not itself be explained as an instance of rule-following, and any account of the conflict would make use of some other method of explanation. Similarly, a demographer could explain why in a given group a high proportion of the married women went out to work by indicating that they were trying to raise their standard of living – and so far were conforming to a set of conventions. If their appearance in the work force resulted in technological changes, then he might wish to answer a new question, namely, 'Do these changes prevent population growth from making such changes in the future impossible?' This question is not one to be dealt with in terms of rule-following. It concerns the unintended, and perhaps unforeseen, effects of rule-following.

Often, however, the question whether a particular social convention or group rule or social norm is present is exactly the one at issue. A typical way in which the problem arises is illustrated by an investigation made of the reasons why a tenants' organization was supported by some divisions of a housing area and not by others. After classifying the activity and attitudes of all the residents with respect to the organization, the authors are led to say:

[1] *Ibid.*, p. 86.

96

What may we conclude from this analysis of the patterns within Westgate and within Westgate West? Do we as yet have any evidence for asserting the existence or non-existence of group standards? With regard to Westgate we can clearly say that there was no group standard for the project as a whole. There were obviously opposing subgroups within Westgate with regard to both attitude and activity. Can one, however, maintain that there were group standards within each court? At this point this conclusion would seem plausible although it is by no means unequivocally demonstrated. We must, however, find some explanation why different courts, each composed of the same kinds of people in the same kind of circumstances, reacted so differently from each other toward the organization and why, in spite of different reactions from different courts, there was relatively homogeneous behaviour within each court. We at least are led to suspect that group standards or group norms were operating.[1]

Now when a social scientist discovers that some particular activity can be explained in terms of rule-conforming, his problems have only begun. He will want to know, for example, under what conditions various types of norms develop, how they are transmitted within a group and from one group to another group, and what the relationship is between the production and diffusion of specific kinds of norms and the structural features of social organization. These problems cannot usually be dealt with by means of rule-following explanations. A further example is one taken up in the study of the Westgate tenants, namely, 'What are the social conditions which permit people to resist the adoption of group standards?' As the authors point out, some people resist conforming to the conventions of a group because they do not consider themselves to be members of it. But they can also refuse because they are in fact conforming to the conventions of some other group. The question then to be answered may be 'Why has the one group received their allegiance rather than the other?' Whatever answer this evokes is not likely to refer to an instance of rule-conforming, though it may do so. It is not likely, because the two groups must be in some sort of competition in order for the question to arise, and in this circumstance the agent can be led to accept the standards of one group and not those of the other for a variety of reasons. Of these *reasons*, his adherence to the norms of still another group is merely one. In any case, the question 'Why one group rather than the other?' must at some stage receive an answer which does not amount to saying 'Because of adherence to a third group'; for at some point a reason must be given why the standards of the very first group were accepted as against those of another.

We have already argued for the unimportance of intention-explanations in the social sciences. It must now be emphasized that rule-conforming explanations are standard only in the sense of being trivially

[1] L. Festinger, S. Schachter, and K. Back: *Social Pressures in Informal Groups*, 1950, pp. 85–6.

common. If we could not explain any behaviour or thoughts of any agents in terms of their adherence to social conventions, this could only be because there were no conventions, that is, no society. For we logically could not, on the one hand, have social norms, and, on the other hand, have no agents who either professed to follow or did in fact conform to them. Part of the meaning of 'social norm' is 'standard of behaviour or thought conformed to by some group of people'. Hence, social norms without social agents are a logical impossibility. The fact that we do have societies and social norms ensures that we can provide some explanations of people's acts in terms of their conformity to social rules. Such explanations are in this sense inescapable.

To say, then, that social scientists depend heavily upon the notion of rule-conforming behaviour is to utter a platitude. Reference to rule-conforming behaviour is not less an explanation for that reason, but as in the case of referring to intentions, a social scientist has little need to make explicit reference to a convention as a means of explaining a particular act or kind of act. Commonly, the conventions, when known to the investigator, are set forth in summary fashion as part of an account which embraces more than the conventions alone; unsanctioned acts, motives, and intentions, are also considered. So is a great deal else, including the interplay amongst all these elements. From this the interested reader can construct a suitable explanation of a piece of social behaviour. But social scientists, no less than physical scientists, demonstrate in their practice that they are not expecially concerned with the explanation of specific events – Batamedi's ploughing or John's fall from a tree – however useful their explanations may be in accounting for these events. Scientists are concerned with general types of events, and social scientists show this by the fact that they use accounts of specific events mostly in order to illustrate the operation of a general factor. They show their concern with increasing the scope of their explanations, as well, in the rapidity with which they advance from questions that permit an answer in terms of rule-following to questions that do not. In exactly the same way that the investigator cannot solve the problems which confront him by means of intention-explanations alone, so he cannot rest content with those referring to norms. In each case he is impelled to ask 'Why this intention. . . . ?' or 'Why this rule . . . ?' and the chain of answers will soon enough depend on refer-ring to neither goals nor rules for its explanatory power.

VIII

REASONS

1

EXPLANATIONS in terms of reasons are a good deal like explanations in terms of intentions. Both play a large part in everyday life, but not in social science.

In the same way that we can speak of a group of people having an intention, so we can speak of a group of people having its own reasons for an action. This is a slightly abbreviated way of asserting that the members of the group have the same reasons in common. A country's cabinet, a trade-union executive, an army's general staff, are all common examples of such groups. But there are other groups whose composition is much vaguer. In explanatory statements referring to these, the only information supplied about the members is that they all have in common the same reason for taking what action they did take. A typical example is this one:

The occasion for the weakness in gilt-edged stocks was the rise in the United States Treasury bill rate last week above the United Kingdom Treasury bill rate for the first time in six years.
This event raised the possibility that American funds, which had moved here to take advantage of our higher interest rates, would be repatriated and that the authorities here might then try to check any such movement by raising Bank Rate. The mere contemplation of the possibility has been enough to drive buyers away from gilt-edged.[1]

The group referred to here is that of stock buyers, though the only characterization given of them is that their suspicion that Bank Rate might rise was the reason why they refused to buy gilt-edged stocks. This is obviously incomplete as an explanation. It assumes that the reader knows that the stock buyers in question are profit seekers, and that he also knows that the raising of the Bank Rate will make the prices of gilt-edged stocks fall. Given this knowledge, the reader will be in possession of an explanation when he learns that the stock buyers suspected that the Bank Rate might rise and thus depress the value of

[1] *The Observer* (London), 30 August 1959, p. 2.

their stock holdings. The more complete explanation of the buyers' avoidance of gilt-edged stocks has the form: 'Stock buyers seek profits; stock buyers believed that a rise in Bank Rate would depress the value of gilt-edged stocks; stock buyers believed that a fall in value would cost them profits; stock buyers believed that the Bank Rate might rise; therefore, stock buyers avoided purchasing gilt-edged stocks.' The four assertions incorporating the phrase 'stock buyers' make up a set of reasons for the action referred to in the conclusion. Since they are also the premises of an argument, it is being claimed that an argument of roughly this form – with appropriate substitutions of tense and the elimination of the phrase 'stock buyers believed' – is the argument which causally influenced the buyers in their action. It is to claim that the stock buyers were familiar with this argument and accepted it as the relevant one. But it is *not* to claim that any one of the stock buyers actually rehearsed the full argument, for he may have articulated only a part ('Bank Rate may rise and depress my stock values') and presupposed the rest, e.g. 'Stock buyers (including me) seek profits'. Nor need any of the stock buyers have deliberated about what to do by comparing one line of action with another; all of them may have taken both the truth of their beliefs and the soundness of the argument on trust, and this would not have prevented the argument from influencing them to a course of action.

What has been explained by this argument in terms of investors' reasons is the deliberate refusal on the part of some investors to purchase gilt-edged stocks. It is a separate question whether the 'weakness in gilt-edged stocks' was due to this refusal to purchase. The explanation asserts that it was. If anyone were to challenge this assertion, however, the connection between this refusal to purchase and the fall in stock prices would have to be shown by an additional argument. In any event, the question is hardly open to an answer in terms of some agents' own reasons. The question is whether failure to purchase on the part of certain investors caused 'the weakness in gilt-edged stocks', and to this causal question the reasons advanced by investors for their actions have no direct relevance.

In considering how reason-explanations are used by social scientists we must remember two points. One is that explanations of this type are provided only for *actions*, whether of individuals or of groups. We remarked previously on the fact that a large number of the explanations offered in the social sciences do not explain actions. We said that they deal with such things as 'differences between classes of actions, or with increases in the members of a class of actions, or with rates of increase and comparative rates'. They also deal, we said, with the 'causal relationship between changes' in various sets of factors. To explanations of any of these sorts an account in terms of agents' reasons has very little to contribute. The other point is this. All actions for which the agent has his own reasons are also actions which he intended – or intends – to perform. Some of the same limitations, then, that we found to apply to intention-explanations apply to those stated in terms of the agent's own reasons. There are, in addition, features of reason-statements which make their use in explanatory contexts even more limited than that of intention statements.

An obvious limitation shared by intention and reason-explanations is this: each can be employed only in those cases where the agent believes that his action is a means to a known end. The reasonable use of these explanations, therefore, is limited to those cases for which there is evidence that the agent holds such beliefs. Yet we have already argued that the 'bulk of explanations in social science do not make use of conscious ends', and we have appealed to our previous examples in support of this claim. Hence, our earlier remarks on the modest place occupied by intention-explanations in the social sciences will also hold true of reason-explanations – in so far, that is, as the modesty of the role is determined by the volume of employment.

There is another restriction common to both methods of explanation. It arises when either intentions or reasons are attributed to a group of agents in such a way that no indication is given as to which members of the group have them. Group assignments of reasons, for example, are vague in that we do not know whether every one in the group holds these reasons. If they are not held by all members of the group, we then have the task of finding out which members, or what proportion of members, hold the reasons that were decisive with respect to the action taken. If we tried to explain why the United States declared war on Japan in 1941, we could say 'All Americans thought that the Japanese attack on Pearl Harbour was sufficient reason for an American declaration of war'. But this (partial) explanation might be quite misleading. Perhaps only a section of the American population thought about the matter at all. The proper use of the notion of group-reasons is restricted to situations in which reasons can be assigned to some individual members of the group. It may not matter whether all members share the same reasons, but it matters a great deal whether the investigator knows this or not.

A third restriction which applies to intention and reason-explanations alike is their logical independence of functional (causal effect) explanations. The truth of the statement 'His reason for taking her home was to indicate that he no longer cared for her' is logically independent of the truth of the statement 'The function of taking her home was to indicate that he no longer cared for her'. Even if his reason (his intention) was to indicate that he no longer cared for her it does not logically follow that he managed to produce this effect. Nor does the fact that the function (effect) was present ensure that it was his reason for taking her home. Of course in the other sense of 'function statement' – the purpose sense

– a function statement is certainly not logically independent of either a reason statement or an intention statement. For 'The purpose (function) of his taking her home was to indicate that he no longer cared for her' and 'His reason for (intention in) taking her home was to indicate that he no longer cared for her' are synonymous. Both sentences are used to refer to the agent's goal; both report that a particular action was knowingly taken to achieve a particular end. It should be observed that the phrase 'his reason for' can have the same sense as 'his intention in'. When it does, no *reason-explanation* need be present, though it may be. In other words, speaking of a person's reason is sometimes merely speaking of his intention alone, with no explanation in terms of reasons, no argument, being referred to or presupposed.

Now it does not follow that two sentences of these types, when employed in explanations, produce synonymous explanations. A reason-explanation, as we have noted, gives more information than an intention-explanation. The former entails the latter. That is, one answer to the question 'What was his reason for using penicillin here?' might be 'He knew that penicillin kills pneumococci, that they were present here; and he wanted to kill them. His intention was to do this by the use of penicillin'. The other answer – the intention-explanation – might be 'He intended to use penicillin to kill the pneumococci'. The latter does not entail the former; it is only a part of the first explanation. Obviously, however, we could expand intention-explanations so that they gave the same information as explanations in terms of reasons. For example, we might have an explanation like 'He intended to use penicillin to kill the pneumococci which he knew to be present here, which he wanted to kill, and which he knew to be killed by penicillin'. If this were to be called an 'intention-explanation' it would not differ from a function-explanation in the purpose sense, for it could be put as 'The function (purpose) of his using penicillin was to kill . . .'. The other, or effect, sense of 'function' could not be substituted here without change of meaning. 'The function (effect) of his using penicillin was to kill . . .' does not entail the statement that he intended to use penicillin, even though he wanted to use it. An agent can want to do something without intending to do so, just as he can intend to do it without wanting to do so. Again, the assertion that the agent intended to use penicillin does not entail the assertion 'The function (effect) of his using penicillin was to kill . . .' unless the phrase 'intended to use penicillin' is expanded by the addition of the words 'and did'. Otherwise, it could be objected that the agent's intention might never have been put into effect, and so the entailment would not hold. The addition of the phrase, however, only incorporates into the assertion what is already suggested by the question, namely, the information that penicillin was used here.

Reason-explanations resemble intention-explanations in a way which we have not yet noted. If we ask why an agent (or a group of agents) performs certain acts for particular reasons of his (or their) own, the answer can take two forms, but only one of them will be a reason-explanation. This parallels, in part, the situation in the case of intention-explanations; as we have seen, they cannot always be accounted for in terms of further intentions. In the case of reasons, one form of answer is a statement subsuming people who offer a reason-explanation of their own action under the wider category of people who offer reason-explanations of a certain general type. Thus a person who explained his failure to buy stocks by saying that he believed a fall in their value to be imminent might have this question asked about him: 'Why does he act for this reason, why does he have this goal?' And the answer might be: 'Because he belongs to the class of people who are influenced by reasons of power, whose goals are those of financial power and commercial success.' The other form that can be employed in accounting for a reason-explanation is a general or universal statement which correlates a class of people having certain properties, such as particular desires or dispositions, with those people – or that class of people – who hold the reasons to be explained. 'All people who are habitually influenced by reasons of power – whose chief goals are financial power and commercial success – are people who suffered emotional deprivation as children' exhibits the simplest form that the statements take. Clearly, if we continue to press for an explanation in the case of the first form of answer we shall be forced back sooner or later upon the second form. If we ask a question like 'Why are some people influenced by reasons of power?' we must eventually give some answer like 'They are people who suffered emotional deprivation as children'. We must do this because our procedure of subsumption will very quickly produce categories that are too general for use in explanation. Under what category, for example, can 'people who are influenced by reasons of power' be subsumed? A category general enough to serve will be so general as to be vacuous. 'People who are influenced by reasons of self-preservation' might be put forward as a candidate; yet it will hardly allow us to distinguish amongst different classes of people. And that, after all, is what we wish to do here in seeking explanations in terms of the agent's own reasons.

2

We can now summarize the conditions which restrict the employ-ment of reason-explanations: (1) they apply only to actions intended by the agents, (2) they must be assignable to individual agents or to individual agents as members of groups, (3) they are logically independent of functional – in the sense of 'causal effect' – explanations, (4) they require evidence concerning (a) the agent's goal (b) his ability to formulate the relevant argument, and (c) the decisive effect of that argument upon his action, (5) they can be used only to a limited extent in the explaining of other reason-explanations.

When we keep these restrictions in mind we can understand why this method of explanation has a very small role in the social sciences. We give some examples which will illustrate this point.

'A boy would be a good warrior. He would help me with the field work, settle down in my house or nearby, and support me in my old age. He would be strong and back me up in all the quarrels with other people.' These were some of the reasons why Jokagaibo desired a boy rather than a girl.[1]

Direct quotation is the most obvious way of supplying the agent's own reason for his action or wish. In the present case we do not have enough of the context to know whether an explanation is being offered by Jokagaibo; he may be simply giving information. His reason *could* be put forward as an explanation, however. The fact that the matter is uncertain indicates how little depends upon the distinction between giving information and explaining in this case. What is useful is the hint that his reasons are typical, not merely that he would, if asked in the appropriate circumstances, give the reasons which we have quoted. The social scientist is not concerned here to explain the individual case – that of Jokagaibo. He is concerned with the kinds of reasons which influence the Kapauku in their desire for male children. In dealing with this problem he need not *explain* why they wish to have boys, though he can *inform* us of their reasons. His lack of interest in the example for its own sake represents a general situation in the social sciences. It helps to account for the unimportance of reason-explanations in these fields, as compared to their position in history or law or everyday affairs. The agent's own reasons for his behaviour often form part of the information collected by the social scientist, but they are seldom advanced in explanation of the agent's behaviour. The investigator has his own explanation of that behaviour to offer, and since he wishes to explain all behaviour of that kind, he must, at the very least, concern himself with reasons shared by a class or group of people. Sometimes, of course, he is content both to accept the agent's explanation as correct and to suggest that it is typical. Thus Evans-Pritchard writes:

I was puzzled to know why Badobo and the other witch-doctors meekly submitted to this bombast. The reasons which they gave were that they hoped to get out of him medicines which they did not know themselves, as they had not had the opportunity to visit Bakaland; that Bögwözu was only a bird of passage and would not trouble them for long; and that their own medicines were quite powerful enough to deal with him when the time came, and would prevent the successful accomplishment of his schemes. I asked Badobo why he remained servile to a man who so freely insulted him. He replied that Bögwözu had acted according to the custom of witch doctors, though, it was

[1] L. Pospisil: *Kapauku Papuans and Their Law*, 1958, p. 35.

true, his own methods were different, for if someone gave him spears, then he would show him all the medicines without further trouble . . . if he had asked Bögwözu why he had come here to trespass on his (Badobo's) ground he would have picked up his things and gone home, and all chance of acquiring new medicines would have been lost. If a well-known witch-doctor like Bögwözu comes to dance in your neighbourhood you invite him to your house and make him a gift when you shake hands with him there. Bögwözu would treat him in the same way if he were to visit him in Rikita's country (where Bögwözu lived). Then if Bögwözu has medicines which you do not possess, you take advantage of his presence to acquire them. Also, even though he was always asking for things, well, there was no shame in the sale of medicines.[1]

The situation in which an account of this sort can be useful does not often arise in economics, demography or sociology. It was suggested earlier why this should be so, and in the present chapter the matter was touched upon once more when we noted that reason-explanations are applied to *actions*. But a large number of the explanations offered in the social sciences, we said, do not explain *actions*. There is, however, another point of interest. Much of the information collected by sociologists and demographers is obtained in the form of answers to questionnaires and census sheets, or as answers given in surveys, polls or panels. Often the informant is asked to indicate which of a set number of reasons offered by the investigators is the one which influenced him in his decision, his choice, his action, or his belief. The answers of all the informants are then tabulated and classified. Sometimes the results are used to explain why some event has taken place or will take place. Sometimes the results themselves are the subject of an explanation. In both cases the explanation will often not be phrased in terms of the agents' own reasons. Why should this be so?

Consider, first, a case in which the results are the subject of the explanation, that is, in which an explanation is given of why certain groups of people hold particular reasons for their views. A sociologist investigated the attitudes of a white population at the edge of a city area into which negroes were moving. He classified the area into five geographical zones, number 1 being the nearest to the negro population and the other zones progressively more remote. Number 5 was several miles away. He then examined the reasons given by the white informants for wishing to bar negroes from living in each of the five zones. Given two sets of such reasons, the percentage of informants in each zone who held them varied in this fashion: (1) Negroes are personally unclean, diseased, smell bad, are physically unpleasant to associate with: zone 1 – 5%, zone 2 – 15%, zone 3 – 16%, zone 4 – 24%, zone 5 – 25%. (2) Don't want children associating with negroes, fear social mixing and

[1] *Witchcraft, Oracles and Magic Among the Azande*, n.d., pp. 223-4

inter-marriage: zone 1 – 22%, zone 2 – 14%, zone 3 – 14%, zone 4 – 13%, zone 5 – 10%.

Of these results Allport says in explanation: 'In Zone 1, where residents encounter more negroes, we find fewer complaints that they are personally and physically unclean or diseased. In Zone 5, where there is little knowledge-giving contact, this stereotype is more common. On the other hand, a more realistic problem comes to the fore in Zone 1. What will happen when the children play together? The probability of love affairs and mixed marriages is bound to increase. Granted the state of social opinion today, such an eventuality is viewed quite realistically as fraught with potential suffering for the children. In Zone 5 this issue is mentioned much less often, since white and negro children in this region have not yet met.

'From this study we learn that *approaching* residential contact is viewed as a threat by the dominant group, but that the nature of the complaints and perceptions varies with the immediacy (or distance) of the threat.'[1]

Now Allport's explanation of the differences in response amongst people of the five zones is very sketchy. It is that experience with negroes modifies the reasons put forward by the whites for barring negroes from living in the white residential areas. The amount of this experience is taken to coincide, at least approximately, with the geographical distance of the two groups from each other. In other words, the white population's reasons are altered by personal contact with negroes. But however vague this factor of personal contact is, no one can correctly say that it forms part of a reason-explanation. *The* reason for these differences is not the white population's own reason, for they have none. They did not deliberately and intentionally alter their reasons, and so no explanation in terms of their reasons for the change can be given.

There are cases, of course, in which people have their own reasons for changing their views or their reasons for actions. Yet such cases, like all cases of reason giving, will not attract the attention of the social scientist very often. He will be interested in the unexplained and inexplicable events of social life, not those for which the agents themselves can provide a correct explanation. If he has doubts about its correctness, then he may wish to indicate how unconscious or unnoticed factors have exerted an influence, and how the correct explanation differs from that given in terms of the agents' own reasons. In supplying a new explanation, though, he will usually be showing that the reason-explanation needs to be replaced by some different type of explanation. The chief case in which he will not be doing this, but will, instead, merely be altering the reason given, is that of lying on the part of informants. With this exception, the general tendency of sociologists, when confronted by

[1] Adapted and quoted from *The Nature of Prejudice*, 1958, pp. 257–8.

dubious reasons from informants, will be to find another method of explaining both the original action and the dubiousness of the agents' own reasons for that action.

Much the same considerations hold when the results obtained by means of surveys are used to explain why some event has taken place. If the question is simply one of information, then voters, for example, can be asked to give their reasons for voting as they did. But if the outcome of the poll is unexpected and puzzling, then collecting the voters' reasons may or may not be a way of obtaining a satisfactory explanation. It will not be if the voters are not aware of why they voted in the way that they did. It can be if the voters' reasons are the correct reasons. The problem of discovering whether they are correct is not a simple one, however. Suppose that in a large group of voters, some say that they voted for A because he is a capable, experienced man, and some claim that it was his integrity which influenced them. The remainder say that it was his likable personality that drew their vote. Suppose it is also known that none of these voters has ever voted for any candidate except one from the party to which A belongs, or that they are all members of his religious denomination. Then the investigator will be strongly tempted to study the relationship between voting for A and the voter's religious or political affiliation. Or he will look into the connection between these affiliations and the kinds of reasons which voters give for the votes that they cast. Or, again, he will investigate how close the relation is between actual voting behaviour and the reasons given for that behaviour, e.g. between voting for A and later saying that A obtained the agent's vote because A seemed sincere.

Now, there are many familiar reasons why voters' explanations are suspect, but this problem is part of the more general problem of why, in general, the reasons given by agents for their own conduct must often be carefully scrutinized. When they are examined, the resulting explanation may not remain one which can be put in terms of the agents' own reasons. For the investigator will then be looking for something like a causal connection between two or more factors, and not for additional reasons on the part of the agents. In other words, if the investigator wishes to test the correctness of a reason-explanation, as he must in making sound predictions, he will have to proceed beyond this method to other methods, and, hence, to other questions. Often this will lead him to eliminate his original explanation. Only if the answers to surveys were accepted uncritically, would the social investigator be inclined to give a majority of his explanations in terms of the informants' own reasons for their actions. Whether their reasons are correct or incorrect, any investigation of this point will quickly lead to the use of some method of explanation other than that of the agents' own reasons, and this method may be applied to the original problem.

In accepting other peoples' reasons for their behaviour we tacitly assume that they are asserting what they believe to be the truth and that they are correct. Our belief in their truth-telling commits us to believing that there is a high positive correlation between what they do and what they say, or more specifically, between their actions and what they claim are their own reasons for those actions. Once our belief in this correlation is attacked, we can establish that there is such a correlation only by investigation. And to do this is *not* to adduce more of the agents' own reasons. It is to look for a generalization. True enough, there are two important possibilities: (1) that the correlation will be established and will count as good evidence for the truthfulness of the agents, (2) that it will not be established and that this will count against the truthfulness of the agents. If the first holds, then the original reason-explanation will remain. If the second holds, the explanation will need to be changed, either into a new version of a reason-explanation or into some other type. Yet assuming in either case that the explanation offered is still phrased in terms of the agents' reasons, the question of its correctness will then arise. The agents may speak what they take to be the truth about their own reasons, and yet be mistaken about them. Thus the same problem will arise about their correctness as arose about truth-telling. In the establishment of their correctness we shall have to look for a generalization as supporting evidence. And once again this will lead the critical investigator to reconsider both his original question and his original answer in terms of some different method of explanation. This exactly parallels the transition which takes place between intention-explanations and other sorts. Reasons, like intentions, apply to behaviour which is rather sophisticated, and which does not often present itself to the social scientist as requiring explanation in either of these two ways. Furthermore, the disadvantages of reason and intention-explanations – which we have already commented on – will become even more apparent as we turn our attention in the succeeding chapters to function-explanations and explanations by means of laws, respectively.

IX

FUNCTIONS

1

IN the chapter entitled *Social Explanation* we distinguished two interpretations of the query 'What is its function?' One, we said, takes the form 'What is it intended to do – what purpose does it serve? This interpretation presents no problems different from those already discussed in the chapter on intentions. It is the other interpretation which now concerns us, the one which takes the sense of the question to be 'What part does it play in the operation of the system?' A typical example is: 'The function of the heart is to circulate the blood.'

Function statements differ from purpose statements in that the latter assume the presence of an agent, an agent who believes in a connection between his goal and some action which he can take to reach it. This is not true of function statements. No agent need be presupposed in their use. They may be so used as to misleadingly suggest the presence of an agent or of a design, but they do not in fact refer to them or assume their presence.

Now in the same way that purpose and function statements do not entail each other, so law-like and function statements do not. The statement 'The function of the adrenalin produced by the adrenal medulla is to enable the organism to counteract the effects of trauma' is not synonymous with the law statement 'Adrenalin produced by the adrenal medulla counteracts the effects of trauma in the organism'. Neither entails the other, for the function statement does not inform us that the adrenalin actually does counteract the effects of trauma, whereas the other statement does so inform us. In point of fact, we should not make the first unless we believed the second to be true, although we might easily believe the second without believing the first, i.e. we might believe that these effects of adrenalin were quite secondary, and that some of its other effects were primary. In that case we should want to assert that adrenalin is produced in order to enable the organism to do something other than counteract the effects of trauma.

What this example suggests is threefold: first, that function statements

109

in science provide us with a condition causally connected with the maintenance of a system, or part of a system, and thus indirectly with a system; second, that function statements in these cases are used so as to emphasize the importance of those conditions connected in some way with the maintenance of systems – that is, we can use function statements in such contexts as show that we wish to emphasize the importance of the property; third, that the use of function statements is somewhat different from that of law-like statements. To the first two points we can add that function statements are testable in so far as we can bring evidence to bear on whether the causal connection claimed to be present is so in fact. But the emphasis we have placed on this connection is not testable – is neither true nor false – though the possession of new information may lead to a change in emphasis. When one effect among many is picked out as the function of something, a tacit recommendation is being given as a practical guide to dealing with it, or in the case of manufactured articles, reference is being made to the most important job for which it is built. In testing 'Adrenalin is produced by the adrenal medulla in order to enable the organism to counteract the effects of trauma', we only test the statement that adrenalin produced by the adrenal medulla counteracts the effects of trauma in the organism. We do not test the emphasis laid on this counteraction.

2

Now it is clear enough that functional relations are a sub-class of causal ones. For suppose we say that there is a system S – a given community – in which the introduction of metal axes (T_1) has the causal effect of creating unemployment amongst the knappers (T_2). We could not rightfully claim that *the function* of T_1 in S was the maintenance (or elimination) of T_2. The two states of affairs would be causally but not functionally related. The difference between the two sorts of relations is that functional relations hold only between traits within a specified system of a certain type – a self-persisting one – while the class of causal relations is much larger. It includes these and others as well – relations holding between traits of different systems, for example, or holding within systems which are not of this required type, that is, within systems which are not self-persisting with reference to the given traits. Functional relations, then, are certain causal ones which operate within self-persisting systems.

A self-persisting system is commonly taken to be a system which maintains at least one of its properties in an equilibrium position despite variations in the other properties, either inside or outside the system, to which the presence of the first property is causally related. This ability to maintain a property in a steady state while its causal factors vary within certain limits depends upon the system containing certain devices. These must be self-regulators in the sense that they must register any significant variations in the state of the property which is being maintained and must compensate for these variations in such a way as to preserve the property within a range of permissible values. The simplest example, and the one most favoured by recent authors, is the thermostat which increases or reduces the heat throttle according to whether its thermometer registers above or below a set value. Another example is the speed governor on an engine; its revolutions are kept constant by allowing the number of revolutions to govern the throttle setting. Any change in revolutions affects the fuel supply and hence, the number of revolutions, i.e. engine speed, in the desired direction. Thus, displacement from an equilibrium position generates forces that tend to restore the position with a certain time-lag.

A self-adjusting mechanism of this sort is now known to everyone as one having negative feed back. A system containing a device for negative feed back with respect to at least one of its properties differs in various important ways from one that does not possess negative feed back. The difference in which we are interested at the moment is that relevant to the use of function statements. For it has been pointed out that they have a use only in connection with self-persisting systems. Thus Ernest Nagel has written that 'functional statements are regarded as appropriate in connection with systems possessing self-maintaining mechanisms for certain of their traits, but seem pointless and even mis-leading when used with reference to systems lacking such self-regulatory devices'.[1]

If we think of simple systems that do not possess these devices we quickly notice how difficult it is to apply function statements to them in the required sense. Our previous example, that the function of introducing metal axes was to create unemployment amongst the knappers, is a case in point. If we assume that they were introduced in order to create unemployment, we seem then to be referring to a self-regulating mechanism which ensures (or ensured) that the volume of unemployment amongst knappers varies (or varied) within a permissible range. No such mechanism is present, however. Up to a point, an increase in the supply of metal axes causes an increase in unemployment and a decrease in the supply, a decrease in unemployment. But there is no device which maintains the unemployment at an equilibrium position by registering these changes and compensating for them. The changes merely occur. On the other hand, if there were some economic mechanism such as a high tariff which came into operation whenever the number of metal axes imported went beyond a certain level, and a tax incentive for importers when the number fell below that level, then this might act so as to keep unemployment amongst knappers within a certain range.

[1] Logic Without Metaphysics, 1956, pp. 251–2.

111

If so, this would be a system with negative feed back, and one of which we could correctly say 'The function of the tariff is to maintain unemployment below, e.g. the 5 per cent level'.

The class of stable systems – those reaching equilibrium positions – and the class of systems having feed back devices overlap but do not coincide. There are stable systems without feed back for given properties, as in the case of a billiard ball at rest in the corner pocket of a table, and there are badly designed feed back systems which display oscillation instead of equilibrium: for instance, the tax and tariff scheme of our previous example might result only in wild oscillation between full employment and no employment if the importers tried to fill their quotas as quickly as possible in order to apply for a tax incentive set at a very low level of imports. In the first stage, unemployment amongst knappers might be high, and in the second stage it might sink to the vanishing point, only to rise as the importers responded to the incentive to import metal axes.

There are various types of negative feed back: that in which the restoring force is proportional to the displacement at the moment; that in which the restoring force is proportional to the time rate of increase in displacement at the moment; and that in which the restoring force is proportional to the average value of displacement over some time period. In these three common types, then, the correction is proportional to the error in the first, proportional to the time derivative of the error in the second, and proportional to the time integral of the error in the third. It is an empirical question, of course, as to which social systems display these types of feed back, and in what mixture they are displayed in any given system, for the same system can display all three types with respect to the same property. Our interest lies in the fact that (a) when function statements are used they refer to systems having one or more types of negative feed back with respect to particular traits, (b) the systems referred to need not be stable ones, (c) the rephrasing of function statements so as to eliminate expressions which either refer to or presuppose such systems does not provide us with statements that are synonymous though non-functional. These three features are some of the conditions of the correct use of function statements. It will be worth while for us to look at some attempts to use function-explanations in the social sciences and at some of the difficulties raised by these conditions.

3

Let us consider an example taken from social anthropology. Assume the question to be: 'Why among the Tallensi people is witchcraft believed to be hereditarily transmitted only by women and not by men?' And suppose one answer to be as follows: 'The notion of maleficent secret malice is incompatible with the structure of the localized lineage. The occurrence of witchcraft within a lineage would poison the mutual confidence of agnates, disrupt their corporate relationships, and throw social life into confusion. As it is, the pegging of witchcraft to the uterine line serves to circumvent any danger it might be to the community. An accusation of witchcraft does not implicate the lineage.'[1]

There are various difficulties involved in taking this explanation to be one couched in terms either of laws or of intentions. Can it be interpreted, then, in terms of functions? Instead of saying either that there must be a law statement of the form 'Members of lineages of such-and-such sort avoid disrupting the confidence of agnates', or that we are committed to asserting the truth of 'Tallensi lineage members intend to achieve and maintain the confidence of agnates', can we truthfully claim that the function of 'pegging witchcraft to the uterine line' is the maintenance of confidence amongst agnates – or the avoidance of lack of confidence?

Now, there are several kinds of objections which can be raised to any given function statement. One is that the statement is not well founded on evidence, and another is that the statement is misapplied. Consider the first point in connection with the present case. It could be argued that what we have done in giving the function of the custom is to report the custom's effects, namely, the preservation of confidence among agnates, and that such confidence is necessary for the maintenance of the lineage system. However, even if we possess a law-like generalization about the incompatibility of malice and confidence among lineage members, the custom – taking witchcraft to be hereditarily transmitted only by women – is neither a necessary nor sufficient condition for the preservation of agnatic confidence. And if the Tallensi view about witchcraft is not necessary for the preservation of agnatic confidence – if confidence could be preserved in some other fashion – then the presence of the Tallensi custom has not been explained. For an explanation would tell us that the custom is present because only it can preserve agnatic confidence and, hence, the lineage system. If other customs will serve as well, we are entitled to conclude no more than that the presence of any one of these customs is explicable – and predictable. The difference is that between the two arguments: (a) 'Only if agnatic confidence is preserved, does the lineage system maintain itself; this custom preserves agnatic confidence; therefore, whenever the lineage system maintains itself, this custom will appear.' (b) 'Only if agnatic confidence is preserved, does the lineage system maintain itself; only this custom preserves agnatic confidence; therefore, whenever the lineage system maintains itself, this custom will appear.' The first argument is invalid, the second is valid.

[1] Meyer Fortes, *The Web of Kinship among the Tallensi*, 1949, pp. 34–5.

At this point it may be objected that we have by-passed an obvious difficulty. It may be said that even if we assume that the Tallensi custom is necessary for the preservation of agnatic confidence, we still do not explain the presence of the custom. The question to be answered is 'Why is the custom present?' This is a different question from 'What evidence is there for asserting that the custom is present?' The function statement can answer the second question but not the first. Yet it is only the first question which requires an explanatory answer. To state what evidence we have for thinking that something is the case is quite distinct from explaining why it is the case. Our evidence for asserting that the custom is present may be the existence of agnatic trust. Its presence, however, does not explain the earlier occurrence of the custom; we have not explained what made the custom occur.

The briefest reply to this criticism is that it assumes what is to be shown: that a function statement cannot be employed to *explain* a state of affairs because the statement refers to the effects of the explicandum rather than to its causal antecedents. But the explanation given by a function statement explains why part (or process) A occurs instead of some other. It does this by indicating that A is necessary for the maintenance of a particular system which is known to exist. A occurs because the system is in operation and A is necessary to that operation. From this information it logically follows that the maintenance of the system is a sufficient condition for the presence of A. In other words, from the law-like statement 'Only if this sort of custom occurs is agnatic confidence preserved', and the statement 'Agnatic confidence is preserved here', we can deduce 'This sort of custom occurs here'. The objection to calling this deduction schema an 'explanation' can only be that it does not supply us with the antecedent conditions – the causes – of the custom. But in answer to this demand we need only point to all the scientific laws which are expressed as functional equations and not as causal laws. Do the former not explain equally as well as the latter? If they do, then the present objection to function-explanations cannot hold.

One criticism of any attempt to provide a law-explanation for the present case is that we are given no satisfactory generalization about the maintenance of confidence, that a candidate like 'Members of lineages of such-and-such sort avoid disrupting the confidence of agnates' is both vague and logically irrelevant to the explanation of why members of one lineage believe that members of other lineages cannot inherit witchcraft ability through the male line. Yet this is the same unsatisfactory generalization whose truth is presupposed by the assertion of the function statement that 'The function of pegging witchcraft to the uterine line is the maintenance of confidence amongst agnates'. If the generalization were not assumed to hold – if lineage members did not avoid disrupting the confidence of agnates – then this could not be the condition to which pegging witchcraft to the uterine line contributed; the function statement could not successfully be used to explain the presence of a custom (pegging witchcraft to the uterine line) if it did not contribute to the equilibrium state of a system, namely, the state of mutual confidence among agnates. Thus, the dependence of the function statement upon an unsatisfactory generalization rules out the former as a well-founded explanation of witchcraft inheritance amongst the Tallensi. The statement of the custom's effects cannot be supported except by referring to a generalization which forms part of the scheme that provides the cause of the custom. In no sense, then, can the function-explanation replace the law-explanation here. Far from supplanting the latter, the former cannot be made in its absence.

This relationship holds quite generally. Thus the valid argument, given earlier, about the appearance of the Tallensi custom consists of three generalizations each of which could be put into universal form, e.g. 'Only if agnatic confidence is preserved, do lineage systems of such-and-such type maintain themselves'. A sound function-explanation can be phrased in a variety of ways. All of them, however, require either the explicit statement or the implicit assumption of two such generalizations: one asserting that some condition is necessary for the maintenance of a system, and another asserting that some trait is necessary for the fulfilment of this condition.

The second kind of objection which can be taken to function statements concerns not the soundness of their supporting statements, but the propriety of using function statements in certain contexts. This question is closely bound up with explanation by means of laws, and the detailed examples to which we now turn will illustrate some of the issues arising from this connection.

Ethnographers had reported from North America, Oceania, and Africa instances of a custom by which persons standing in certain relationships resulting either from kinship, or more usually from marriage, were permitted or required to behave towards one another in a disrespectful or insulting way at which no offence might be taken. Such relationships came to be called 'Joking relationship' . . . thus arose a problem of comparative sociology: what is there in all these relationships that makes this type of behaviour appropriate, meaningful, and functional?[1]
. . . privileged 'joking' with the wife's brothers and sisters, can be regarded as the means of establishing and maintaining social equilibrium in a type of structural situation that results in many societies from marriage. In this situation we have two separate and distinct social groups, families or lineages, which are brought into connection with one another through the union of a man of one with a woman of the other. The husband is outside, and usually separated from, his wife's group. Through his relationship with her he is in

[1] A. Radcliffe-Brown: 'A Further Note on Joking Relationships', *Africa*, Vol. XIX, No. 2, 1949, p. 133.

an indirect or mediated relationship with individuals of her group. What is required for social equilibrium is that, as far as possible, he should not enter into conflict with his wife's group, but be obliged to maintain with that group or its members a 'friendly' relation . . . and the 'joking customs' are the means by which this situation is socially regulated.[1]

In this example it is not clear which statements are presupposed though not asserted in the explanation, and it is these which are of special importance to us. If we consider only the quoted sentences there is no explanation given by means of laws. We merely learn that privileged joking is the 'means of establishing and maintaining social equilibrium' in certain situations, but the remainder of the example indicates that privileged joking is neither a sufficient nor necessary condition for producing this kind of social equilibrium. It seems to be achieved in some societies by other means. And there are other disturbing influences in such situations than those tensions which privileged joking is said to alleviate. The joking relation is simply one of various conditions which if taken together may be sufficient; but since the additional conditions are not supplied to us we cannot state the relevant law that would connect privileged joking with social equilibrium. We have to adopt a lengthier explanation and the difficulty of presenting a schema here makes this plain. Even at first glance it is obvious that the following is not an acceptable outline in terms of laws, where the statement to be explained is 'Joking relationships occur in some societies'.

(a) All human societies avoid social dis-equilibrium (law statement).

(b) Conflict between husbands and their relatives-in-law is one kind of social dis-equilibrium (definition).

(c) People between whom a joking relation holds in personal encounters are not in conflict on those occasions (definition).

(d) All people between whom such joking relations hold in personal encounters do not conflict otherwise (law statement).

Clearly, from these four statements we cannot infer that joking relationships occur in some societies. We can infer that conflict between husbands and their relatives-in-law is avoided in all societies. We can also infer that people in a joking relationship are thereby avoiding one kind of social dis-equilibrium. Neither of these helps us, however. In any case, there is a further difficulty and it is this one which mainly concerns us now.

How are we to interpret the generalization (a) 'All human societies avoid social dis-equilibrium'? One major problem is knowing what sense to give here to the expression 'social dis-equilibrium', or for that matter, 'social equilibrium'. The original explanation required that the

[1] *Ibid.*, p. 135.

116

conflict of husbands and relatives be one kind of social dis-equilibrium. Obviously not *all* infractions of the manners, ethical and legal rules maintained by a group of people are to be classified as examples of social dis-equilibrium, even if some of the rules countermand each other. The phrase 'social equilibrium' is supposed to refer to a state of balance. Yet it has often been pointed out that the notion of a state of *social* balance is far from clear. An equilibrium point is the point of balance resulting from counteracting forces. It is a state of rest for these forces or variables in the sense that they will remain in it unchanged if not disturbed by outside influences having more than a given magnitude.

In physics many kinds of equilibrium are recognized. There is, first, an over-riding distinction into stable equilibrium, as in the case of a stone pyramid, and unstable equilibrium, as in the case of a ball balanced on a vertical rod. The pyramid will return to its position if disturbed by small forces, the ball will not. Then there is hydrostatic equilibrium in which, for example, the pressure on a drop of mercury at the bottom of a U-shaped tube filled with mercury from one side and water from the other, is such that the drop has no tendency to move. There is thermal equilibrium: a heat source within a furnace may maintain its immediate area at a constant temperature even though the furnace loses heat to the surrounding air; the entire apparatus is in a steady state but not all of it is at uniform temperature. In thermo-dynamic equilibrium, on the other hand, an alloy of copper and zinc at high temperature will exhibit both uniform temperature and no energy changes. Similarly, gas at uniform temperature in a closed container is said to be in dynamic equilibrium when the average velocity of all the moving molecules is constant, that is, when the energy of the gas is constant. Again, materials in a state of no further interaction are in a state of chemical equilibrium if their chemical processes are balanced at a given temperature and pressure. Thus nitrogen and hydrogen can form ammonia at a rate which will balance its rate of dissociation into nitrogen and hydrogen. Now in all these forms of equilibrium we know what properties are said to be in equilibrium, how they are to be measured, and what conditions are held constant.

The same holds true of the notion of equilibrium when it is used by economists. The intersection point of a supply curve and a demand curve on a graph is the price level or equilibrium state of supply and demand. If turnips are being sold in a single market, then the determination of the momentary point of equilibrium of supply and demand will require that certain conditions be kept constant. The obvious ones here are the prices of all commodities that are (*a*) substitutes for turnips in consumption, (*b*) substitutes for turnips in production, (*c*) complements of – associated with – turnips in production, e.g. turnip greens, (*d*) complements of turnips in consumption, e.g. margarine dressing. The conditions to be held constant will vary according to the length of time for which the equilibrium state is to be determined. In finding it for the short run, economists assume that there is no variation in fixed investments, whereas they take account of such variations in determining equilibrium for a commodity in the long run. In either case there are assumptions which can be stated, just as the factors in equilibrium can be identified and, of course, their means of measurement be stated, at least in principle.

A physical body, we have said, is in equilibrium if the forces applied to it so balance one another that they do not change its state of motion or rest. In economics, a price level is said to be in dis-equilibrium if demand exceeds supply; and this is said even though the price level be stable, for it may be held at a certain point by governmental authority and producers may restrict their output to a figure below what they would otherwise try to reach. It may appear, then, that the social situation resulting from marriage will be in equilibrium if the actions of the relevant people are so balanced against each other that they do not change the situation. But on the analogy of physics this equilibrium is a balance of conflicting actions (counteracting forces) not the absence of conflict required by the explanation. If all that is required by the explanation is that the two groups of marriage relatives associate without conflict, there is no need to introduce the notion of social equilibrium. It is *not* the same as social harmony or the absence of conflict. If, on the other hand, the explanation is supposed to indicate that the system of relationships amongst the two groups is a self-maintaining one in which privileged joking acts so as to provide negative feed back, then a number of difficult questions will have to be answered.

First and foremost will be the question 'What property is being maintained in a steady state?' Is it friendly relations between the husband and his wife's relatives? If so, it will have to be a particular kind of friendly relation, since it would be unreasonable to claim that privileged joking was sufficient – or necessary – to maintain *all* relations amongst these relatives in a friendly state. But which relations can these be that are so maintained? They will have to be specified. And, secondly, if we are to determine when they are in equilibrium – when the point of no relevant change has been reached – they or their effects must be measurable in terms of degrees. Otherwise we should not know when the equilibrium point on a scale has been reached. We must, for example, have some way of knowing that the energy of the gas in a closed container is constant; that the heat source in a furnace is maintaining a constant temperature; and that at a certain point of price the amounts supplied and demanded of a commodity are equal, that a stationary price and quantity have been attained. Thirdly, an answer will have to be given to the question 'What conditions are assumed to be constant?' If certain relationships amongst relatives are thought to be maintained in a steady state by privileged joking, then this effect will not occur despite *all other* causal influences. Some, like famine, war, death or disaster, may disrupt the system entirely. Some may simply destroy the feed back effect of privileged joking. A particular explanation which makes use of the notions of social equilibrium and feed back will have to indicate what are the special conditions under which they are thought to operate, and what are the ranges and values of these variables under whose influence the system maintains itself. This will be difficult.

All these objections to the use of the phrase 'social equilibrium' are, of course, objections as well to the use of our suggested generalization 'All human societies avoid social dis-equilibrium'. There are additional objections to the generalization, however.

Granted that by the phrase 'social equilibrium' we are not referring to a self-maintaining system, but only to an absence of overt conflict between marriage relatives, the claim will then be that societies avoid overt conflict of this sort. The word 'conflict' will need to be defined in terms of the society's rules of behaviour, so that we can interpret the generalization as asserting that members of human societies avoid rule infractions. (We leave aside the issue of conflicting rules.) The generalization does not commit us to asserting the success or failure of people in their efforts, but, equally, the term 'avoid' is so vague that we cannot tell what will or will not count as avoidance of overt conflict. The prospective law becomes useless. If we replace 'avoid overt conflict' by 'have a tendency to avoid overt conflict' we must give up hope of obtaining a logical derivation from our schema. A tendency statement will not permit us to derive the statement we wish to explain, namely, 'Joking relationships occur in some societies'. We might drop our generalization from the schema and try replacing it. But the problem of finding a suitable replacement is not easy. Privileged joking is only one means, if it is a means, of avoiding conflict between marriage relatives, and the mere fact that a group wishes to avoid such conflict will not in itself explain why privileged joking occurs among them.

Thus what our quoted explanation tries to account for is not why joking relationships occur in some societies and not in others – for as we have seen it cannot answer that question – but what effect privileged joking has in the society in which it does occur. In short, the explanation is not an unsuccessful law-explanation; it is an unsuccessful function-explanation. It attempts to explain the presence of a custom in terms of its effects within a system of relationships. The weakness of the attempt is that none of the conditions necessary for the successful employment of a function-explanation are met. The kind of system and the internal and external variables are left unspecified; the variables are unmeasurable; and nothing is said of the conditions which are to be taken as constant. Hence, this example is one of the improper use of function statements. For in the absence of the requirements that we have listed, there can be no proper employment of a function statement as an explanation.

Let us now consider an example in which the schema is more explicit than most: it has the dual advantage of allowing us to decide unambiguously what generalizations are being used, and of combining law and function statements in an interesting fashion. The question asked was 'What are the functions of alcohol in primitive societies?' The answer is given in brief.

... the primary function of alcohol is reduction of anxiety. The greater the amount of alcohol consumed, other conditions being equal, the more completely anxiety is reduced; and conversely, the greater the initial anxiety, the greater the amount of alcohol required to reduce it. Anxiety-reducing acts are inherently rewarding and, therefore, tend to be habit-forming. Since anxiety is a universal reaction to certain conditions of social life, all peoples to whom alcoholic beverages are available are potential habitual drinkers. But since anxiety is the agent of inhibition, anxiety reduction tends to reduce inhibition and release previously inhibited responses. Inhibitions are themselves the results of punishments imposed by society, according to its cultural tradition, for certain proscribed forms of action (especially sexual and aggressive acts). Release of such behaviour tends to reinvoke the original punishments, which then produce responses in opposition to the rewarding act of drinking. To these punishments may be added others, self-inflicted, or socially administered, resulting from alcoholic impairment of physiological functions ...

From this very general theory we derived the following set of theorems, from which concrete prediction of anthropologically observed behaviour could be formulated.

(1) The drinking of alcohol tends to be accompanied by release of sexual and aggressive impulses.

(2) The strength of the drinking response in any society tends to vary directly with the level of anxiety in the society.

(3) The strength of the drinking response tends to vary inversely with the strength of the counter-anxiety elicited by painful experience during and after drinking.[1]

From (2) and 'Subsistence insecurity and acculturation are anxiety-provoking conditions' we derive 'The customary degree of insobriety is positively associated with subsistence hazards, including hazards due to acculturation'.[2] If to (3) we add the assumption that 'the punishment for pre-marital sexual behavior can be taken as an index of the probable (but not reported) punishments for sexual responses released by alcohol'[3] then we can infer 'Drinking will be inversely associated with the strength of punishments for pre-marital sexual behavior in those

[1] D. Horton: 'The Functions of Alcohol in Primitive Societies' in *Personality*, ed. by C. Kluckhohn and M. Murray, 1953, pp. 681–2.

[2] *Ibid.*, p. 683.

[3] *Ibid.*

societies in which the level of subsistence anxiety is not high'.[1] 'The counter-drive elicited by punishment of sexual responses is not strong enough to compete with high subsistence anxiety.'[2]

Clearly, this explanation, if correct, is sufficient to answer a wider question than the one concerning primitive societies. It will also answer the question 'What are the functions of alcohol in any society?' Our task now is to decide whether the explanation can serve in this capacity.

The three 'theorems' are tendency statements, but rather loosely phrased so that our knowledge of what could confute or confirm them is also vague. For example, theorem (2) is 'The strength of the drinking response in any society tends to vary directly with the level of anxiety in the society'. Yet it is doubtful whether a precise use can be given to the two phrases 'strength of the drinking response in any society' and 'the level of anxiety in the society'. No indices are provided for either of these properties. Moreover, from a tendency statement (theorem 2) that does not even tell us to what extent the strength of the drinking response *tends* to vary directly with the anxiety level, and the additional statement that subsistence insecurity and acculturation are anxiety-provoking conditions, we cannot derive, as the explanation attempts to do, the statement that 'The customary degree of insobriety is positively associated with subsistence hazards, including hazards due to acculturation'. The verb 'is' must be replaced by the phrase 'tends to be', since that is all theorem (2) authorizes us to conclude.

And what is 'the customary degree of insobriety'? Is it the proportion of the society's members who become drunk every day, or the proportion who become drunk on ceremonial occasions? Or is it the proportion who are certifiable alcoholics? Or would an index be constructed by determining the amount of alcohol consumed per person during a given period of time? These are practical issues, apparently, but a neglect to deal with them – and similar questions arising elsewhere in the explanation – will make it difficult to decide whether the explanation is in principle capable of being applied. If no suitable answers can be given to such questions, then obviously the theorems are too vaguely expressed for their intended employment. And in that case they are not false; they are untestable.

The problem from which we began was that of 'the functions of alcohol in primitive societies', and the first answer provided was that 'The primary function of alcohol is the reduction of anxiety'. This function statement was supported by a number of law-like generalizations on the effects of alcohol. But what reason is there for employing the function statement when the remainder of the explanation in which it appears is couched in terms of laws?

There seem to be three possible reasons. One is the desire for a

[1] *Ibid.*
[2] *Ibid.*

grading judgment. Another is that the author may have wished to play upon both senses of 'function' simultaneously – to suggest that some consumers take alcohol with the purpose of reducing their anxiety whereas some take it without knowing why they do so. The effect (in the other sense of 'function') is the same in both cases, and the expression 'primary function' permits this deliberate use of the 'purpose' sense and the 'effect' sense on the same occasion.

A third reason is this: alcohol drinking may have been thought of as an element in a system, either that of a personality or of a social group. In terms of the maintenance of the system, a high degree of anxiety would be a disrupting influence. Hence, the consumption of alcohol might be viewed as a feed back mechanism which served to keep the anxiety level within a certain range, as the inflow and outflow valves in some artificial pools automatically keep the water at a given level. If this were the view taken of alcohol drinking, then we should need to have all the information about the system, the variables, and the conditions assumed to be constant, which we have already discussed. The problems of supplying them for the present example are clear enough; and this may help to explain why, in this case as in so many others, the author is content to suggest that a system is somehow involved without committing himself further.

Generalizations of a law-like sort can be supplied for the behaviour of a system whenever we know that some properties are the necessary or sufficient conditions, or both, of other properties. Thus when a function statement gives the explicandum, e.g. alcohol consumption, privileged joking, witchcraft inheritance, as a sufficient condition of the explicans (anxiety reduction, friendly relations, agnatic confidence), a law statement can easily be framed on this basis. The explicans is then the necessary condition of the explicandum: the presence of friendly relations amongst marriage relatives is necessary to the presence of witchcraft inheritance in the female line. And this also can be stated as a generalization.

Similarly, when a function statement gives the explicandum as a necessary condition of the explicans, a law statement can supply the latter as a sufficient condition of the former. In either case, formulating these conditions in law statements will be useful, because in a law-explanation we are trying to explain the presence of the explicandum in terms of its sufficient and (sometimes) necessary conditions. The first piece of information – the sufficient condition of the explicandum – will be entailed by a function statement which (a) has the form 'The function of X is Y' and (b) gives the explicandum as a necessary condition of the explicans. The second piece of information – the necessary condition of the explicandum – will be correspondingly entailed when the function statement gives the explicandum as a sufficient condition of the explicans. We can make use of either of the conditions supplied by functional statements in this way. When neither sufficient nor necessary conditions are supplied the situation is different, of course. The matching generalizations cannot be framed.

These considerations show that certain function statements and law statements can supply some of the same information, namely, in those instances where necessary or sufficient conditions, or both, are supplied by a function statement. But most function statements are not in this special category. They merely cite a condition – which is neither necessary nor sufficient by itself – of the presence of some event or process in a system. To claim that the function of X is Y is, in the majority of cases, simply to claim that usually X, but not only X, produces or helps to produce Y. For most cases, then, function statements give us less information than laws or law-like statements do; and for all cases their use is somewhat different from these. Function statements are dispensable in that there are statements of different types, which though not synonymous with them, provide us with much the same information. 'The function of incest taboos is to consolidate the nuclear group' has, *in this sense*, its equivalent in: 'The chief effect of incest taboos (in those social systems which possess them) is to consolidate the nuclear group.'

Not all examples are of this kind. The statement 'Incest taboos and exogamy rules appeared in order to make social co-operation compulsory' has its counterpart in 'The appearance of incest taboos and exogamy rules had the effect of making social co-operation compulsory'. The phrase 'in order to make' is too ambiguous for rephrasing. If a legislator is ruled out, then the phrase may or may not mean that the taboos and rules would still have appeared in the absence of the 'need' to make social co-operation compulsory. Nor is it clear what kind of need this can be. Whose need is it? If there is no need, what is the force of 'in order to make'?

4

We have been relying until now upon a distinction referred to at the beginning of this chapter, a distinction between the purpose sense of 'function' and the effect sense of 'function'. It would be an obvious mistake, however, to assume that the distinction is always easy to draw. In many explanations it is not, and this is especially true of the work of political scientists. They sometimes talk about the functions of governmental organs as though the functions had been laid down in toto by legislative planners. Political scientists have considerable use for purpose or intention explanations: they often wish to explain the actions of a person or a party in terms of what the actors were consciously trying to achieve – the state of affairs, e.g. forcing a debate in parliament – the actors attempted to bring about. And since the goals of an organization are often apparent, being those ends upon whose pursuit the members are agreed, it is, on occasion, quite easy for political scientists to explain the behaviour of a group by accepting these professions at their face value. Sometimes indeed, the articles of a charter list the purposes which are relevant to the explanation of the activities of an 'interest group'.

But it is abundantly clear that, in general, social institutions produce unforeseen consequences and perform unsuspected jobs however careful the designers have been. Conversely, some institutions develop in an unplanned state for a long time before any attempt is made to plan their functioning or control their effects. The term 'function' is often used by political scientists in such a way that it is difficult to say whether the function at issue is purposeful or not. It may be a mixture of both. This mixture can be illustrated by an example concerning the British Cabinet.

For the combination to come about and to work it is necessary for prospective cabinet ministers to make up their minds – not necessarily from enthusiastic love – to serve under Mr X and for Mr X to shape his program so that his colleagues in the cabinet will not too often feel like 'reconsidering their position', as official phraseology has it, or like going on a sitdown strike. Thus the cabinet – and the same applies to the wider ministry that comprises also the political officers not in the cabinet – has a distinct function in the democratic process as against Prime Minister, party, Parliament and electorate. This function of intermediate leadership is associated with, but by no means based upon, the current business transacted by the individual cabinet officers in the several departments to which they are appointed in order to keep the leading group's hands on the bureaucratic engine.[1]

Some of the activities carried on by the Cabinet are the result of design and some are not. Some of its functions have simply grown until people have become aware of them. Thus the question 'What is the British Cabinet intended to do, what purposes does it serve?' can be given an answer, but this answer will not tell us all the functions that it serves. Not all of them are intended; indeed, some of them may be both unintended and unwanted by the participants. If the Cabinet became the habitual scapegoat for the sins of the party executive, then this activity might be called one of the functions of the Cabinet. It would not, however, be one of its purposes. To sort out these two kinds of functions is often difficult, and the use of the ambiguous question 'What are its functions?' does not help in the sorting.

The matter is made even more complicated by the tendency of political scientists to have paid little attention, in the past, to the difference between prescribing functions for political institutions and describing the functions which they actually possessed. The form taken by this neglect is well known:

There are many political institutions for which either no generally accepted plans exist, or for which the plans, though accepted by those with the authority

[1] J. Schumpeter: *Capitalism, Socialism, and Democracy*, 1950, p. 278.

to fulfill them, and by society generally, are too vague to specify the actual activity of the institutions. When political scientists use the language of function to describe these institutions – among which are the most important of all, parties, interest groups, the courts, the legislature, the executive – they vacillate between descriptive uses of 'function' and uses in which endorsement and prescription are implied. In certain contexts to insist that the function of the independent regulatory agencies is to protect consumers is at the same time to *endorse* the purpose for which the agencies were allegedly set up and to *condemn* the practice of staffing them with people more easily influenced by the industries they are supposed to regulate than by consumers' interests.[1]

Some cases in which functions are prescribed do not allow any other interpretation; they are openly recommendations: (*a*) 'The first function political parties should perform in a democracy', Goodnow believed, 'is to assure responsibility of government to the people.'[2] (*b*) 'In the kind of government Croly envisaged the sole function of the legislators would be that of translating the broad policies commanded by the governor and or the people into workable pieces of legislation.'[3] But there are less simple cases as well. In these, careful study of the context may be required in order to determine whether a recommendation or a report is being given, or whether both are being offered together. If each of the following three examples is taken in isolation from its original context, we shall probably not know which interpretation is correct. (*c*) 'Once it establishes the responsibility of the political side of the government to the people, Goodnow continued, the next function of party is to enable politics to control administration. . . .'[4] (*d*) 'In the United States in particular . . . the nature of the formal governmental structure is such that political parties are called upon to perform certain functions which do not fall to them, for example, in England.'[5] (*e*) 'Thus Goodnow believed that the kind of parties needed to perform the many functions that fall to parties in the American system are those with strong leadership capable of providing unity and discipline within their ranks.'[6]

To say, as these quotations do, 'that the next function of party is' or 'parties are called upon to perform certain functions' or 'parties needed to perform the many functions that fall to parties' is not to assert that the functions have ever been fulfilled in practice. However great the need, the response may have been inadequate. Yet none of the quotations asserts that a function has gone unfulfilled. In point of fact, the

[1] D. Braybrooke: 'The Relevance of Norms to Political Description', *The American Political Science Review*, Vol. LII, No. 4, 1958, p. 996.

[2] A. Ranney: *The Doctrine of Responsible Party Government*, 1954, p. 96.

[3] *Ibid.*, p. 144.

[4] *Ibid.*, p. 96.

[5] *Ibid.*, p. 97.

[6] *Ibid.*, p. 99.

question 'Report or recommendation?' does not arise in this fashion. It arises in connection with a much larger body of material:

The prescriptions conveyed in talk about 'functions' do not come one by one, entirely independently. They are generally connected with one another, in what might be called normative *models*, which may be more or less elaborately developed in the case of different writers, and may also vary in explicitness. In such models, ideal functions will be designated for a number of actual or possible institutions, in a way co-ordinated by some more or less coherent set of value judgments. The models have the effect on associated descriptions of politics of encouraging stress upon the points at which observed phenomena depart from the prescribed standards; in other words, upon the ways in which the described institutions fall short of successfully performing what would ideally be their functions. This is the effect deliberately sought by Robert Dahl, whose description of the American political system in *A Preface to Democratic Theory* is oriented by the carefully stated model of 'polyarchal' democracy which he develops; and this is the way in which Schattschneider, in *Party Government*, works back and forth from his ideal of a system in which parties would be both disciplined and responsible to a description of parties as they are.[1]

Clearly, these cases of prescription do not in themselves present us with any problem concerning function-explanations. For a question like 'What are the functions of the British Cabinet now, considering that the party executives are so powerful?' cannot sensibly receive the reply 'Its functions ought to be those of intermediate leadership'. This reply would not answer the question unless it was understood that the questioner wished to know something about the disparity between the functions as planned and the functions as practised.

Thus the question 'What is its function?' has three possible interpretations, depending upon the circumstances in which it is employed. It can mean (1) 'What should it do – what purpose should it have?' (2) 'What does it actually do – what effects does it have in fact?' (3) 'What purpose does it serve?' The complication which may arise in choosing among the three alternatives is this: an inability to determine whether the function is merely recommended will create an additional difficulty in answering the query 'Purposeful or not?' For if a certain function is merely recommended, the query does not apply to it. From the point of view of the agent there is no difference between 'What purpose should it have?' and 'What effects should it have?' His recommendation that a certain function be present is the same as his recommendation that a certain goal be pursued. Once his recommendation has been given it is unnecessary to ask of *that* function the question 'Purposeful or not?' It is a question which can have only one answer. Hence, a failure to distinguish between the report of a function and the recommendation of a function will make it more difficult to distinguish

[1] Braybrooke: *op. cit.*, pp. 996–7.

between the purpose and effect sense of that term. And we hope that the importance of this distinction has already been sufficiently displayed.

However, the principal difficulty with the use of the term 'function' in political science is not that of making these distinctions, though it is a related one. The difficulty lies in knowing what information is given when functions are used as a means of explaining some event or process. We have claimed that any genuine employment of function-explanations presupposes a feed back system. The extent, then, to which this employment will be successful must depend upon the extent to which the details of the relevant system are specified. But it is an open secret that in the work of political scientists these details are generally not supplied. The three questions that must be answered if we are to explain in terms of functions remain unanswered and, often, unanswerable. They are: 'What property is being maintained in a steady state?' 'Which internal properties are the variables, how can they be measured, and what are their values and ranges?' 'Which external conditions are assumed to be constant and which to vary within specifiable limits?'

Now two sorts of reply may be made to this complaint. One is that political scientists, like other social scientists, take the background system for granted, that they could specify it if they wished – at some cost of time and trouble. Or as a variant of this retort it may be said that some social scientists *have* done it already. The second reply is more radical than this. It is that function-explanations do *not* always presuppose feed back systems, and that sometimes to give the function of an institution or a custom (or anything else) in explanation is only to refer to the work that it performs, the job that it does. Let us consider these two objections in order.

The first is easily settled. If it is true that at least some political scientists can specify the feed back systems to which they refer, so much the better. Let them do it. Or if it has been done, let these systems be compared with those which still remain unspecified, so that we can decide which function statements are genuinely explanatory and which are not. Surely, they cannot all be so? In any event, no explanation can be given when the background system is simply taken for granted. That will be useful only if the *auditor* knows what is being taken for granted, and the literature of the social sciences is well stocked with examples that preclude such knowledge. How, for instance, would the system in which the British Cabinet has the 'function of intermediate leadership' be specified? Or the system containing 'independent regulatory agencies'? Or that in which the 'function of party is to enable politics to control administration'? If these systems can be specified, then function-explanations can be offered. If the former cannot be done, then neither can the latter. Until the systems are produced, it is false to claim that because they could be, function-explanations have been supplied. The system and the function must be put forward together.

The second objection denies this conclusion. However, the suggestion that a reference to functions is merely a reference to work done or a job performed is not very helpful. Either this is only another way of talking about the role played by the explicandum in a system, or it is a resurrection of the view that function statements are simply a variety of causal statements. The latter view has already been given treatment, and the former requires none. Yet it may be argued that a third interpretation is possible, that in specifying the planned functions of organs of government – the Post Office or the Department of Primary Industry, for example – we are merely reporting on the reasons for which they are devised and maintained. This is quite true. This kind of explanation, however, is one in terms of intentions and purposes, for then the question to be answered is 'What purpose does it serve – what is it intended to do?' And, once again, no problems are raised here which have not already been considered in connection with the problem of how we explain when we cite intentions.

5

Now there is a familiar problem to which the general progress of our argument is relevant. The problem is whether it is more useful in the social sciences to concentrate attention on producing function-explanations as a means to finding law-like ones, or whether the former will be more easily obtained after the latter have been discovered.

Though identifying functions may therefore not reach so far as stating full fledged causal laws (which involve the notion of necessary and sufficient conditions), it is nevertheless a useful step toward doing the latter, and at least approximately locates the causal relationships that need to be studied. There may even be psychological advantages in postponing direct attempts at causal laws and in trying instead for functional descriptions as a first step – in asking, given an institution, 'What does this contribute to the persistence of the whole system?' 'What would be left undone if this were discarded?', or 'If this entirely succeeded in doing what it now does in part, what other activities would it help or hinder?'; or, knowing that in one society there is a specialized institution for doing F, in asking what institutions there were for doing it in this other one.[1]

Durkheim, on the other hand, argued that social scientists must look first for causes, since their discovery will help in determining functions – or effects.

For example, the social reaction that we call 'punishment' is due to the intensity of the collective sentiments which the crime offends; but, from

[1] Braybrooke: *op. cit.*, p. 995.

another angle, it has the useful function of maintaining these sentiments at the same degree of intensity, for they would soon diminish if offenses against them were not punished. . . . And again, in proportion as men are obliged to furnish more highly specialized work, the products of this work are multiplied and are of better quality; but this increase in products and improvements in quality are necessary to compensate for the expense which this more considerable work entails. Thus, instead of the cause of social phenomena consisting of a mental anticipation of the function they are called to fill, this function, on the contrary, at least in a number of cases, serves to maintain the pre-existent cause from which they are derived. We shall, then, find the function more easily if the cause is already known.[1]

Obviously, it is pointless to ask a question like 'What does this contribute to the persistence of the whole system?' unless there are grounds for believing that a system is actually present. The chief way of learning this is by discovering such features as correlations between changes in properties, changes which are in partial independence, at least, of outside conditions: and, as a special case of this, the self-maintenance of properties with respect to outside conditions. To obtain this information, however, we must conduct exactly the same kind of investigation as we should if we were trying to find laws. There is no difference between them, for in seeking laws we note dependency effects amongst variables, look for negative feed back mechanisms which serve to maintain properties in a steady state, and notice which conditions affect the variables so slightly or indirectly that they can be referred to as 'outside the system'. If we are successful in finding laws of the operation of some type of *negative feed back system*, then we can also state some functions that are carried on within that kind of system. The law that 'If X then Y' allows us to say that Y is a property being maintained in the system, i.e. a property which is a necessary condition of the maintenance of a given system.

It has been suggested previously that the discovery of function relations will lead to the discovery of laws only if the former supply necessary conditions, sufficient conditions, or necessary and sufficient conditions. When these are not supplied no laws can be stated. We have seen also that the search for knowledge of functions presupposes a belief in *some* laws or law-like statements. In believing, for instance, that the function of incest taboos is to consolidate the nuclear group, we are also committed to believing that the absence of these taboos will result in some changes elsewhere in the properties of the system, e.g. consolidation of the group by political means. But to believe this is simply to believe a law-like statement of the form 'If incest taboos are removed, then group consolidation will take place by political means'.

Moreover, as we have already said, we can only predict and explain in terms of functions when the explanations contain law-like generaliza-

[1] E. Durkheim: *The Rules of Sociological Method*, 1938, p. 96.

tions from which the required deductions – predictions and explanations – can be made. If, for example, a pint of blood is removed from a healthy donor, the loss is made good by the body within twenty-four hours or so. Hence, we have grounds for predicting what will happen in given cases if we know under what conditions a donor is healthy, and also know something about the normal operating range of the relevant system. The removal of four pints of blood may be too great a disturbance to the system. It may take it so far beyond the limits of self-maintenance that the system will break down completely, or the limits may be exceeded just far enough for the result to be permanently crippling. In either case, the possibility of predicting what will happen depends, as it does for manageable disturbances, upon our knowing that the system is self-regulating within given limits. Once we know this and know, in addition, which certain internal conditions are necessary for the preservation of the system, we can talk legitimately about the function of particular traits; that is, we can explain and predict their presence in terms of their functions within a self-maintaining system. But for other kinds of systems – ones without self-regulating devices – we have no basis for either *functional* prediction or *functional* explanation since we cannot rely upon the system maintaining itself (within limits) even after disturbances.

In view of these relationships, it is curious to say, as Durkheim does, that we shall 'find the function more easily if the cause is already known'. For in the case of punishment he is referring to a causal relation of a reciprocal type: collective sentiments produce punishment and it, in turn, produces the sentiments. To say that we can find the function of punishment (production of collective sentiments) more easily if we know the cause of punishment (presence of collective sentiments) is indisputable but uninteresting.

The same point holds of the relationship between expensive specialized work and the production of better quality products. When the causal relation is reciprocal, it is little more than a tautology to assert that the knowledge that A causes B will help us to find out that B causes A. And if it is said that the investigator does not know beforehand that the relation is a reciprocal one, then how can his knowledge that A causes B help him? Whether or not he possesses this information he still has to find out that B causes A. The only aid he can obtain from his information is the hint that the relation *may* be reciprocal. Surely this hint is of no more value than the other hints which he can pick up from knowing other relevant causal laws?

Thus neither of these two views about the order of investigation in social sciences has much to recommend it, and for the same reason: the problem is not a genuine one. In the investigation of a system the same questions will be asked by scientists interested in establishing laws as those asked by scientists who are interested in establishing functions.

The two groups will sometimes be satisfied, as we have indicated, by different types and amounts of information. Each group will find the information collected by the other as useful as its own. Or to put it a little differently, there are not two groups but only one. Its members may, of course, spend more time investigating functions at a given period than they do at another. This, however, will depend upon the progress of their particular work, and not upon any difference in the kind of scientific knowledge that they are seeking, namely, knowledge of laws.

The social sciences in which function-explanations may be found, as even a casual glance will show, include sociology, anthropology and political science, but not economics. The most general answer to the question 'Why should this be so?' is that they are not needed. Most often in economics, laws are sought. Economic actions are commonly performed on the basis of rational purposes; the agents – a board of directors, for example – know their interests and take what they believe to be effective means to their goal, e.g. maximization of profits in the long run. The sense of 'function' which would apply to such cases is the purpose sense. Any explanation of their activities or of economic institutions, therefore, is likely to be one in terms of intentions and not one in the effect sense of 'function'.

Moreover, the economic intentions of a firm or a trade union or a government agency are so well known and so obvious, as a rule, that there is little use even for intention-explanations. Thus there is no need to assert, for instance, that the function of price-cutting is to stimulate sales at the expense of competitors. Under conditions of perfect competition, it is assumed that private and social interests coincide, and these interests can in principle, at least, be specified exactly, as when they are measured in terms of money. Given this identity of interests, it is pointless to try to explain why some business firms are more successful than others in terms of the social functions (purposes) they respectively fulfil. The firms all have the same purpose, maximization of private profit or benefit; and if they pursue this they will also be pursuing public or social benefit. There is no difference in function which will explain their difference in performance. Under conditions of imperfect competition, e.g. monopoly, or those in which an unpaid social benefit is produced by an agent (as when farm land increases in value because of private development nearby), function-explanations are still not useful since both private and social interests are known and measurable. That is to say, intention-explanations of a trivial sort can be given. But if we wish to explain why the value of the farm land has risen – as a consequence of neighbouring improvements – we cannot say 'The function of such improvements is to raise the value of neighbouring property'. It is not the purpose of the improvers to do so in this case, and there is no feed back system present to legitimize the causal sense of 'function'.

At present, function-explanations in the social sciences are more often invoked by name than employed in fact. This is because their developed use requires that a number of rather stringent conditions be met, and social scientists are seldom in a position to do so. They are, however, often able to make use of function statements to construct an undeveloped form of explanation whose usefulness, nevertheless, is considerable. When an investigator has reason to believe that some sort of self-persisting system is present, he can employ a crude type of function-explanation as a stop-gap. He can use it to summarize his information, to indicate the relative importance of the various causal factors, and to refer obliquely to possible laws. His hope, of course, is that later he will be able to replace this primitive explanation by one in which the set of laws that describe the workings of the system are made explicit, that is, by a function-explanation in its developed form.

X

EMPIRICAL GENERALIZATIONS

IT is often asserted that the social sciences have not established any genuine laws. But this assertion can be taken in two quite different ways. It may be understood as claiming that the universal hypotheses put forward have not been well tested. Clearly, it is only the social scientists who can decide whether this is so. For the critics' competence to do this is open to serious doubt, since the answer to the question 'What constitutes being well tested in this particular case?' does not depend merely on logical and methodological requirements common to all the sciences. The answer depends also on the body of knowledge that is relevant to the particular problem; and there is every reason for supposing that the social scientist has a better command of this body of knowledge than have his critics.

However, the charge that the social sciences have produced no genuine laws, i.e. ones that stand up to tests, need not be an attack on the quality of the evidence available. It may be interpreted as asserting the rather different view that no hypotheses of the appropriate kind – hypotheses which if they stood up to tests would be genuine laws – have in fact been advanced by social scientists. This view claims that the candidates put forward do not possess the necessary *logical* qualifications for being submitted to serious testing. Now this assertion may seem to be so obviously false as to be not worth making.

Consider a random list: (1) 'Magical belief and ritual fortify confidence and reduce anxiety', (2) 'The imposition of direct taxes produces a higher degree of satisfaction in the taxed than the imposition of the levy by excise taxes', (3) 'People who participate in high involvement relationships show high ability to empathize', (4) 'The higher the cohesiveness of a human group, the higher will be the correlation between popularity rank and perceived leadership rank', (5) 'Industrial workers strike for higher wages only if (a) they believe that they can maintain themselves during a period of unemployment (b) they believe that their employers are able to pay higher wages', (6) 'The strength of the drinking response varies directly with the level of anxiety in the society.'

Whether or not any one of these statements has been well tested, each of them, when given in its complete form, may seem to be open to proper testing. For each of them appears to have the structure represented by the formula 'All As are Bs' and to be testable by taking As and considering whether they are Bs. A more refined version of this is 'For any X, if X were to have the property A, then X would have the property B.' The same kind of formula will serve when more than two qualities or relations are associated. We can use the most complicated member of our list as an example. It becomes: 'For any human group, if such a group were to have the property of cohesiveness, the higher its cohesiveness, the higher the correlation between popularity rank and perceived leadership rank.'

Statements of universal hypotheses can be correctly phrased in a number of ways, and it does not much matter here into which of the various forms they are cast. We need only reiterate that universal hypotheses are assertions about relationships. They do not unconditionally assert the existence of the objects, states, or events which are said to be related. They assert that if certain kinds of things exist, then certain relations must exist among them; that if, for example, properties A and B are present, a given change in A will always be accompanied or followed by a given change in B; or they assert that if certain events occur, then so will certain others. Hence, to argue that none of the hypotheses proposed by social scientists are appropriate candidates for laws will be to argue that no claim to have discovered an invariable relationship has in fact been made by social scientists.

One familiar way of discussing invariable relations is in terms of necessary and sufficient conditions. We can remind ourselves that universal hypotheses are commonly thought to assert of two properties A and B, that (1) an instance of property A is a necessary condition for an instance of property B, (2) an instance of property A is a sufficient condition for an instance of B, or (3) an instance of property A is a necessary and sufficient condition for an instance of property B. It is important to emphasize that these are conditions of causal and not of logical connections. To say, for example, that A is both a necessary and sufficient condition of B is to claim that they are in fact *always* associated. On the view that, roughly speaking, causal connection amounts to invariable association, the relationship between A and B is a causal one. It is not a relationship of entailment: the existence of property B cannot be logically deduced from the existence of property A. The terms 'necessary condition' and 'sufficient condition' are, of course, often used in this logical sense. Mathematicians speak of a set of necessary and sufficient properties when they mean that the presence of other properties logically follows from the presence of the set. But we are concerned only with the former sense of the terms and not with this latter sense. The difference between the two senses parallels that between the logical sense of 'proof' (entailment) and the empirical sense of 'proof' (overwhelming evidence). Our question, then becomes: 'Are those statements which assert such empirical relations represented on our list? Would any social scientist be prepared to say that our examples provide sufficient conditions or necessary conditions, or both? If he would, then we should have to consider whether there was any logical or methodological reason for refusing to admit his candidates to examination. If he would not, we should have to answer the question 'Why not?'

Let us return to the examples on our list. If magical belief and ritual are sufficient to fortify confidence and reduce anxiety, then these effects *must* occur whenever the belief and ritual are present. If the striking of industrial workers for higher wages is a sufficient condition for the presence of their beliefs about self-maintenance and the ability of employers to pay, these beliefs have to occur when the strike occurs. Conversely, the fortifying of confidence and the reduction of anxiety will be necessary conditions for the occurrence of magical belief and ritual – conditions in whose absence the belief and ritual cannot occur. In the same fashion, the strikers' beliefs will be a necessary condition of their striking. This is so, we may recall, because A is a sufficient condition for B if and only if B is a necessary condition for A. One benefit, therefore, of picking out the necessary and sufficient conditions expressed in statements is that it immediately becomes obvious that expressions like 'depends on', 'varies with', and 'contingent upon' are too vague for scientific purposes. Each of them can be interpreted as stating that A is a sufficient condition for B, or that B is a sufficient condition for A, or that A is sufficient for A and A for B. The example which asserts that the strength of the drinking response varies directly with the level of anxiety in the society lends itself, in the absence of further information, to all these interpretations. The same ambiguity is displayed by the other generalizations that we listed. Is magical belief necessary to fortify confidence, or merely sufficient? Or both? Or do none of these apply? And we do not know whether it is being asserted that an increase in the cohesiveness of a human group is sufficient and necessary for an increase in the correlation between popularity rank and perceived leadership rank. Perhaps the first increase is only a sufficient condition of the second increase.

It seems, then, that if we maintain that universal hypotheses should provide us with either necessary or sufficient conditions or both, our examples of generalizations are open to reasonable criticism. We do not know whether any of them claims to provide us with sufficient or necessary conditions, whether any of them is to be taken as doing so only if amplified in certain ways, or whether any of them is to be understood as asserting neither sufficient nor necessary conditions. In brief, the view that no hypotheses of the appropriate form have been advanced by social scientists may not be so absurd as it seems at first sight.

There is still another point of attack on the ability of social scientists to produce laws. It is simply this: even if we assume that well tested hypotheses of the appropriate type do exist, it is nevertheless true that they are of the most elementary type. They are nothing more than crude empirical generalizations, empirical not in the sense in which it is contrasted with logical, but in the sense of not being theoretical. They resemble in origin and form the assertion that if anything were made of refined gold, then that gold object would be ductile. The account merely includes the case in question within a given class which has a certain property. Similarly, any person who participates in a 'high involvement relationship' is included within the class of people who 'show high ability to empathize'. Hypotheses of this type, it is said, merely generalize from known cases to all cases. They explain the behaviour of a thing only in the sense of classifying it with other things which behave in that way. But, the argument continues, genuine sciences begin where social science stops: physics and chemistry *begin* by explaining empirical generalizations in terms of theoretical laws and their associated theories, whereas the most that social scientists, except perhaps economists, can do is to derive empirical laws from more general ones of the same kind. It is doubtful whether this process of derivation can even be said to explain, since the very same question arises concerning the last generalization as arose concerning the first. If the original question was 'Why did those people show high ability to empathize?' the answer might be 'Because they were participating in high involvement relationships, and all people who do that show such ability'. Yet the same question reappears as 'Why do all people who participate in those relationships exhibit that ability?' Hence, the critics conclude, any such classifying hypothesis cannot be used as an explanation, since it does not dispel the original puzzle.

There are two different charges, then, with which we can deal here. The first is that none of the hypotheses advanced by social scientists is properly framed; and the second is that while some are properly framed they are no more than empirical, i.e. non-theoretical, generalizations. It will be economical to consider the two claims jointly. This really amounts to considering the second charge, because it contains the contradictory of the first. If we can discover a well-framed hypothetical generalization we shall falsify both charges at once.

2

Let us begin by reminding ourselves of the kinds of hypotheses which, according to their critics, social scientists ought to put forward. They ought to be concerned with either (1) the regular association of properties, whether these be in sequence or simultaneous, or (2) the relations between properties, measurable directly or indirectly, such that changes in some of the properties are mathematically expressible as functions of changes in other of the properties. This, in general, is said to be the form taken by laws in the physical sciences; and the social sciences – if they are sciences – ought to display generalizations with these features. Our problem now is to find out whether they do.

One difficulty is that the hypotheses are often not clearly stated. It is left to the reader to pick out the generalizations upon which the argument depends. Thus in a study[1] of fertility rates amongst different socio-economic classes in the United States, it was found that specific lines of work were not significantly correlated with fertility rates. If, however, larger classes of these occupational groups were formed a 'consistent rank order' emerged. The class consisting of the three occupational groups of professional workers, clerks, and proprietors, had the lowest rate of fertility in the sample drawn; service and craft workers had rates from 13 to 26 per cent higher than those of the first class; operatives and labourers had rates from 28 to 51 per cent higher; farm owners and farm labourers had, in general, rates from 43 to 72 per cent higher than the rates of the least fertile class. It was found, in addition, that within each class there was some variation over a period of time in the fertility rank of occupational groups. In 1910 and 1940, for example, the clerks in the North-east region had a slightly higher rate of fertility than the professional people in that same region. In 1940 this position was reversed for the Western region.

Suppose, then, we take this variation within such a narrow range to be a puzzle worth explaining. How can we do so? The suggestion is that the variation be taken as evidence that the class consists of groups 'having the same general values and modes of living, and thus the same level of fertility'.[2] The word 'thus' in the phrase is a sign of an attempted generalization; it asserts a connection between certain modes of living, with their associated attitudes, and certain levels of fertility. But do clerks belong in this class, then? They do not, after all, have the same economic or social status as proprietors or professional people. The answer to this is that clerks 'might be classed with other white-collar groups since they tend to imitate their patterns of living. It is possible for clerks to have the same general attitudes and the same general style of living as professionals and proprietors, although unable to express this style of living and its associated attitudes on the same social and economic plane as the people whom they imitate.'[3]

For our purposes it does not matter whether the generalization connecting modes of living with fertility levels was held before the occupational groups were formed into classes, or whether the differences

[1] R. Dinkel: 'Occupation and Fertility in the United States', *American Sociological Review*, Vol. 17, No. 2, April 1952.
[2] *Ibid.*, p. 183.
[3] *Ibid.*

amongst the four classes suggested the generalization. In either case, this generalization and the classifying of the four occupational groups affected each other, since the explanation given of the smallness of the variation found within the least fertile class was that its three groups share the same pattern of living. This could hardly be an explanation unless a generalization which related pattern of living and fertility rate were presupposed. Its soundness would provide, in turn, a reason for retaining the classification system: different fertility rates could be explained in terms of occupational class and the associated style of life.

Now the statement that clerks have the same 'mode of living' as professional persons and proprietors is a statement of one of the initial conditions. We have to produce evidence that members of these groups do in fact share the same pattern of living. In order to do this we have to define 'pattern of living' in such a way that we provide criteria for classifying occupational groups into their appropriate patterns. Only if we can give such criteria shall we be in a position to frame a generalization connecting the different patterns with different rates of fertility. An obvious criticism of the study, therefore, is that since no criteria of 'pattern of living' are specified, no testable generalization has been put forward. The result is that no scientific explanation of the change in relative position within one class has been offered. All that has really been advanced is a proposal to look at the association between mode of life and fertility rate. But this cannot be done until we substitute some testable properties for those vaguely referred to by the phrase 'mode of life'.

Thus the need for a generalization has arisen, but it has not been successfully met. It arose because an attempt was made to explain why clerks fell into the same fertility class as proprietors and professional people. The generalization failed because it was improperly framed. The upshot of our discussion of the present example, then, is simply this: there is in the social sciences a class of studies which to the casual reader appear to contain explanations in terms of law-like statements, whereas in fact, they do not. What they do contain are hints as to which properties or situations or events may be connected and, hence, ought to be investigated. Such studies are actually prolegomena to future generalizations.

Untestability is a defect not confined to any particular field of social science. For example, a similar vagueness is displayed by the following generalizations, the first of which is taken from political science, and the second from economics. (1) 'When the need for protection against external pressure is removed, the suppression of internal freedom produces (as in Poland) an unbalance, chemically explosive and impossible to be maintained except by direct force.'[1] (2) 'A substantial increase in the

---

[1] G. Catlin: 'Political Theory: What Is It?', *Political Science Quarterly*, Vol. 72, No. 1, March 1957, pp. 14–5.

quantity of money within a relatively short period is accompanied by a substantial increase in prices.'[1] These two differ in an important respect, however. The economic generalization can be made more precise; the 'substantial increase' needed depends upon a number of factors which can be partially specified, e.g. the volume of the increase as compared to the total amount of money, and the counter-inflationary measures taken by the government, such as a rise in the bank rate. But it is difficult to see how this can be done for the other generalization. Is the first clause to be interpreted as referring to the beliefs of the general population about foreign enemies? Or the claims of the military establishment? And what is the relationship between the suppression of internal freedom and the resultant imbalance?

An hypothesis may be untestable for different reasons, not only because the properties it refers to are poorly defined. The untestability may result from the generalization being – to put it briefly but crudely – 'true by definition'. If it is, there can be no question, naturally, of submitting the hypothesis to tests. The social sciences are filled with instances of analytic statements (ones whose denials can be shown to be self-contradictory) that have been unwittingly treated as empirical assertions. This confusion arises in two familiar ways. Firstly, a particular expression may ordinarily be taken as true by definition and yet not be clearly marked as such. Thus it may be said that a rational entrepreneur tries to make marginal cost and marginal revenue equal. This doesn't look to be merely a definition, but a closer analysis reveals that in fact it is. We can put the generalization in this fashion: 'If: (1) An entrepreneur seeks maximum profits. (2) His marginal cost curve does not fall so fast as (or, rises more rapidly than) his marginal revenue curve. (3) These curves are continuous. *Then:* He operates at the output where marginal revenue equals marginal cost.'[2] Sentences (1), (2) and (3) jointly entail the conclusion. In brief, it logically follows from the definition of 'rational entrepreneur', taken together with such definitions as those of 'marginal cost' and 'marginal revenue', that a rational entrepreneur will seek to equate cost and revenue of this kind. Hence, no empirical assertion is being made by the assertion that he does so.

Secondly, confusion may arise from a statement being taken first as empirical and later as analytic. The commonest cause of this change is the desire to avoid the inconvenience of having a cherished hypothesis open to falsification. The fact that the change has taken place often goes unrecognized for a period of time. Two examples chosen from a large number of cases will serve to illustrate this claim.

There is in economics a well-known case of an hypothesis with this type of chequered career; sometimes the hypothesis has been taken as

---

[1] M. Friedman: *Essays in Positive Economics*, 1953, p. 11.
[2] G. Stigler: *The Theory of Price*, 1947, p. 4.

true by definition and sometimes it has been interpreted as an empirical claim. It is the hypothesis known as 'transitivity of preference' or 'maximization of utility'. The problem arises in this way. Assume that a person's preferences satisfy certain postulates, in particular, the postulate of transitivity. This says that if a person prefers a to b, and b to c, he must prefer a to c. It can be shown that if this postulate is satisfied, we can always define a self-consistent utility function which is always maximized by the person's choice, that is, the person will always choose the alternative with the higher utility for him. If this postulate is not met, we cannot define such a self-consistent utility function. Now suppose the person actually displays intransitive preference such that at one time he prefers a to b, and b to c, but at a later time prefers c to a. Then if we take the postulate to be an empirical one, this case is a counter-example. However, we can always escape this conclusion by saying that at the first time he would really have preferred a to c, but at the second time his taste had changed and so he preferred c to a. With this stipulation the postulate becomes analytically true. We can state the general point thus: if certain parameters are so defined as to make mathematical formulae true by definition, then the application of these formulae beyond the area of their definition will require an empirical assumption. This will be the assumption that the relevant parameters are stable over a period of time. But the question whether they are stable or not is clearly one of fact. If we wish to avoid the possible falsification of this assumption, we can always do so by asserting that the parameters have changed. Then, of course, we shall be interpreting the formulae as analytically true. Both these positions have been taken by economists in the past, and some of them did not realize that there were two positions between which they were oscillating as convenience dictated.

Another example of an expression which has given rise to problems of interpretation in the past is that produced by Keynes. He said that '$S \equiv I$' where S = savings and I = investment. But it was not immediately realized that savings and investment are equivalent in this expression by definition, and that this is the result of Keynes taking 'investment' to include involuntary investment, e.g. unsold stock, as well as planned investment in stocks and machinery. When involuntary investment is excluded, savings and investment are not equivalent; the relationship between them becomes a matter for empirical investigation. Economists are well aware of this, however, and have taken that interpretation – empirical or analytic – which best suits their purposes at a given time. No confusion has arisen from this policy because they now mark the difference by calling the Keynesian interpretation 'ex-post savings and investment' and the other 'ex-ante savings and investment'.

Somewhat different problems appear when efforts are made to produce social generalizations in the form of mathematical relations between measurable properties. Thus an attempt has been made to supply numerical values for two of Aristotle's generalizations. One of them is put thus: 'Whenever a separation of political and economic power results from the fact that economic power is vested in the wealthy few, whereas *real* (not necessarily *nominal*) political power resides with the many, the holders of political power, in an attempt to eliminate the concentration of economic power in the elite, probably will advocate a revolution.' The other hypothesis is put in this fashion: 'Whenever a separation of political and economic power exists because economic power has shifted to the many, whereas *real* (not necessarily *nominal*) political power is retained by the few, the few, in order to regain their economic power, will probably resort to a civil war.'[1] The obvious deficiency of these generalizations is their vagueness. We do not know when power of either sort has shifted from one group to the other. If there were some means of measuring these shifts, we should be able to test the hypotheses. Hence, the notion of a 'concentration ratio' is introduced. It is supposed to give 'numerical values for the critical points in the separation of political and economic power; i.e. it specifies that if the separation of political and economic power has proceeded beyond certain values (above or below 0·5), political disturbances will ensue'.[2] If the value is above 0·5 a revolution will be likely; if the value is below 0·5 a civil war is probable. The concentration ratio, P, is calculated by the equation $\rho = \dfrac{1}{2a-1}$. The constant a gives the slope of the curve of distribution of income obtained by Pareto's law $N = \dfrac{A}{\chi^a}$. 'N represents the number of people whose income is equal to or higher than income denoted by χ; A is a constant, depending upon the size of the economy; a is a parameter.'[3] Its values can vary from infinity to 1, those of P from 0 to 1. When the value of a is high, there is high equality of income; when the value of a is low, there is great inequality of income. An a value of 1·5 with P at 0·5 is taken to indicate a *stable economy*, and this, in turn, is taken as a reliable sign of political stability. Economic, and hence political, instability appear as these numerical values are departed from, that is, when income is either highly concentrated or very widely distributed. What the use of the concentration ratio amounts to, then, is a measure of the stability of an

[1] F. Kort: 'The Quantification of Aristotle's Theory of Revolution', *The American Political Science Review*, Vol. XLVI, No. 2, 1952, p. 492.
[2] *Ibid.*, p. 493.
[3] *Ibid.*, p. 489.

economic system with respect to political disturbances. For 'a revolution is a political disturbance that is created by an under privileged majority; a civil war is a political disturbance that is initiated by a privileged minority'.[1]

Now it is clear enough that any attempt to use the ratio will require that certain difficulties be acknowledged. The nub of the equation is the constant a, since it is a measure of the equality of income. But there is no other *measured* property referred to in the employment of the equation. The other properties which enter into the hypothesis (or hypotheses) are unmeasured. High concentration of income is apparently assumed to be a sufficient condition of economic instability and so is very wide dispersion of income. No measurable criterion of economic instability – or of stability – is produced except that of equality of income. And the causal connection between this and economic stability is the point at issue. It is not obvious that a certain kind of income distribution is the invariable accompaniment of a certain degree of economic stability or instability. Nor is it even clear what is meant by the phrase 'stable economy'. It presumably does not mean 'fluctuations in gross annual income over a period of time are small'. If that were so, any expanding economy would be an unstable one and thus prone to political disturbance. Economic stagnation cannot be the identifying mark of political peace, for there are a great many counter-examples to this proposition. If 'economic stability' is interpreted as meaning that the system has reached an equilibrium state to which it returns after outside influences have disturbed it, then there need be no reason why this economy should exhibit a certain kind of income distribution. Equilibrium states can display various sorts of income dispersion. In any case, until we know what 'stable economy' means we cannot learn much by being told that a certain income distribution is its sufficient condition.

Moreover, since the hypothesis assumes that economic stability is a sufficient condition (or reliable sign) of political stability, the same kinds of problems arise once again. True, 'political stability' is definable as 'the absence of revolution or civil war'. However, there are obvious difficulties connected with the use of the term 'revolution'. Its vagueness ordinarily leaves open the question whether, for example, a political movement that does not aim at an economic revolution can yet be called a 'political revolution'. In the present case the hypothesis itself answers the question in the negative: '. . . the holders of political power, in an attempt to eliminate the concentration of economic power in the elite, probably will advocate a revolution.' This will be an *economic* revolution to change the income distribution. Therefore, to say that economic instability is a sufficient condition (or reliable sign) of

[1] *Ibid.*, p. 491, footnote.

political instability is to say, in part, that economic instability has this same relation to the revolutionary attempt at changing the income distribution. Where economic instability occurs, so will revolution. Part of the definition of 'political stability', then, will be: 'the absence of a revolutionary attempt to change the income distribution'. The other part, of course, will be: 'the absence of any attempt to create a civil war – to change the distribution of political power'. Joining the two parts together we have as our definition of 'political stability': 'the absence of any revolutionary attempt to change the income distribution or of any attempt to change the distribution of political power'.

Now 'being a sufficient condition of' is a transitive relation. If A is sufficient for B, and B for C, then it logically follows that A is sufficient for C. The same is true of the relation 'being a reliable sign of'. It is for these reasons that we are entitled to conclude that it follows from the present argument that a certain income distribution (where $P = 0.5$) is sufficient to produce the absence of revolutionary economic or political changes. This hypothesis, it should be noted, differs somewhat from those of Aristotle, but it has the advantage of eliminating the need for connecting economic stability with either income distribution or political stability. The problem is simplified to one of discovering whether measurable patterns of income distribution are sufficient conditions of certain economic and political changes. Nothing has been done, of course, to provide a measure of these changes, and unless that is done the testing of the hypothesis can only be as precise as the definition of 'economic and political revolution'. In short, no relation between measurable properties has been advanced, and certainly no mathematical relation between such properties has been formulated. The measurement of one property only cannot ensure either of these results. On the other hand, the hypothesis does refer to the regular association of properties. One of these is measurable at present and the other is not. Even if both became measurable, however, it would not follow that the relationship between them could be mathematically expressed as a function relationship. The former is merely a necessary condition of the latter, not a sufficient one.

The two generalizations derived from Aristotle are rather more complex than our revised hypothesis and they present problems of their own. There is, first, the difficulty that the concentration ratio gives the concentration of income whereas Aristotle's hypotheses are represented as referring to 'economic power vested in the wealthy few'. The point here is simply that high concentration of economic power may co-exist with high equality of income. The chairman of a large corporation or the Minister of a government department may have great economic power, but neither need have incomes much greater than those of other people.

Secondly, Aristotle's hypotheses are so stated as to blur the distinction

143

between two different states of affairs: (*a*) the situation in which economic and political power are held by separate groups – the few and the many, (*b*) the situation in which economic or political power has *shifted* from one group to the other so that the two kinds of power are held by separate groups. It is not clear whether it is the mere fact of separation that is supposed to be responsible for civil war and revolution, or whether it is the separation preceded by a shift that is thought to be responsible. The two situations are obviously distinct. A civil war might occur if economic power shifted from the few to the many while political power was still held by the few. But it might not occur if economic power had long been held by the many and political power by the few. It would be a matter for empirical investigation to discover whether civil wars occurred under the one set of conditions or the other, or both – or neither.

Finally, the concentration ratio is said to specify 'that if the separation of political and economic power has proceeded beyond certain values (above or below 0·5), political disturbances will ensue'. And this is taken as implying that 'the qualitative relationship which Aristotle formulated has been restated in quantitative terms'.[1] Yet has this been done?

The concentration ratio specifies the concentration of income, not the separation of political and economic power. If P is greater or less than 0·5, nothing at all follows about the separation of powers even if it is assumed, contrary to our earlier criticism, that high concentration of economic power and high concentration of income are either identical or sufficient conditions of each other. It is not the separation of economic and political power that has deviated from a value of 0·5; it is, at most, concentration of economic power that has deviated. The only way in which Aristotle's hypotheses can be made to incorporate the concentration ratio is not as a measure of separation of power.

We can make this point by stating the hypotheses in some fashion such as this: (1) 'Whenever $P > 0·5$ to a certain degree, whereas political power is held by the majority, then the latter probably will advocate a revolution.' (2) 'Whenever $P < 0·5$ to a certain degree, whereas political power is held by the few, then the latter probably will advocate a civil war.' The values of P give no information about the size of the group that holds political power. Only if they did – only if P were also a measure of the distribution of political power – would it be correct to claim that the concentration ratio measures the separation of economic and political powers. In fact, the ratio measures the same property as it did in the case of our revised hypothesis. The difference here is that Aristotle introduces at least one additional feature, the holding of political power by the few or the many. The result is that to the previous difficulties of defining and measuring those changes which

[1] *Ibid.*, p. 493.

144

we call 'revolution' and 'civil war', we must now add the difficulty of defining 'political power', and of measuring its distribution. No more than in the previous hypothesis has the relationship advanced in the present hypothesis been stated in quantitative terms. But as in the earlier case, a generalization has been put forward about the regular association of properties, one of which is measurable and the others of which may be roughly testable.

4

There is no doubt that all the examples so far considered – the well formed and the ill-formed alike – are empirical generalizations, that is, they are all derived from or based upon *observations*. They contain no references to the existence of abstract or theoretical objects, processes, or states. For social scientists, it is said by their critics, have no *theories* with which to explain their empirical generalizations. Their efforts are spent upon producing more and more general forms of empirical hypotheses from observation and experiment, whereas in the more advanced sciences this is not so. In them, laws are obtained by deduction from theories, or by deduction combined with transliteration into the vocabulary of experimental work; it is by the latter method that empirical laws are obtained in physics and chemistry. Scientists in those fields are primarily interested in the theories which allow them to explain empirical laws, and not, in contrast to social scientists, in the production of such laws.

This is, in outline, what one common complaint about the use of empirical generalizations in the social sciences amounts to. We shall argue against this complaint that in fact there are both well-framed hypotheses and theories in the social sciences. We shall argue, further, that the presence of abstract or theoretical objects is irrelevant to the question of whether there are such hypotheses and theories. We begin by listing some examples of well-formed hypotheses:

(1) 'Societies in which marriage is allowed or preferred with mother's brother's daughter but forbidden or disapproved with father's sister's daughter will be societies in which jural authority over ego male, before marriage, is vested in his father or father's lineage, and societies in which marriage is allowed or preferred with father's sister's daughter but forbidden or disapproved with mother's brother's daughter will be societies in which jural authority over ego male, before marriage, is vested in his mother's brother or mother's brother's lineage.'[1]

(2) 'For men, the length of sickness absence decreases directly with the length of employment service.'

[1] G. Homans and D. Schneider: *Marriage, Authority, and Final Causes*, 1955, p. 51.

(3) 'Labour turnover increases directly with the distance of worker's residence from work and inversely with the level of unemployment.'

(4) 'The trade cycle (rise and decline of employment, prices, profits, and income) is caused by the "alternating excess and deficiency of investment in relation to saving by the consuming public, and the amount spent by industrialists with the Government on new investment".'[1]

(5) 'A rise in the price of any one good will result in a fall of demand for that good provided all other prices and money income remain unchanged.'

(6) 'If the price of a good rises the supply of that good forthcoming will be increased – other things being equal.'

(7) 'If there is unemployment it can be decreased by decreasing taxation of the poor and increasing taxation of the rich.'

(8) 'A country can improve its deficit on the balance of payments by devaluing its currency.'

Do these generalizations meet the requirements of invariable association, universality, and testability? Does each assert that a property – or state or situation or process – is either a necessary or sufficient condition of some other, or a necessary and sufficient condition of another? Clearly, all the statements listed might in fact be false; none of them need have its truth determined merely by definition of its terms or by logical demonstration. At least, all of them can be so interpreted that they are not analytic statements. It may be thought that numbers (5) and (6) are suspicious; that, for example, the phrase 'other things being equal' in number (6) will allow so many qualifications to be made that the statement will become logically true and, hence, unassailable. This need not be the case, however, for while such conditions as the presence of a market – sellers, consumers, supplies, etc. – are assumed, once these are stated, it is still open to test whether under such circumstances a rise in the supply of a good is the result of a rise in its price. Similarly, a rise in the price of a good is claimed to result in a fall in the quantity bought – if all other prices and money income remain unchanged. These latter conditions do not logically ensure that a rise in price will result in a fall of expenditure, since consumers could, if they wished, devote a larger proportion of their income to the purchase of the good in question. What the hypothesis claims is that they do not.

None of the statements on our list, we have said, need have its truth determined by definition of its terms or by logical demonstration. Nor will the truth of any of them be decided by direct observation. Each generalization refers to an unlimited number of cases, past, present, and future; that is, each is a universal hypothesis which refers to events or things of a certain kind and not to particular instances. It is asserted that any country can improve its deficit balance of payments, that any

[1] E. Durbin: *Problems of Economic Planning*, 1949, p. 165.

unemployment can be decreased, that for any group of men belonging to a class with certain properties, the length of sickness absence decreases with service. Naturally, qualifications may have to be made concerning the kinds of country, unemployment, and man, of whom these statements hold. But the statements will remain universal ones because no particular country or period of unemployment or set of men will be mentioned. The hypotheses will apply to any objects that fall into the appropriate category, and no finite set of direct observations will be sufficient to provide a test for every one of an infinite set of cases.

Again, it will not be correct to say that any of our generalizations is too vague for testing. Each is briefly stated, but each can be so expanded as to permit us to formulate the conditions which would test it. Thus no one believes that a rise in the price of one good ever occurs in isolation from a rise in all other prices. The influences which raise its price also raise the prices of other goods at the same time. Yet if such a single rise *were* to occur, then according to our hypotheses, the supply of the good would increase and the quantity bought decrease. Testability in principle is all that we can require of any scientific hypothesis. Otherwise we shall eliminate from the sciences a large array of important statements about such things as frictionless surfaces and ideal gas molecules. A claim like 'If two perfectly elastic bodies were to collide, the total kinetic energy of the system would be the same before and after the impact' is testable in principle though not directly testable in practice. In this respect it is exactly like our economic example. The other examples do not even raise this problem. They are straightforward cases which can be directly tested once certain assumptions are made clear. It would not be reasonable, for example, to interpret statement number (2) as asserting that the length of sickness absence decreases directly with the length of employment service even under conditions of forced labour or in concentration camps. But qualifications such as these hold of all scientific generalizations. In the natural sciences it is quite common to speak of these as qualifications forming a 'text' which accompanies all hypotheses. The 'text' includes a number of different kinds of qualification, some of which apply only to hypotheses framed as equations; others apply to the kind of statement found on our list. The first kind is illustrated by an example of Bridgman's:

. . . if I set up the mathematical theory of a body falling under the action of gravity, I have the equation $\frac{dv}{dt} = g$, but I have to supplement this by a 'text', saying that v is a number describing a property of the moving body which can be obtained by a certain kind of measurement, which is specified, that t is the time obtained by another kind of measurement, etc. . . . it must also specify the connection between the different symbols in the equation . . . the text specifies that the s and the t are the distance and time obtained by *simultaneous* measurements. The equation itself has no mechanism for demanding that s

and t be simultaneous, and in fact this demand cannot be described in the language of the equation.[1]

The second sort of qualification laid upon a scientific hypothesis by its 'text' includes the definition of its terms and an accurate statement of the limits within which it is supposed to hold. Neither of these need appear in the generalization itself, and however obvious each is, critics of the social sciences often speak as though hypotheses of the type that we have listed are deficient in not containing such qualifications on their face. It is worth the time, therefore, to remind ourselves that the generalizations of the natural sciences do not differ on these points from those of the social sciences. One instance – that of Galileo's laws of projectile motion – is referred to by Holton, and his remarks are sufficient to indicate how similar the 'texts' are in the two fields.

We find in his work a thorough examination of the major limitations involved; for example, he points out that the trajectory will not be parabolic for extremely large ranges because then the acceleration of gravity, being directed toward the center of our round earth, will no longer be parallel for different parts of the paths assumed in our equations. Of course this failure applies, strictly speaking, even to small trajectories, but in such cases it is by theory and test permissible to neglect it for our purposes, just as we have already neglected the effect of air resistance, rotation of the earth, variation of the value of g over the whole path, etc. . . . if we were required to deal with actual motions in which these secondary factors are not negligible, we are confident that we would surely be able to discover the laws guiding those smaller effects, and add them to our calculations.[2]

The eight examples on our list differ amongst themselves in the extent to which their scope has been accurately determined. They also differ amongst themselves in the degree to which a given investigator might feel 'confident that we would be able to discover the laws guiding those smaller effects' – those effects which have been deliberately neglected in the statement of the hypothesis because they do not substantially alter the major effect, or else complicate the hypothesis unduly, or both. The situation in the social sciences is more often the second alternative than the first. In other words, if we are required to deal with the actual price movements of goods where secondary factors like the rise in other prices are not negligible, we find it very difficult to discover the laws guiding those effects and add them to our calculations. But neither of these differences amongst the members of our list is peculiar to the social sciences; a list of hypotheses drawn from the natural sciences would show a similar variation with respect to our knowledge of their scope and our confidence that laws governing the 'smaller effects' could be discovered.

[1] P. Bridgman: *The Nature of Physical Theory*, 1936, pp. 59–60.
[2] G. Holton: *Introduction to Concepts and Theories in Physical Science*, 1952, p. 270.

If it is true, as we have been arguing, that all the generalizations on our list seem to meet the three requirements of universality, testability, and uniformity of connection, is it also true that all our hypotheses give either necessary or sufficient conditions, or both? The briefest answer to this is that the question is somewhat misapplied.

Suppose we ask the same question of generalizations in the natural sciences. Take the simplest possible case like that of Boyle's Law. It states that at a given temperature the volume and absolute pressure of a gas vary inversely. But when we first learn about it we also learn that there are conditions under which it does not hold. Similarly, there are conditions to which Snell's Law does not apply. In those conditions it is not true that if a light ray is incident at a surface separating two transparent media, then it is also bent so that the ratio of the sine of the angle of incidence to the sine of the angle of refraction is constant for those media.

If we simply look at the statements of these laws, as we did at our list of social hypotheses in the opening pages of this chapter, then we shall find it difficult to answer the popular questions: 'Necessary condition? Sufficient? Or both?' Under some circumstances not mentioned in its statement, Snell's Law gives the sufficient conditions of the bending of the light ray in the manner indicated. Under other conditions it does not. When we know only what is given in the form of its brief statement we cannot answer the questions about necessary and sufficient conditions. And the same is true of Boyle's Law: for one, the type of gas has to be specified before we can correctly assert that such and such are the sufficient conditions for the pressure and volume of an enclosed gas to vary inversely. Hence, it is not a fair criticism of an hypothesis to say, in the absence of its 'text', that we do not know whether it is to be interpreted as asserting necessary conditions or sufficient ones, or both. It may be that the hypotheses on our first list are defective in not providing us with such conditions, but we shall never be able to show this merely by examining them without their accompanying glosses.

The generalizations of the social and natural sciences are exactly similar in this respect. Boyle's Law, we may recall, is accurate only for gases of very low density. It assumes an ideal gas – one without internal friction since its molecules are supposed to have no extension and to exert no forces on one another. As the density of an actual gas increases the accuracy of the law decreases, for when the molecules are nearer to each other the forces of attraction amongst them are greater; and the result of this is that the pressure is reduced. Yet the law's range of accuracy, while available to the interested student, is not usually included in the statement of the law itself. Nor is the scope of the hypothesis 'The higher the cohesiveness of a human group, the higher will be the correlation between popularity rank and perceived leadership rank' included in its statement. The question whether the relevant information *could* be made available to the interested auditor is an important but different one. The charge that it could not be, if substantiated, would mark the distinction between a proto-hypothesis and a fully developed one. Our claim, then, is that whatever the status of the examples on our first list, those on our second are supported by 'texts' at least as respectable – considering the difference in subject matter – as those of generalizations in the natural sciences.

Now let us examine the credentials of several of our generalizations in more detail. We begin with some remarks about the one concerning popularity and leadership rank, for it is drawn from our first, and, apparently, weaker list. What exactly docs it assume? It takes cohesiveness to be 'the total of individual members' identifications with the group' and to depend 'upon the degree of member attachment resulting from the satisfaction of self-needs they have experienced through membership'.[1] Under conditions of low identification with the group a person will be receiving little satisfaction from it. 'He may then be expected to like or dislike fellow members purely on the basis of personal preference. However, when he is deeply concerned about the welfare of the group, he may then be expected to like most those members whom he perceives as making the most valuable contributions to the group.'[2] This is substantially what the hypothesis claims about members of small groups. Four such groups were tested for cohesiveness and ranked. The index numbers for the groups were these: group A = 82, group B = 52, group C = 63, group D = 41. The most cohesive group was A, the least cohesive was D. The index was constructed on the basis of direct answers to questions put to members about their enjoyment of meetings, their liking for each other, and their willingness to sacrifice for the group. Then members' responses to two questions about the other members' popularity and the value of their contributions to the group were scored and correlated.

One result was that group A had a linear correlation of ·94 between the perceived leadership of any member ('amount of valuable contributions') and his popularity; group B of −·19; group C of ·66; group D of ·20. This is support for the view 'that through time leadership and popularity roles may either merge or differentiate, depending on whether cohesiveness is increasing or decreasing, with specialization of these roles a function of low cohesion'.[3] Obviously, the negative correlation of ·19 for group B is anomalous and requires explanation. Equally obvious is the fact that the generalization does not present us with a mathematical relationship – even though all three properties are measured. Nothing is said about the functional connection amongst

[1] G. Theodorson: 'The Relationship Between Leadership and Popularity Roles in Small Groups', *American Sociological Review*, Vol. 22, No. 1, February 1957, p. 59.
[2] *Ibid.*, p. 60.
[3] *Ibid.*, p. 67.

these properties. We do not know how closely the correlation between popularity and leadership varies with cohesiveness. But it does seem to be claimed that the presence of a higher (or lower) cohesiveness in one group than in another group, or at different periods in the same group, is always *sufficient* for the presence of an increased (or decreased) correlation between the other two properties.

Clearly, no information is given about the change in cohesiveness as a *necessary* condition of the change in correlation between leadership and popularity. Does this distinguish the present example from the cases of Boyle's Law and Snell's Law? Do they, in conjunction with their glosses, provide us with necessary conditions as well as sufficient ones? For Boyle's Law the answer is 'Yes'. Roughly speaking, there are four conditions which are both sufficient and necessary for the volume and absolute pressure of a gas to vary inversely. These are: (*a*) the gas must be of low density, (*b*) the gas must be compressed at constant temperature, (*c*) the temperature of the gas must be well above its liquefaction point, (*d*) no chemical association or dissociation must take place in the gas. Given these conditions, Boyle's Law holds approximately. If greater accuracy is required, van der Waal's Law can be employed.

Thus it is a difference between Boyle's Law and the hypothesis about group cohesion that the first is expandable so as to supply necessary conditions while the second is not – at present. Is this difference also exhibited in the case of Snell's Law? A moment's consideration will show that it is. What we must take into account are the conditions which change the velocity of light, that is, change the electromagnetic properties of media. The chief conditions affecting these properties are the colour (or wave length) of the light; the temperature variation within the media, especially the temperature of gases; any elastic strain to which the media are subjected; and in the case of crystalline media such as quartz and feldspar, the orientation of the direction of incidence with respect to the planes of the crystal. All these conditions affect the operation of Snell's Law: it does not hold under certain states of temperature change and elastic strain, or for certain kinds of light rays or for transparent crystals. Taken jointly, then, these four types of factors are the ones from which we can draw both the necessary and sufficient conditions required for Snell's Law to hold.

The question which now confronts us is whether *any* of the texts of the generalizations on our second list supply us with similar sorts of conditions. In the case of the anthropological example the situation is as follows. The hypothesis claimed that: 'Societies in which marriage is allowed or preferred with mother's brother's daughter but forbidden or disapproved with father's sister's daughter will be societies in which jural authority over ego male, before marriage, is vested in his father or father's lineage, and societies in which marriage is allowed or preferred with father's sister's daughter but forbidden or disapproved with mother's brother's daughter will be societies in which jural authority over ego male, before marriage, is vested in his mother's brother or mother's brother's lineage.' The phrase 'jural authority' means 'legitimate or constituted authority, and a person holds jural authority over others when, according to the stated norms of his group, he has the right to give them orders and they have the duty to obey'.[1]

The authors go on to make it clear that the presence of jural authority in conjunction with cross-cousin marriage is to be taken as a roughly sufficient[2] condition for the existence of a particular form of marriage. 'From our general theory we argued that, if the locus of jural authority over ego, before marriage, is his father, then, provided unilateral cross-cousin marriage is allowed at all, the matrilateral form will be the rule, and if the locus of jural authority over ego, before marriage, is his mother's brother, the patrilateral form will be the rule.'[3] The difficulty with taking this hypothesis as a statement of the *necessary* conditions for the matrilateral and patrilateral forms is simply that all anthropologists know of societies which have both forms of cross-cousin marriage and only one locus of jural authority. In these societies it is obvious that the two forms of marriage cannot have as their necessary conditions the two loci of authority required by the hypothesis.

We have on our list some well-known examples drawn from economics, and a brief consideration of them will tell us something of their status. One asserts that a rise in the price of a good will produce a fall in its consumption. But no economist believes that a price rise is always sufficient to produce this effect. For if the good in question cannot easily be dispensed with, the consumers – being poorer – may decrease their purchases of luxury goods and increase their purchases of the necessity. This substitution will result in a rise in demand rather than in a fall. This may occur even though 'all other prices and money income remain unchanged', as the hypothesis demands. A more common situation is a rise in consumption for a particular luxury good after its price has been raised; the rise in price may accompany an increase in the prestige of the good and so increase its consumption. Hence, a price rise is not sufficient for a decrease in consumption, and certainly not necessary for such a decrease, since sometimes a price decrease produces a fall in consumption. A luxury good may lose prestige by having its price lowered and thus lose part of its market.

The same general conclusion holds of some of our other economic generalizations. We cannot take the price rise of a good to be sufficient to increase its supply. Sometimes the price may increase but the supply

---

[1] Homans and Schneider: *op. cit.*, p. 21.

[2] 'Roughly sufficient' because the authors may be correct in believing that they have found a counter-example to their hypothesis. *Ibid.*, p. 57.

[3] *Ibid.*

decrease, as in the case of a labour force that stops work once a particular level of real income has been reached. Any price rise that adds to their income will merely decrease the amount of the good which they need to produce in order to reach their desired standard of living. Again, unemployment may not 'be decreased by decreasing taxation of the poor and increasing taxation of the rich'. If the rich are taxed their incentive for investment may diminish and nullify the effects on unemployment of increased consumption by the poor. Similarly, a country may not improve its deficit on balance of payments by devaluing its currency. A country which devalues its currency hopes to improve its deficit in two ways. It expects import prices to be higher and export prices to be lower. Hence, it expects the country's imports to drop and its exports to rise. Neither of these effects may take place, however. Economists have shown that under certain conditions of demand the increase of exports and the decrease of imports may not be sufficient to produce the desired result.

These three generalizations are alike, then, in not actually providing sufficient conditions, though they may be interpreted as attempting to do so. Nor does any of these hypotheses supply necessary conditions. In each case – that of increased supply of a good, change of taxation, devaluation of currency – the presumed result can take place in the absence of the specified condition. The supply of a good can increase through many other means than by an increase in its price. Decreased taxation of the poor and increased taxation of the rich does not wait upon unemployment for its stimulus. A country could conceivably decide to revalue its currency for other reasons than that of affecting its balance of payments.

Now it is not likely that any economist ever believed that necessary conditions are provided by the economic generalizations on our second list. In the past, some may have believed that sufficient conditions are supplied in these cases, but the present view, certainly, would be that the hypotheses as stated merely assert strong tendencies and not perfect correlations or constant conjunctions, although the actual statements of the hypotheses are universal in form.

One question which we have been trying to answer is whether relevant information about necessary and sufficient conditions could be drawn from the texts of our sample hypotheses. The answer is an equivocal 'Yes'. Some cases have a settled answer and some cases do not. To ask, for instance, what sort of conditions the hypothesis about jural authority gives us is to ask the question of someone who might employ it professionally – some anthropologist. In this particular case the authors' words seem to indicate that they take the hypothesis to supply a roughly sufficient condition. Our reason for believing that they do not take it as supplying a necessary condition as well, is simply that we credit them with knowing what some other anthropologists also know, that there are societies with the required types of marriage and without the required types of jural authority. But if it so happened that the authors were not familiar with these examples, then they might wish to treat the hypothesis as supplying a necessary condition of a certain kind of marriage. Since a different investigator might treat the statement as supplying neither necessary nor sufficient conditions, it is not enough in such a case to ask 'What does the generalization assert?' We have to ask 'What was the generalization used to assert on such-and-such occasions?'

However, in contrast to these, there are also hypotheses for which there is a settled interpretation. Boyle's Law is an instance of this type and so is Snell's Law. There is no need, therefore, to distinguish in such cases between the question 'What does the generalization assert?' and 'What was asserted by it on that particular occasion?' The interpretation does not change from one occasion to another, at least not in the way that the interpretation of a new hypothesis can change. Of course both laws have undergone such changes in the past. Boyle knew nothing about the factors of gas density and Snell nothing of the effects of elastic strain. Their original statements gave only some of the necessary conditions and part of the sufficient conditions, e.g. in Boyle's case the compression of the gas at constant temperature. With further work additional conditions have been provided, that is, the scope of the hypotheses has been more accurately determined and agreement on them reached by physicists.

There are, on our lists, generalizations with a history and status similar in these respects to those of Boyle's Law and Snell's Law. Economists are generally agreed upon the scope of the Laws of Supply and Demand, and the criticisms that we have raised of the two on our second list (numbers 5 and 6) are familiar to every economics student. They are, in fact, criticisms without an edge, since they are usually taken by economists as limits to the scope of the laws. It would be quite possible to qualify the generalization about rising price and increased supply so as to take account of the diminished output from certain labour forces. This is not necessary for the same reason it is not necessary that Boyle's Law incorporate a provision about chemical action or Snell's Law a proviso concerning temperature changes in the media. It would be extremely cumbersome to write into the statements of these laws all the qualifications which are understood to apply to them. In the same way, the generalization about taxation to relieve unemployment and the one about devaluation of currency resemble generalizations in the natural sciences. In both the natural sciences and the social sciences there are generalizations whose texts are generally taken as providing well-known limits of range and accuracy. In both fields, there are hypotheses which lack such texts, either because not enough is known, as in the case of high involvement relationships and ability to empathize, or because there is no general agreement as to what is known.

We have been trying to show – in part by bad example – the dangers of asking of hypotheses the questions 'Necessary condition? Sufficient? Both?' in the absence of accompanying glosses or texts. If we are correct, it is equally dangerous in such circumstances to make more than a preliminary judgment about some of the other features of hypotheses – their universality, testability, and invariability. The lack of precision for which we criticized the generalizations on our first list should be a warning to us. No generalization in any science can be expected to withstand criticism of this kind. Nor will any critic be able to determine by simple inspection whether a sentence like 'Any country can improve its deficit on balance of payments by devaluing its currency' is habitually interpreted by economists as a universal hypothesis about all countries, or as a tendency statement whose limitations are well known. If the knowledge is available, it is always possible for investigators to choose between stating their hypotheses in a simple form that may mislead outsiders and stating them in a more complicated and accurate fashion which enlightens the bystander while inconveniencing the worker.

There is a further point to be stressed here. The distinction between necessary and sufficient conditions has well-known limits of usefulness. It is helpful in that it leads us to ask what exactly is asserted by the employment of a particular sentence. But the aid given by the distinction always depends upon it being understood that the conditions called 'necessary' and 'sufficient' are not complete, that all sorts of possible influences are not specifically mentioned when these two kinds of conditions are listed. We do not have to state that one of the necessary conditions for Boyle's Law to hold is that molecules do not radically alter certain of their properties; or that it is necessary for the truth of the hypothesis 'Labour turnover varies inversely with the level of unemployment' that the labour force be willing to work for a reward. True, if such conditions are not met, these hypotheses will not hold. But the fact that such conditions are taken for granted is an indication of how much is left unsaid when we claim that certain conditions are necessary and sufficient for an occurrence. It is usually declared, and correctly so, that the conditions which are taken for granted are those that have their origin outside the system in question. If there were no longer any scarce goods in the world, many laws of economics would no longer be applicable. This contingency affects the problems of economists very little, however. They proceed under the assumption that goods will remain scarce in this world. Their subject deals with problems arising from a scarcity of goods, and the question whether that scarcity is a sufficient or necessary condition for a given hypothesis to hold is not one that ordinarily arises. The result is that of any generalization we can always truthfully assert that it leaves unheeded some essential qualifications. So long as these are incorporated into a gloss or are standard presuppositions of workers in the field, no harm is done. Only when they are not accounted for in either of these ways, does their absence from the statement of an hypothesis form a serious criticism.

5

We have now reached the point of saying 'Of course there are well-formed hypotheses in the social sciences; and our examples show us that the hypotheses can take the form of a regular association of properties'. But we have not yet said what is equally true, namely, that there are also generalizations which are expressible as equations. Most of these fall within the field of economics. We give two familiar examples.

The first is the well-known equation: $D_1 = f(p_1 . . p_N y t)$ where $D =$ demand, $p =$ price, $y =$ income, and $t =$ time. The equation says that the demand for a good is a function of price, income, and time. The fact that substitution of numbers in this equation, as in many others of economics, does not usually allow us in practice to accurately predict individual situations, only shows us that there is interference from other factors. It does not show that the factors represented in the equation are not measurable; nor does it indicate that the equation is incorrect as far as it goes.

Our second example can be put thusly: 'International trade will equalize factor prices if $\frac{X_{11}}{X_{12}} \neq \frac{X_{21}}{X_{22}}$, where $\frac{X_{11}}{X_{12}} =$ the ratio of the quantity of labour and capital (factors 1 and 2) used in the production of good one, and $\frac{X_{21}}{X_{22}} =$ the ratio of factors 1 and 2 used in the production of good two'. The entire generalization reads: 'International trade will equalize factor prices if whatever factor prices might be, it will never be efficient to produce both goods with the same factor proportions.' This generalization holds under the assumption that there are two countries, two goods, two factors of production, and the same production functions. It also assumes that in a reasonably perfect market the price of a given commodity tends to be the same in all parts of the market – that the market is in or near equilibrium. Here again, there are two interpretations possible. If these assumptions are written into the generalization it becomes analytic. If the equilibrium condition is dropped, then the hypothesis is empirical. In this case the additional assumptions which are needed in order for it to hold with even rough accuracy are these: (a) the profit motive must be widespread, (b) many markets must be statically stable and sufficiently independent of other parts of the economic system so that most of the time they are near their equilibrium positions, (c) in many markets people must be well informed about prices, for they must be able to take advantage of price

156

disparities, that is, undertake arbitrage operations, (*d*) either consumers or commodities must be sufficiently mobile.

Now there are difficulties of deviation in our economic examples, and these deviations from the claims made by the hypotheses can make any given substitutions in the equations only a rough and ready basis for predicting the actual course of events. But this in no way differs from the situation with respect to some of the elementary laws of physics or chemistry: for example, Henry's Law that 'the mass of gas dissolved by a given volume of solvent at a constant temperature is directly proportional to the pressure'.[1] The conditions under which this law holds and does not hold have been more accurately determined than have the corresponding conditions of our economic equations. There is no difference in kind, however, for in both fields separate treatment must be given to the deviations. Thus an introductory text of physical chemistry is careful to indicate the limitations of Henry's Law in much the same way that an economics text would indicate – to the limit of the information available – the boundaries of an economic generalization. Just as the latter holds only under certain assumptions, and not otherwise, so the former does not hold, for instance, over the larger pressure ranges of carbon dioxide in water. For 'at room temperature carbon dioxide concentrations in the gaseous phase differ widely from those calculated using Boyle's Law'.[2] There is also the deviation resulting from the difference between the molecular states of a liquid and its gaseous phase: 'In the case of hydrogen chloride in water, deviation from Henry's Law is very marked over any range of pressures and is due to the almost complete dissociation of the molecule in aqueous solution up to high concentrations. In a non-ionizing solvent the behaviour of hydrogen chloride agrees with Henry's Law as accurately as most other gases.'[3] This is analogous to saying that deviation from the hypothesis about factor prices is marked when the profit motive is not widespread or when there are more than two goods.

Having given an affirmative answer to our first major question – 'Are there well-formed hypotheses in the social sciences?' – we turn to our second question – 'Are any of the hypotheses of the social sciences more than mere empirical generalizations?' That is, are they simply generalized observations or do they include some theoretical element as well?

Now we shall not be able to answer this question until we take up the topic of theories in the next chapter. For while we have not claimed that the generalizations which we have put forward as examples are anything more than generalized observations, we cannot decide whether they are the sole occupants of the field of social laws without also considering the problem of the existence of abstract hypotheses in social

[1] L. Angus: *Physical Chemistry*, 1954, p. 77.
[2] *Ibid.*, p. 80.
[3] *Ibid.*

science. What we *can* do here, however, is to indicate the point of the second question and thus show why it arises. What, after all, is the matter with '*mere* empirical generalization'?

We have already mentioned the kind of dissatisfaction felt by many people about these generalizations. We said that the gist of their complaint was that such generalizations do not really *explain* what they purport to; that only theoretical or abstract hypotheses explain in the sense of thoroughly clearing up a puzzle. The use of empirical generalizations in order to explain something only produces a series of puzzles, each puzzle being similar to but more general than the previous one. This series cannot be terminated except by ignorance or by a theoretical explanation. Hence, it is a basic weakness in a science if its workers do not have access to such explanations, though they may either be taken from other disciplines or generated within the science itself.

The criticism which we are considering can be amplified in the following manner. The standard account of explanation in terms of laws argues that prediction and explanation are simply different uses of the same schema. In prediction we are said to be in possession both of the hypothesis and the statement of initial conditions from which the prediction-claim is derivable. In explanation, on the contrary, the explicandum is assumed to hold, and we attempt to find the statements of initial conditions and the hypothesis which jointly entail it. We can employ one of our earlier examples in order to illustrate the difference between (1) *explanation*:

(Generalization sought)	'All scopolamine causes rapid dilation of the human pupil.'
(Initial condition sought)	'Ruth put scopolamine crystals in her eyes this morning.'
(Results known)	'Ruth's pupils are dilated this morning.'

and (2) *prediction:*

(Generalization known)	'All scopolamine causes rapid dilation of the human pupil.'
(Initial condition known)	'Ruth put scopolamine crystals in her eyes this morning.'
(Results predicted)	'Ruth's pupils are – will be – dilated this morning.'

Thus according to this view, if we can justifiably predict that an event will occur, e.g. the dilation of Ruth's pupils this morning, then we can also give an explanation of *why* that event occurred, e.g. why Ruth's pupils dilated this morning. The explanation and prediction are supported by exactly the same information, namely, the relevant generalization and the statement of initial conditions. Given this characterization of explaining and predicting in terms of laws, it is self-contradictory to say that we can predict the occurrence of an event but not explain it, or that we can explain its occurrence but not predict (or retrodict) it.

To this account of explanation and prediction it has been objected that the two are often independent of each other, and that we are all familiar with situations in which we can predict something without being able to explain why that event took place. For example, it may be said that the following schema predicts but does not explain its conclusions: 'All husbands are mean; Albert is a husband; Albert is mean.' Surely we do not learn *why* Albert is mean by learning the two premises? And yet with the information supplied by these premises we can certainly predict that Albert will be mean.

This is the same objection, of course, that we have been dealing with, namely, that mere generalization does not explain anything. The answer to this has been touched upon before. It is that the giving of an explanation always takes place in a context. If the questioner is unfamiliar with the premises, then in learning both of them he has been given an explanation of why Albert is meaner than some other men: he is a husband and they are bachelors or widowers. The questioner has not received an explanation of why Albert is meaner – if he is – than all other men, unless it is being assumed that he is the only husband and that no men but husbands are mean. Nor has the questioner been told why husbands are mean; nor why Albert is a husband. These are additional questions whose answers may not be required for clearing up the original puzzle. For it is the context of the question that determines what will count as an explanatory answer. If the person knows either that Albert is a husband or that all husbands are mean, but not both, then in learning the other premise he may be receiving an explanation. And if he is already familiar with both of them taken together he can still be given an explanation – provided that he has not previously drawn the required conclusion. In each case the person has received an explanatory answer to a different question. Knowing that Albert is both mean and a husband, the questioner may wonder why Albert is mean when some other husbands are not. The answer 'But all husbands are mean' dissolves the puzzle, for it denies a necessary presupposition of the question. Or the query may take the form: 'Why is Albert mean when some other men are not?' Here the answer 'But all husbands are mean (and some men are not husbands)' accounts for the difference between Albert and some other men. Similarly, anyone who knows that all husbands are mean can be puzzled about Albert's meanness for various reasons. Once again, he can be given an explanation by learning the other premise – that Albert is a husband. As in all cases, he can but need not be. The questioner's puzzle may be one to which these particular premises are not an appropriate answer. He may wish to know about Albert's psychological history, how Albert's meanness came to develop, and to this question a different reply will be needed.

In the same way, a person ignorant of metals is given *an* explanation of a coin's ductility when he is told that it is made of gold and that gold is ductile. He has not been told why every piece of gold is ductile; he has only been told why this particular piece of metal is ductile. If he does not know why gold is ductile he may wish to ask that question next. Of course, if he knows that answer already, he will certainly have obtained an explanation of why this piece is ductile in learning that it is gold. To suggest, then, that we do not obtain an explanation under conditions such as these is to lodge a mistaken complaint. It is to assume that questions like 'Why is Albert mean?' have only one explanatory answer, that they spring from a social vacuum. In fact, there are many possible answers. Which answer is the relevant one will depend upon the puzzle of the questioner.

The 'symmetry' between law-explanations and predictions has also been attacked from the other side. It has been said that in quantum physics we can explain a single micro-event without being able to predict its occurrence.

It is perfectly true that, *given* any single quantum phenomenon P (for example, the emission of a β particle from a radioactive substance or the scattering of a γ-ray photon by an electron), P can be completely *explained* ex post facto; one can *understand* fully just what kind of event occurred, in terms of the well-established laws of the composite quantum theory. . . . These laws give the *meaning* of 'explaining single micro-events'. The philosopher should not legislate here; he must note what *counts* as explanation in microphysics, and then describe it precisely. But it is, of course, the most fundamental feature of these laws that the *prediction* of such a phenomenon P is, as a matter of theoretical principle, quite impossible.[1]

The obvious question to be asked here is 'What does quantum theory explain in the case of P?' For to understand or explain what *kind* of event took place is not to understand or explain why the *particular* event P took place. If quantum theory can explain the occurrence of a kind of event then it can predict the occurrence of that kind of event. But it is clearly a mistake to argue from the difference between (a) explaining the occurrence of a type and (b) predicting the occurrence of an instance, to the difference between (c) explaining and (d) predicting the occurrence of an instance. The error is displayed even more distinctly in this passage from the same argument:

. . . there can be nothing, save position, to distinguish, for example, the nuclei of a cluster of atoms of carbon 14. At any time *t*, then, all C14 nuclei are absolutely identical. But C14, being an unstable isotope of carbon, decays randomly. Fundamental particles are emitted in a wholly unpredictable way

[1] N. Hanson: 'On the Symmetry Between Explanation and Prediction', *The Philosophical Review*, Vol. LXVIII, No. 3, July 1959, pp. 353–4.

(as the uncertainty relations require); certainly it is not the case that *all* the nuclei of the cluster decay at once. But then any particular nucleonic decay must be an 'uncaused' event. For if all the nuclei are identical until the time some one of them breaks up, then there can be no causal reason for the decay, since there is nothing to distinguish the context in which the event did occur from the context in which it did not, save the occurrence itself.[1]

If this passage accurately represents the case, then in terms of quantum theory it makes no sense to speak of *explaining* why a particular nucleus decayed at a particular time *t* any more than it makes sense to speak of *predicting* that a particular nucleus *N* will break up at some particular time *t*. Prediction and explanation are perfectly symmetrical here in that neither procedure can be applied to the occurrence of single micro-events. If it is true that 'there is nothing to distinguish the context in which the event did occur from the context in which it did not, save the occurrence itself', then it is logically impossible for a law-explanation to be given of the single event. An explanation in terms of laws picks out those features in the context of an event which explain its occurrence rather than its non-occurrence, or *its* occurrence rather than that of some other event. Hence, to say that all the contexts of this kind of event are identical is to say that there are no such features. And when this possibility is ruled out so is the possibility of explaining (in terms of scientific laws) why nucleus *N* decays at time *t* and not nucleus N_1. Given this situation it is only to be expected that the possibility of predicting the decay of *N* will follow suit. This merely confirms – rather than discredits – the view that if we can provide an explanation of an event in terms of laws we can by that same means predict its occurrence.

One conclusion drawn from the objection that we have been considering is that there are two distinct activities: *predicting* by means of a generalization and *explaining* by means of deduction from a theory. The argument in support of this distinction has been made in terms of an example from physics:

It can be established by empirical observation that, all else being equal, the intensity of illumination on a plane surface varies inversely as the square of the distance of the surface from a constant light source. From this empirical generalization one can predict what will happen if, for instance, the distance from the light source is doubled or trebled; one would say that the change in distance causes a change in illumination, but it would surely be odd to say that the change in distance *explains* the change in illumination except in the rather loose sense where one might answer the question of a naive observer, 'Look, the brightness has changed, how do you explain that?' with the rejoinder, 'Well, look, I have altered the distance between the light and the screen'. A sort of explanation or a phenomenon can be given by subsuming it under an empirical generalization, but this way of explaining is generally held

[1] *Ibid.*, p. 357.

to be not very satisfactory in a science. The change in illumination is explained by reference to a formal model, the sort of system which Professor Toulmin compares with a map. One considers the model in which rays of light travel in straight lines, the source of light is a point source from which a fixed number of rays emerge, uniformly distributed in all directions. Intensity of illumination is defined as the number of rays impinging on a surface per unit area. By considering a spherical surface with such a point source at its centre one deduces that the total illumination (luminous flux) over the sphere is invariant for changes in its size, since all the rays impinge on it somewhere. But the intensity of illumination on any segment of the sphere of constant area varies inversely with the surface area of the sphere, and hence inversely with the square of the radius of the sphere, i.e. the intensity of the illumination varies as the reciprocal of the square of the distance of the surface from the light source. This I think we would normally call an explanation of the dependence of intensity of illumination on the distance from the light source.[1]

It may be thought that the author of this quotation is not asserting that the explanation and the prediction of the occurrence of the *same* event are different. However, another and slightly later remark of his seems to indicate that he does wish to refer to the same event: '. . . it is clear that the sufficient conditions for predicting changes in illumination with distance are different from those from which an explanation of those changes can be derived. Sufficient conditions in the first case can be established simply by observing what happens when the distance between light source and surface is varied, keeping other factors constant, and by having a suitable means of measuring intensity of illumination. Sufficient conditions for being able to explain the inverse square law, however, involve showing that the property to be explained is entailed by the properties of the model in the way previously elucidated. . . .'[2]

Now it is quite obvious that the supporters of this argument have confounded two separate problems. One problem concerns the distinction between predicting the occurrence of a particular event and explaining its occurrence in terms of a law-explanation. The other problem concerns the distinction between explaining the occurrence of an event and explaining the empirical generalization which applies to that event. All that the argument shows is that there is a difference between the prediction of a particular event or set of events (the illumination will change on *this* screen as it is moved with respect to the light source), and the explanation of an empirical generalization (the theory of light rays which explains the generalization that 'the intensity of illumination on a plane surface varies inversely as the square of the distance of the surface from a constant light source'). But this difference

[1] P. Dodwell: 'Causes of Behaviour and Explanation in Psychology', *Mind*, Vol. LXIX, No. 273, January 1960, pp. 6–7.
[2] *Ibid.*, p. 7.

is not in question. Moreover, its existence certainly does not demonstrate, as the argument is intended to do, that the law-explanation and the prediction of the same event or set of events are logically independent of each other, for in the case cited what is explained and what is predicted are different. The argument only emphasizes what no one doubts, that there is an important difference between the causal connection which is asserted by an empirical hypothesis and the logical connection which holds between a theory and those empirical hypotheses that are derivable from it. In sum, the argument is misplaced. It does not deal with the question at issue; nor does it provide any new reason for withholding the label 'explanation' from the use of empirical generalizations to account for particular events. The sole reason that the argument can possibly offer is the same as our previous one: explanation in terms of a theory puts an end to a series of questions of the same kind, whereas explanation by means of an empirical hypothesis does not.

The argument has been thought to apply to empirical generalizations in exactly the same way as it does to particular events. Generalizations receive an explanation only when they are deduced from a theory and not when they are entailed by another empirical generalization. The approved relationship is that holding between Newton's first law of motion which, in some formulations at least, has no instances – is a theoretical law – and Galileo's laws of projectile motion which have instances – are empirical hypotheses – and, when other laws are added to Newton's, are deducible from it. The disapproved relationship can be illustrated by an example of this sort: the empirical generalization 'water is denser than ice' is deducible from the laws that (a) 'below 4°C. water expands as the temperature drops' and (b) 'the freezing point of water is, under constant pressure, constant', combined with the analytic statement that water freezes at 0°C.[1] On the view being considered, the greater density of water is not *explained* by this account, for we can go on to ask 'Why does water expand below 4°C. . . . ?' and 'Why is the freezing point of water . . . constant?' The account gives us simple generalization.

But why does a theory of the right sort put a stop to such questions? One answer can be developed from a point made by Campbell, though the answer should not be attributed to him: the dynamical theory of gases does not explain the properties of gases merely because these properties 'are shown to be the consequences of the subjection of molecules, of which the gases consist, to the general laws of all moving bodies'. What makes the theory an explanation is that it 'states that there are such things as molecules' which are not 'discernible to direct perception' . . . 'and that gases are made up of them'.[2] In other words,

[1] Given by A. Pap: *Elements of Analytic Philosophy*, 1949, p. 151.
[2] N. Campbell: *What Is Science?*, 1952, reprint, p. 85.

we may argue that a theory of the required kind asserts the *existence* of indiscernible or unobservable entities, states, or events; and that, therefore, the theory prevents the development of a question-series because we cannot sensibly ask why natural objects exist.

Now if we are told that light rays and molecules exist, the question 'Why do they?' has a variety of interpretations. Perhaps the most natural one is 'How did they come to exist?' 'How did they originate?' This is a question which requires an historical (or cosmological) answer. It is very different from the question 'Why does water expand below 4°C. . . . ?' which, if pursued, demands an answer in terms of universal hypotheses and theoretical entities. The second question can lead to a series of 'why' questions and to a series of scientific answers. At some point, however – the argument proceeds – the question 'Why this?' will no longer be applicable or have a possible answer. To ask it will be to ask why brute existence is as it is, why the laws and fundamental features of nature exist instead of not existing. And when we exclude historical explanations and religious ones, there is nothing left to say but 'That's the way things are – the way of the world'.

One of the tasks of a scientific theory, then, is to direct questions into the series which terminates with an assertion of the existence of something. Only an assertion of this kind, the argument concludes, can supply an explanation, for only it confronts the questioner with the brute facts of life. This is why the question 'Are there any theoretical hypotheses in the social sciences?' is thought to be of such importance by some writers. And it is one reason why we now need to turn our attention to the various kinds of theories present in the work of social scientists.

XI

THEORIES

1

DREARINESS and a numbing confusion are characteristic features of discussion by social scientists about theories in their fields, and this is particularly true of discussion about sociological theories. The situation may arise, in part, because many social scientists, while making use of several different types of theories, are unclear about the differences between the types. It is worthwhile, therefore, to distinguish some of the kinds of theories present in the work of social scientists, and to comment on a few of the issues raised by the examples we shall give of each kind. We can then concentrate our attention upon the type which most concerns us in our efforts to answer the question 'Are there hypotheses in the social sciences which are anything more than mere empirical generalizations?'

It is common information that the term 'theory', like the term 'explanation', can be variously employed. There is, firstly, the colloquial sense of 'theory' in which it refers to an untested explanation whose status is doubtful. And there is, secondly, the sense in which theory – a body of principles or rules or propositions – is opposed to practice. The first sense has no special interest for us. However it, like the second sense, reminds us of a number of relevant points. It reminds us that any explanation, or any part of it, may be called a 'theory'. In brief, the terms 'theory' and 'explanation' are often used synonymously. In the following quotation, for example, the two words are interchangeable: 'Stemming from these pregnant observations was his theory that magical belief arises to bridge the uncertainties in man's practical pursuits. . . .'[1] This explanation, as we know, can be interpreted either in terms of functions or in terms of empirical generalizations. Both versions may be called 'theories'.

But 'explanation' and 'theory' are not always synonyms. Quite often we distinguish an explanation-schema or an explanatory hypothesis from the theory of which it is a part. Before attending, however, to those cases

[1] Merton: *op. cit.*, p. 102.

in which it is important to separate, rather than to amalgamate, theories and explanations, we shall need to take notice of still another sense of 'theory', one which is less closely related to the topic of explanation than is the sense that we shall take up later. The sense to which we now turn our attention refers to a set of procedural rules and principles of policy on the one hand, and to a schema of terminology and classification, on the other. We shall remark on both these elements in turn.

When a social scientist begins his professional remarks by speaking of his 'basic orientation' or of his 'methodological approach' or of his 'general theory', he often has in mind a set of procedural rules which he claims to follow, a set which he usually wishes to recommend for dealing with what he takes to be the major problems of his field. Obviously, a theory of this kind has a close connection with the terminology and system of classification adopted by its supporters. Hence it is common for social scientists to refer both to a set of procedural rules and to a classification system under the one title of 'frame of reference'. It is one of the standard deficiencies of these frames of reference that while they supply elaborate vocabularies for discussing social problems, these vocabularies lead to few, if any, generalizations.

Examples of procedural rules are not difficult to find. Thus in his book *The Rules of Sociological Method*, Durkheim argues that 'The determining cause of a social fact should be sought among the social facts preceding it and not among the states of the individual consciousness'; that is, 'The function of a social fact ought always to be sought in its relation to some social end'[1]. He claims that 'The first origins of all social processes of any importance should be sought in the internal constitution of the social group',[2] rather than in the psychology or physiology of individual members of the group. In directing us to examine 'the internal constitution of the social group' for the sources of social behaviour, Durkheim is advancing a procedural rule. If he were to justify the use of this rule he might well begin by defining such terms as 'social fact' and 'internal constitution of the social group'. By this means we should be led from the rule to the terminology and classificatory system of which it is an expression. We should then be confronted with the rather general beliefs which – given certain goals – are supposed to justify the rules. For instance, the claim that 'The cause of a social or individual phenomenon is never another social or individual phenomenon alone, but always a combination of a social and an individual phenomenon'[3] can be plausibly interpreted, on occasion, as an injunction to look for causes of a particular kind. If we ask why we should seek causes of this sort rather than those of another sort, the reply seems to be in terms of the general

[1] Pp. 110–11.
[2] *Ibid.*, p. 113.
[3] Quoted from W. Thomas's 'The Polish Peasant' in H. Barnes: *An Introduction to the History of Sociology*, 1948, p. 800.

belief that all social change is 'a product of a continual interaction of individual consciousness and objective social reality' [1]. This, in distinction to the rule which it supports, embodies a truth-claim about society, one which, however vague, is supposed to provide a sound reason for following the rule. In its present form it obviously does not. The conclusion presented is that since all social changes are caused by interaction, the causes of 'individual and social phenomena' are also interaction. Yet this conclusion cannot be drawn unless individual phenomena are classified as social changes. And we have not been shown that they can, or ought to be.

While we cannot test rules of procedure for truth or falsity, we can find either that they are helpful or that they are not. Marx's 'theory of class struggle' includes the remark that 'The history of all hitherto existing society is the history of class struggle'. This sentence summarizes the passage from which it is drawn; for that passage is designed to draw attention to a particular topic – class struggle – and to assert its indispensability in the explanation of certain widespread features of economic history. The commonest reason for rejecting such a precept, of course, is that it is based upon a false belief – based upon it in the sense that if the belief had been known to be false the precept would not have been advanced. In Marx's case, it might be argued, the false belief is that all important social changes are caused by changes in the means of production. Nevertheless, the falsity of a belief does not ensure the uselessness of the precept or the interpretation which it supports. Thus the principle of Least Action in its various forms was adopted to great advantage by such scientists as Euler, Lagrange, and Hamilton. But the justification for the adoption was often only a belief in the parsimony of Nature or the skill of a Heavenly Designer.

Now a rule of procedure not only embodies the preferences of its author, preferences as to the kind of problems considered to be important, it also assumes a 'methodology' for dealing with these problems. A typical example of a methodological view is that of 'sociological holism'. On this view 'social systems constitute "wholes" at least in the sense that some of their large-scale behaviour is governed by macro-laws which are essentially *sociological* in the sense that they are *sui generis* and not to be explained as mere regularities or tendencies resulting from the behaviour of inter-acting individuals. On the contrary, the behaviour of individuals should (according to sociological holism) be explained at least partly in terms of such laws (perhaps in conjunction with an account, first of individuals' roles within institutions and secondly of the functions of institutions within the whole social system)'[2].

This example is typical because it attempts to persuade us to follow a

[1] *Ibid.*

[2] J. Watkins: 'Historical Explanation in Social Science', *The British Journal for the Philosophy of Science*, Vol. VIII, No. 30, August 1957, p. 106.

particular course of action, that course being a search for macro-laws rather than laws about the behaviour of individual people. It is typical also in that it is defended, in part, by means of a belief whose truth is thought by critics to be questionable. The belief here is that social groups have structural and functional properties which are not reducible (not logically equivalent) to those of the individual participants. One of the methodological conclusions to be drawn from this view is that 'any attempts at scientific prediction of group behaviour must employ some scheme of measurement of group characteristics and performances, i.e. of traits of the group as a whole'.[1] Group properties like 'accuracy of conclusion in committee-like debate on given data; reduction of strength of pull when tug-of-war rope is electrified (a "morale" variable); time to construct a large wooden structure to given specifications'[2], are measurable 'without any observations on the *internal* interaction of the group'.[3] Hence, supporters of 'social holism' can argue that their proposal is based upon the fact that group characteristics do exist. They can go on to claim, as they do, that no conclusive reason can be given to show that laws connecting such properties with each other are undiscoverable. The argument then turns upon two points: whether such laws can in fact be found in any quantity, and whether they are reducible to laws about individuals. In short, methodological differences resemble what in other fields are called 'differences of policy'.

2

The social sciences have long been rich in classificatory systems. In large part their construction has been the result of efforts to select a limited number of fundamental notions for study, and to establish laws by which they could be related. But this goal has often been combined with a more ambitious one, that of producing a deductive system in which from a minimum number of axioms and definitions there would follow all the scientific laws needed in the explanation of our social activities and institutions, or at least some important part of them. These are two quite different goals. A deductive system in science consists of a set of definitions, axioms and statements. It certainly classifies its subject matter but this is not the purpose for which it is devised. A deductive system is to be contrasted with a classificatory scheme of the sort with which we are now concerned, for the latter is not a deductive system though certain deductions can be drawn from it. For example, if we know the criteria that determine the classes of the system, and also know that

[1] R. Cattell: 'Types of Group Characteristics' in *The Language of Social Research*, ed. by P. Lazarsfeld and M. Rosenberg, 1955, p. 297.
[2] *Ibid.*, p. 299.
[3] *Ibid.*

an item belongs in a particular class, then we can always deduce information about the item's membership (or lack of membership) in other classes. Thus according to the Warner classification, one of the defining criteria for membership in the upper-upper social class is residence in areas of expensive housing. From this it follows that a person of that class cannot live in the slums, but this fact is a discovery not about the world but about the logical consequences of the criteria adopted by the classifier.

Now it is often maintained, more in anger than in sorrow, that most classificatory schemes of sociology and political science, with their associated nomenclature, are of a completely useless variety. They do not aid in the *discovery* of universal hypotheses. Yet instances of the connections between classificatory schemes and testable generalizations are by no means absent in these fields.

Suppose, for example, that we are familiar with two classificatory systems, one dealing with psychiatric disorders and the other with social classes. Suppose, further, that we ask the question whether there is any significant relationship between membership in the class system and the contraction of any particular type of psychiatric disorder. We use a scheme of five social classes, and the criteria that we employ for determining membership in these classes are: the occupation of the subject, his degree of formal education, and his area of residence. If we now choose one of the severe disorders, e.g. schizophrenia, for our study, we shall be able to use the figures of reported cases with some assurance that relatively few cases are unreported. Then by determining the social class of each person who is reported as a schizophrenic, it is a simple matter to correlate the numbers of such cases with the figures of class membership for the patients concerned. When this was done for a 5 per cent sample of the population of an American city it was discovered that the lower the social class the more prevalent was schizophrenia in it. Hence, in this case there was an 'inverse relationship between social class and schizophrenia'.[1]

Ordinarily, however, critics do not have as their targets simple classificatory schemes of this type. They have in mind the more elaborate and far reaching systems of a type long associated with the field of sociology. We can refer, for our purposes, to a classificatory system developed by Talcott Parsons.[2] Its chief technical terms are 'role', 'status', and 'pattern'. All these terms are discussed at some length, but let us here consider only the term 'pattern'.

According to the author, human behaviour in any society is to be classified into three kinds of patterns: (1) Situational (2) Instrumental

[1] This example is taken from A. Hollingshead and F. Redlich: 'Social Stratification and Psychiatric Disorders', *American Sociological Review*, Vol. 18, No. 2, April 1953

[2] 'Toward A Common Language for the Area of Social Science' in *Essays in Sociological Theory*, 1949.

(3) Integrative. The first kind is concerned with the various patterns which are generated by 'the situation in which men are placed, their biological nature and descent, their psychological nature'.[1] Features which give rise to specific patterns within this general category of 'situational patterns' are: infant plasticity, age and sex, kinship, territorial location, and personal qualities. Every such feature is called a 'focus' and a specific pattern is said to 'crystallise' around it, e.g. around the kinship 'focus' have crystallised patterns of courtship and marriage. The second category of pattern-type – that of instrumental ones – has four 'foci'. These consist of the 'content of the differentiated functional roles by virtue of which a system of interdependent units becomes possible'.[2] An instance of such a specific pattern is that of property rights. Other specific patterns are those relating to economic exchange and to authority of different sorts. The third category of patterns contains those which 'bring it about that all the statuses of the society intermesh like a series of interlocking wheels'[3]. Amongst these particular patterns are social stratification, government organization, and ethical views.

To the question 'How does this scheme help sociologists?' Parsons would answer, apparently, that he tried 'to construct a conceptual model which reflects with a minimum of distortion certain important relationships which prevail between the phenomena'. He might well add that the scheme was 'only intended to assist in the organization of material and to suggest a more unified approach to the understanding of human behaviour'.[4] Now a reply in this strain is both instructive and typical. A classificatory system is commonly defended, as this one is, on the grounds that it (*a*) organizes data and (*b*) reveals connections between classes of events. But it is often not clear what relations are thought to exist in a given case between (*a*) and (*b*). To organize data so as to reveal testable connections between certain classes of events or processes is to organize data in the most scientifically useful manner possible. How, then, are (*a*) and (*b*) different? In answer an appeal is sometimes made to the completeness and precision with which a scheme organizes a number of classes. The justification of the scheme is then said to lie in its completeness and precision alone. Something like this justification is obliquely referred to in the following account of the differences between the sense of 'theory' employed by physical scientists and that employed by social scientists.

The trouble is that whereas a Newton could begin with intuitively evident quantities (length as measured by sticks, time as measured by clocks, force as felt in the muscles), the social scientist cannot make such a beginning. The stuff from which human relations and social structure are made is not evident

[1] *Ibid.*, p. 45.
[2] *Ibid.*
[3] *Ibid.*
[4] *Ibid.*, p. 44.

170

intuitively. It must somehow be distilled, or abstracted from innumerable 'events', and the selection of these events depends to a great extent on one's experiences, cultural background, and biases.

Nevertheless, the social scientist does try to select the fundamental entities of his field of interest. This process of selection, however, is so laborious and involved that it often constitutes the bulk of the social scientist's effort, and so he hardly ever gets around to stating 'postulates'. He must first relate his terms to referents. These referents cannot be simply exhibited; they must themselves be abstracted from a rich variety of events, generalizations, and relations. By the time a number of these referents have been so abstracted and christened, one already has a bulky 'system' before the work of seeking out 'laws' has ever begun. Such 'system', particularly in sociology, is sometimes taken to be 'theories'.[1]

Now even if we accept this account of the 'distillation process' engaged in by the social scientist, there remains the problem of justifying the product. Unless data are organized with a view to revealing explanatory connections between classes of events, there is no point in talking about the completeness and precision of the system. These features of it must have some relevance to the chief aim of scientific work – explanation. It is mistaken to suggest that a social scientist can select 'the fundamental entities of his field of interest' independently of their explanatory value. Problems and their answers are so closely linked to the categories and nomenclature adopted by the investigator that all these elements develop concurrently. When someone produces a 'bulky system' he must also answer the implied question 'A system for what?' He cannot merely reply 'It organizes the data'. *Any* criterion will organize data – will order items in classes – but only some systems of classification will be scientifically useful. The work of selecting the 'fundamental entities' of a field is united to the work of finding the answers to its basic problems. If we seek explanations only *after* we have produced a system, we have no reason to believe that we shall discover them. After all, if the scheme of classification was not developed with explanations in mind, why should we?

3

There is, of course, another sense of the term 'theory' and it is the one to which we shall devote most of our attention from this point onward. The sense is that assumed by critics when they assert, disapprovingly, that none of the social sciences except economics contains any formal theories. But the phrase 'formal theory' is used rather loosely. Thus the title 'formal theory' is often applied to a set of empirical generalizations, a set which jointly entails some additional generalization. This kind of

---

[1] A. Rapoport: 'Uses and Limitations of Mathematical Models in Social Science' in *Symposium on Sociological Theory*, ed. by L. Gross, 1959, p. 351.

formal theory, whether put in words or mathematical symbols, is simply the explanation-schema that we referred to in Chapter Three of Part One and again in the previous chapter. If, for example, we take Charles' Law and Boyle's Law to be empirical generalizations, as they originally were, then we can deduce the generalization that the pressure of a gas, when its volume remains constant, is directly proportional to the absolute temperature. But this shop-worn example would never be called a 'physical theory'. All three of these empirical generalizations can be deduced from the conjunction of a particular theory and a particular law, however. The theory is that of the kinetic theory of gases, and it states that there are molecules of gases, that they have certain properties such as elasticity, and that they follow Newton's laws of motion. The law adds to this theory the information that the absolute temperature of a gas is proportional to the average molecular kinetic energy.

The point is that Charles' Law and Boyle's Law were originally put forward as statements of observable regularities, whereas the kinetic theory of gases and the law associated with it could not be. Newton's laws contain, for example, such theoretical terms as 'force' and 'mass'. Each of these two terms can be explicitly defined only with the aid of the other, and not simply in terms of some set of observable properties. The relations of pressure, volume, and temperature to each other in a gas are explained, then, by means of a theory about the existence, movements, and energy of unobservable gas molecules. And it is this kind of formal theory which has attracted the attention and excited the envy of social scientists. They have asked whether in the social sciences, as in the physical ones, there are or can be formal theories of this sort, ones from which empirical generalizations are deducible but which contain statements about unobservable entities and relations as well.

Let us turn to a scrutiny of an empirical generalization that was mentioned earlier. It is a generalization which has attracted wider comment than many in the social sciences.[1] It says that 'Societies in which marriage is allowed or preferred with mother's brother's daughter but forbidden or disapproved with father's sister's daughter will be societies in which jural authority over ego male, [i.e. any man] before marriage, is vested in his father or father's lineage. . . .'.[2] Assume this to be (a) well tested and confirmed, and (b) to assert that the presence of a *rule* of matrilateral marriage under the stated condition is sufficient for the presence of a rule to the effect that jural authority over ego male is to be held patrilineally, and that the presence of the latter rule is also sufficient for the presence of the former rule. Let us take this to be a social analogue of the gas laws, and hence, like them, to cry out for

---

[1] See, for example, D. Emmett: *Function, Purpose and Powers*, 1958, pp. 100–1.

[2] Homans and Schneider, *loc. cit.*

theoretical explanation. We now ask how it is in fact explained by the anthropologists who put it forward.

It is explained in the following way. In some societies the father has jural authority over the son: the former has the right to give orders and the latter has the duty to obey. The two are not closely related by ties of affection. But the relations between mother's brother and ego are close, for the maternal uncle provides help, advice, and goods. He is a 'male mother' to his nephew in a way that his nephew's father is not. In other societies the father has no jural authority over the son. This authority is vested in ego's maternal uncle. In these circumstances father and son have a close relationship while son and uncle have not. Thus in the first situation ego will be 'fond of mother's brother, and as mother's brother and his daughter in the patrilineal complex, the Oedipus Complex if you will, are themselves particularly close to one another, he will tend to get fond of the daughter. Their marriage will be sentimentally appropriate; it will cement the relationship. Or, if women are indeed scarce and valued goods, and ego is in doubt where he can get one, he will certainly be wise to ask his mother's brother, on whom he already has so strong a sentimental claim'.[1] On the other hand, in those societies in which jural authority is held by the mother's brother, ego will become fond of the daughter of his father's sister and marriage with her will be the preferred form.[2]

It turns out, therefore, that the association between the two sorts of prescribed behaviour is explained in terms of the sentiments and emotions of the actors. The explanation makes implicit use of generalizations such as these: (1) a relationship in which are stressed the right of some members to command and the duty of the other members to obey, produces sentiments that inhibit the development of feelings of affection between the members of the two groups, (2) if ego is fond of his mother's brother, and this person in turn, is fond of his own daughter, then ego will tend to be fond of the daughter, (3) if ego is not fond of his father, then he will not be fond of his father's sister nor of her daughter.

The attempt to make these generalizations explicit reveals, perhaps, their inadequacy. But this does not matter. What is important here is that the statement of an observable regularity – the association between jural authority and type of marriage – is explained by means of a set of empirical generalizations concerning the psychology of the people involved. The case at hand is not analogous to the kinetic theory and the gas laws; here one statement of an empirical regularity is simply taken to be derivable from a number of others. And this kind of 'theory', while present in the social sciences, is not what many social scientists are seeking, rightly or wrongly, when they demand theories analogous

[1] *Ibid.*, p. 23
[2] *Ibid.*, pp. 26–7.

to those of the physical sciences. The question, then, is 'Can these demands be met?'

A clear answer to this question requires that we first recognize two different methods by which a formal theory can arise. The difference between them is that of whether or not the theory was developed as an interpretation of a calculus. The point to be emphasized can be made in the following fashion. A deductive system or theory in the *natural* sciences – a formal theory – is couched in words or other symbols, at least some of which describe or refer to a subject matter. The system consists of: (1) a set of axioms which have these properties: their truth is assumed; their truth can be tested only by the testing of some of their logical consequences; they cannot be deduced from other statements within the system; (2) those statements (theorems) that are entailed by the axioms or by the axioms in conjunction with theorems and definitions; such theorems may be either theoretical laws, and so open to testing only by means of certain of their logical consequences, or they may be empirical generalizations and thus open to direct testing; (3) a set of definitions of some of the descriptive (non-logical) terms that appear in the axioms; other definitions may be introduced in the course of proving the theorems, but these will be based upon the earlier ones.

In contrast to this, an uninterpreted calculus is a system of axioms, theorems, and definitions, couched entirely in logical and mathematical symbols which refer only to the arrangement and kinds of other such symbols. These are the subject matter of the system. The axioms and theorems are formulas rather than statements, so that questions of truth and falsity do not arise. It is this sort of formal system which is transformed into an interpreted calculus when rules of meaning are given for certain of its logical and mathematical symbols. These rules of interpretation convert the formulas into statements. Formal scientific theories are a sub-class of the class of interpreted calculi – of interpreted axiomatic systems. Thus a formal theory in the sciences may stem from an uninterpreted calculus. Or the theory may never have passed through such a stage in its history. It may not have been first developed as a logical skeleton, but have sprung forth at birth decently equipped with a subject matter. Since it was never anything other than an interpreted system, to call it an 'interpreted calculus' is merely to say that it has a logical structure which, if exposed, could be laid out in terms of definitions, axioms and theorems. It is not to assert that its order of development was from uninterpreted calculus to interpreted calculus. This difference in the possible history of a formal theory corresponds to the difference between two meanings of the question 'Are formal theories used in any social science except economics?'

One meaning of the question is whether social scientists do and should construct calculi which by a process of interpretation can become empirical theories. Another meaning of the question is: 'Are there – and should there be – theories whose logical structure, when displayed, would be that of an uninterpreted calculus?' It might be the case that while, at present, there were no theories fit for such examination, it was desirable, nevertheless, for social scientists to produce them; and one way of doing so would be for them to construct calculi susceptible of interpretation as empirical theories. Another way would be for social scientists to produce their theories first and worry later about exposing the logical skeletons of those theories.

Before taking up this difference, it will be useful for us to consider several other features of physical theories. These features can be introduced by our stressing this point: the interpreted *axioms* of physical theories are not statements of observed regularities. They are not mere empirical generalizations. This is important because there is a temptation on the part of some social scientists to believe that a set of empirical generalizations which are deductively related – an explanation schema – can be turned by the procedures of logic into the social analogue of a physical theory like the gas theory. They believe that making explicit the logical structure of such a set, laying it out in terms of definitions, axioms, and theorems, is tantamount to producing a formal scientific theory of the kind desired. That it is not is easily seen.

No matter how much effort of this sort is put into a set of empirical generalizations, the sense in which they form a theory is the same as that which applies in the case of the 'theory' about matrilateral marriage. This claim can be supported by our considering how Herbert Simon has rewritten[1] a set of generalizations put forward by Homans in his book entitled *The Human Group*. Some of Homans' generalizations are: (1) 'If the scheme of activities is changed, the scheme of interaction will, in general, change also, and vice versa.' (2) 'If the frequency of interaction between two or more persons increases, the degree of their liking for one another will increase, and vice versa.' (3) 'Persons who feel sentiments of liking for one another will express those sentiments in activities over and above the activities of the external system, and these activities may further strengthen the sentiments of liking.'[2]

The four terms 'interaction', 'friendliness', 'activity', and 'external system' are used by Simon to prepare a list of symbols whose definitions are as follows:

'I – the average rate of *interaction* per member'; 'F – the average *friendliness* between pairs of members'; 'A – the average amount of time spent per member per day in *activity* within the group'; 'E – the average amount of time that would be spent per member per day in activity within the group if members were motivated only by the

---

[1] 'A Formal Theory of Interaction in Social Groups' in *American Sociological Review*, Vol. 17, No. 2, April 1952.

[2] Taken from pp. 102–18 of *The Human Group*, 1950.

external system'. All four of these letters are taken to represent variable quantities; and these variables are interpreted as functions of time (t). The expression $E(t)$ is held to represent an independent variable and $I(t)$, $A(t)$, $F(t)$, dependent variables. Three axioms are then laid down. The first one will indicate their type: 'The intensity of interaction depends upon, and increases with, the level of friendliness and the amount of activity carried on within the group.' In symbols this is: $I(t) = a_1F(t) + a_2A(t)$. Thus Simon writes that 'a_1F may be regarded as the amount of interaction generated by the level, F, of friendliness in the absence of any group activity. That is, if $A = 0$, then $I = a_1F$'.[1] After the necessary and sufficient conditions for stability of equilibrium have been provided, the results of changes can be deduced. For example, we can deduce a generalization not given in Homans' original group. This generalization is the theorem that 'an increase in the activities required of the group by the external environment will increase (when equilibrium has been re-established) the amount of group activity, the amount of friendliness and the amount of interaction. As E decreases toward zero, A, F and I will decrease toward zero.' Or where 'd' represents 'derivative':

$$\frac{dIo}{dEo} = a_1\frac{dFo}{dEo} + a_2\frac{dAo}{dEo} > 0.\;^2$$

If we now compare this theorem with the axiom given previously – from which the theorem is in part derived – we see that the testability of one is as direct as that of the other. Either they are both generalizations of observable regularities, or neither is. They do not differ in the way in which a statement about the molecules of a gas differs from a statement about the volume and pressure of that gas. The molecules of the gas cannot be directly inspected whereas its volume and pressure can be. This important difference, which is thought to be of crucial importance by some critics, is not reflected in Homans' theory, and so, of course, not in Simon's rendering of it.

There are, in addition, some obvious difficulties. Simon points out that it has to be assumed that the four variables can be measured. He also points out that in the first axiom it is assumed that the level of interaction responds almost immediately to changes in the level of friendliness and the amount of intra-group activity. No help is given on these two points by the original generalizations. Moreover, some of these unqualified generalizations are probably not true, e.g. that frequency of interaction increases degree of liking. But most of these defects are repairable in principle. The absence of theoretical axioms is not – according to the view that the particle theories of physics are to be regarded as a useful pattern for the theories of social scientists.

Yet why should they be? Is the absence of theoretical axioms a

[1] Simon: *op. cit.*, p. 204.
[2] *Ibid.*, p. 206.

176

genuine defect? The answer that we are considering is that it is, because only the assertion of the existence of indiscernible entities, states, events, and relations, can terminate an otherwise endless series of 'why' questions; for only an existence claim of this kind rules out any further scientific answer. Surely, however, this reply is simply mistaken, and with it the view about the need for theoretical axioms. The reply is the result of a compound of errors, errors which are also responsible for the charge that social scientists produce 'mere empirical generalizations'. Once it is realized that supporters of such complaints have confused a number of different issues, the plausibility of these criticisms launched against theories in the social sciences vanishes.

4

At the outset it should be noted that even if an existence claim of the required sort were necessary for the termination of a series of 'why' questions, this would still not be sufficient reason for restricting the title 'explanation' to theories incorporating such a claim. An explanation does not cease to be an explanation because it leaves another puzzle in its wake. We judge the soundness of a theory by various criteria, e.g. fertility of testable consequences, economy of means, and compatibility with other knowledge. None of these calls for an end to all future questions originating from the limits of the theory's power to explain. If that were required the results would be unpalatable. First and foremost, no theories except those of atomic and sub-atomic physics could properly be said to explain. Newton's theory of gravitation, classical mechanics and thermodynamics, would fail this test. So would most theories in most other fields of science. But there is no need to elaborate, since the confusion within the argument being examined is sufficiently shown by the fact that it wavers between viewing theoretical laws as those which cannot be directly tested – by inspection of their instances – and as those which make existence claims for indiscernible objects or events or relations. For this reason it can rule out, on the one hand, Newtonian theories as non-explanatory – because they make no atomic claims – and, on the other hand, find that the theories are genuine explanations – because they are more than empirical generalizations, i.e. cannot be directly tested in the required fashion.

The second result of restricting the title 'explanation' in the proposed way would be to eliminate all methods of explaining except one, and to make every explanation of that one kind (theoretical laws) an ultimate explanation. Explanations which refer to intentions, dispositions, reasons, and functions, would no longer properly be called 'explanations'; for while some of them do, on occasion, make existence claims, these claims do not seem to refer to indiscernible entities of the required type. Or do they?

This question underlines the chief cause of the confusion in the argument concerning the nature of theoretical laws. The muddle is caused by a failure to distinguish between two sorts of indiscernible entities. One sort consists of *idealizations* and the other sort consists of *unobservables*. Frictionless surfaces, volumeless molecules, perfect gases and vacuums are imaginary conditions, limiting cases which are extrapolated from the existing values of the relevant variables. These states are imaginary (or ideal) because they assume what, given the present laws of nature, is physically impossible: the total absence of certain properties such as friction and volume. There is no question, then, of these being observable conditions. They are idealizations. In sharp contrast to these are the unobservable particles like mesons and protons, or the larger units like molecules. Claims for the existence of these objects do not assume the absence of certain properties, but the presence of indiscernible ones which are related in complex ways to measurable properties. It is physically impossible to observe the particles, but this is not because physicists assume them to be imaginary objects. Whatever their statuses, a molecule and a volumeless molecule are quite unlike each other.

Now, clearly, an existence claim that is capable of providing an ultimate explanation must be one which, according to the view under examination, asserts the existence of unobservable entities. It obviously cannot assert the existence of idealizations – that would be to assert that they are *not* imaginary, not idealizations. Yet the desired explanation can hardly refer, in the social sciences, to unobservable particles and their properties. It must, then, refer to unobservable entities like the unconscious group-mind or to unobservable social relations like corporate ownership. But since we already possess unobservables of this sort, and it is a matter of fact that they do not perform the desired job, there must be something wrong either with the kinds of social unobservables so far employed or with the demand itself – the demand for this type of ultimate explanation. Now it is a question of fact whether there are unobservable social entities and relations which could play the role required of them. The evidence is surely against there being anything in the social life of human beings that can be said to exist in some sense different from the sense in which the Id exists or love exists, and if these are examples of the sort of entity needed for ultimate explanations, the obvious answer is that we already have such explanations. Yet far from terminating a series of 'why' questions, an explanation in terms of the Id, for example, merely increases our curiosity. We wish to know a great deal about the origin and development of the Id. The same is true in the very different case of physical particles. The discovery of the proton and the meson certainly did not provide the kind of ultimate explanation envisaged by supporters of the present argument.

The truth is that the recurrent charge against the social sciences, the one with which we have been concerned, is the result of conflating three familiar questions. The first is whether there are any idealizations in the social sciences as there are in the physical sciences. The second is a question upon which we have already touched, namely, 'Are formal theories used in any of the social sciences except economics?' The third question we have just now been considering. It is whether there are in the social sciences the kind of explanations that terminate a series of 'why' questions – ultimate explanations. When these questions are run together it is quite natural to conclude that explanation by means of 'mere generalization' is deficient on all three counts: the generalization is directly testable; it is not an interpreted axiom or theorem in a formal theory; it is not part of a formal theory which provides an ultimate explanation by confronting the questioner with an assertion of the existence of a fundamental feature of nature. Let us, then, consider each of these three questions at more length.

The problem of whether social scientists have produced hypotheses that are not directly testable is of little interest in itself. The answer is obvious: 'Yes, they have.' The reasons why hypotheses are not directly testable vary, however. The objects referred to may be observable only indirectly, as in the case of sub-atomic particles, or two properties may be so combined that they are never found separately, and so a statement about the effects of one taken by itself may be testable only indirectly because of the masking effects of the other property. But the reason which has been of interest to social scientists is neither of these. It is that some hypotheses make use of idealizations. The success of these in the physical sciences has encouraged the belief that they ought to be employed in the social sciences as well. Hence, part of the pejorative force of the phrase 'mere empirical generalizations' derives from the feeling that a statement of an idealization should either be substituted in place of the generalization or be joined to it.

The point at issue is whether idealizations are present in the work of social scientists. No one doubts that social scientists sometimes refer to 'ideal types'. It is a question, then, how similar these are to the idealizations of the natural sciences. Here we must recognize the distinction commonly made between 'extreme types' and idealizations. The former are simply the end points of a series that is ordered by certain criteria; that is, any property or set of properties that admits of degree, such as reverence for tradition or social status, will have extremes that may or may not have actual instances. Pure folk societies, for example, do not in fact exist today, but they could exist in the sense that they are not physically impossible. Idealizations, on the other hand, are physically impossible. Perfectly elastic bodies and perfectly straight lines are like perfect folk societies in being the end points of a serial array. The first two, however, differ from the third in that they are known to be extrapolations to the limits of the variables that they represent. It is also known that they cannot exist under present physical laws. 'Extreme types', on the other hand, such as pure folk societies, may or may not exist. When they do not exist it is simply because certain conditions which might well have been met under known laws happen not to have been met.

Thus our answer to the question 'How similar are the ideal types of the social sciences to the idealizations of the natural sciences?' must begin by distinguishing extreme types from idealizations. *Some* of the so-called 'ideal types' advanced by social scientists are extreme types and not idealizations. 'The Dandy', 'The Protestant Sect', and 'Gemein-schaft' are terms which are often used to refer to extreme types, and the similarity of these to an ideal pendulum or to any other idealization is, as we have just indicated, rather slight.

The other and more interesting question concerns the presence of genuine idealizations in social science. Are such notions as a perfect market, a perfect monopoly, and an economically rational agent, instances of extreme types or of idealizations? It has been suggested by some writers that notions of this kind are not idealizations, that they belong to theories which deliberately omit certain variables because they are not relevant. These theories are said to differ from theories which extrapolate to the physically impossible limits of their variables. We are asked to 'consider that it is not disturbing to say that there are no perfect gases or dimensionless points. Nobody ever thought there were. But to say that economic man or the ideal type of capitalism does not exist is to say that certain theories are false, either because they neglect unspecified but relevant variables or because the laws among those specified do not hold.'[1]

The reply to this is clear enough: whoever thought that economic man or ideal capitalism existed? Certainly not Max Weber, the best-known advocate of the use of ideal types. He says that 'An ideal type is formed by the one-sided accentuation of one or more points of view and by the synthesis of a great many diffuse, discrete, more or less present and occasionally absent *concrete individual* phenomena, which are arranged according to those one-sidedly emphasized viewpoints into a unified *analytical* construct (*Gedankenbild*). In its conceptual purity, this mental construct (*Gedankenbild*) cannot be found anywhere in reality. It is a *utopia*.'[2] It is no more disturbing to say that ideal capitalism does not exist than to say that there are no perfect gases. Neither in the one case nor in the other does the falsity of 'certain theories' hang upon the existence of the subject. Naturally, all theories omit variables taken to be irrelevant and only some theories make use of idealizations. This

[1] M. Brodbeck: 'Models, Meaning, and Theories' in *Symposium on Sociological Theory*, ed. by L. Gross, 1959, p. 382.
[2] *The Methodology of the Social Sciences*, 1949, p. 90.

distinction has nothing to do, however, with the problem of whether such notions as ideal capitalism and economic man are genuine idealizations. The only reason for thinking that this distinction is relevant arises from a neglect of the notion of extreme types. It thus becomes easy to believe that our employment of phrases like 'economic man' commits us to the assertion of his existence, since such phrases are thought to refer only to actual instances. Ideal types are treated neither as extreme types which may or may not have existing instances, nor as idealizations which cannot have them. Instead a phrase like 'economic man' is taken to resemble in use one like 'melancholic man' as it appears in the sentence 'There goes a melancholic man'. But while melancholic men walk the streets economic men do not. They exist only in the pages of certain books and journals, and in the professional conversation of economists. Failure to remember this is a result of thinking that economic man is not a physical impossibility, and that therefore he must exist. Yet the very question to be answered is whether notions like that of economic man concern what is impossible in this sense.

It may be well to remind ourselves of the kinds of assumptions which economists have in fact made about economic men. Here are some laid down by Frank Knight in connection with his analysis of perfect competition: (1) All members of the society act with complete rationality, that is, 'all their acts take place in response to real, conscious, and stable and consistent motives, dispositions, or desires; nothing is capricious or experimental, everything deliberate. They are supposed to know absolutely the consequences of their acts when they are performed, and to perform them in the light of the consequences.' (2) Each member 'controls his own activities with a view to results which accrue to him individually. Every person is the final and absolute judge of his own welfare and interests.' (3) 'There must be "perfect mobility" in all economic adjustments, no cost involved in movements or changes.' (4) 'There must be perfect, continuous, costless intercommunication between all individual members of the society.'[1]

It is obvious that each of these assumptions is unsatisfiable – is physically impossible – in our world. The first assumption demands that every person have perfect foresight. The second demands that there 'be no way of acquiring goods except through production and free exchange in the open market'. It also makes it necessary that every person 'be free from social wants, prejudices, preferences, or repulsions, or any values which are not completely manifested in market dealing. Exchange of finished goods is the only form of relation between individuals, or at least there is no other form which influences economic conduct.'[2] The third assumption requires that 'all the elements entering into economic

---

[1] Taken from *Risk, Uncertainty and Profit*, 1921, pp. 77-8.
[2] *Ibid.*, p. 78.

calculations – effort, commodities, etc. – must be continuously variable, divisible without limit. Productive operations must not form habits, preferences, or aversions, or develop or reduce the capacity to perform them. In addition, the production process must be constantly and continuously complete; there is no time cycle of operations to be broken into or left incomplete by sudden readjustments. Each person continuously produces a complete commodity which is consumed as fast as produced. The exchange of commodities must be virtually instantaneous and costless.'[1]

Surely no one would argue, given what is known of individual human behaviour and of the conditions under which societies can be formed and maintained, that any one of these assumptions – much less all of them – can be met. And if they cannot be satisfied, then it is true to say of them that they represent idealizations. As Lionel Robbins put it when writing of the notion of economic man, 'The purpose of these assumptions is not to foster the belief that the world of reality corresponds to the constructions in which they figure, but rather to enable us to study, in isolation, tendencies which, in the world of reality, operate only in conjunction with many others, and then, by contrast as much as by comparison, to turn back to apply the knowledge thus gained to the explanations of more complicated situations. In this respect, at least, the procedure of pure economics has its counterpart in the procedure of all physical sciences which have gone beyond the stage of collection and classification.'[2]

Having echoed what every economist knows – that idealizations are used in economics – we ought to go on to state what most social scientists also realize: that the distinction between extreme types and idealizations is not generally made in the other fields of social science, for it is not needed. It is not needed because a great deal of what is called 'theorizing in terms of ideal types' is usually classifying by means of extreme types. As characteristic specimens we can take the following pairs: folk society and urban society; mechanical solidarity and organic solidarity; gemeinschaft and gesellschaft; status society and contract society. The use of them gives rise to generalizations about their properties, but the way in which this occurs is different from what happens when idealizations are used. The latter are terms which are defined by a set of hypotheses that relate certain properties to each other, namely, those properties represented in a shorthand manner by such idealizations as a perfect market. The working out of the relationships amongst these properties is a logical exercise in the drawing of consequences and results in a deductive system. This deductive system

[1] *Ibid.*, pp. 77–8.
[2] *An Essay on the Nature and Significance of Economic Science*, 2nd edition, 1935, p. 94.

will not be usable in the explanation of *any* occurrence until the system is given application, until, that is, the hypotheses are supplemented in such a way that the hypotheses become empirical statements. It is a perennial criticism levelled at economists that they produce deductive systems or calculi without being able to apply them usefully. The employment of extreme types does not raise this problem. They are classificatory devices. An individual case is assigned a position in a serial array, is classified, for example, as being much more like a contract society than a status society, according to the extent to which the individual case displays the properties taken as defining one or other of the extreme types.

Now when an idealization is used the behaviour of an ordinary market is explained in terms of its deviation from the behaviour of a perfect market. This is done by comparing what is observed of the former with what is deduced from the criteria of the latter. And, similarly, the behaviour of an ordinary contract society can be explained in terms of its deviation from the behaviour of an ideal contract society. Thus we can compare actual behaviour with the generalizations which have been suggested as applying to the ideal, e.g. 'All pure contract societies have developed from pure status societies'. But one point of difference between an extreme type and an idealization is that a person can use the latter as a means of explaining the presence of the former. He would never have occasion, however, to use an extreme type in an attempt to explain the presence of an idealization. It is a set of hypotheses (or the conditions referred to by these hypotheses). Since these conditions cannot exist, they do not require an explanation of their presence or distribution as do the properties referred to by the names of extreme types. For while the latter need not exist, they sometimes do, and then an explanation of their presence may be required. Of course there is no deductive system present in connection with them, and, hence, no problem of making use of it as a system of empirical laws. This point can be made clearer if we consider the example of the folk society.

Robert Redfield characterized the folk society as an ideal type that has these features: 'small, isolated, non-literate, and homogeneous, with a strong sense of group solidarity. The ways of living are conventionalized into that coherent system which we call "a culture". Behaviour is traditional, spontaneous, uncritical, and personal; there is no legislation or habit of experiment and reflection for intellectual ends. Kinship, its relationships and institutions, are the type categories of experience and the familial group is the unit of action. The sacred prevails over the secular; the economy is one of status rather than of market.'[1] The communities of Yucatan were found to display these features much more

[1] 'The Folk Society', *The American Journal of Sociology*, Vol. LII, No. 4, January 1947, p. 293.

than certain Guatemalan societies. In the latter the small, stable, homogeneous society was discovered to have impersonal relationships, formal institutions, weak family organization, secular life, and individuals acting from personal advantage.[1] Such differences between types of society have led investigators to examine the degree to which the properties of the ideal folk society are associated with each other in various actual societies – what causal relations there are amongst them.

Thus 'the ideal folk society' and 'the perfect market' are both phrases which refer to sets of properties. In the case of the perfect market these are imaginary properties, and the statements which assert them are arranged in a deductive system so that it may be seen what consequences logically follow from these assumptions. The relating and explaining of the behaviour of actual markets in terms of their divergence from the behaviour of the perfect market is similar, in principle, to the physicist's problem in relating Boyle's Law to the behaviour of actual gases. The divergence between the ideal case and the actual one is taken by economists, as by physicists, to indicate the need for alterations in the law statements employed. The classification of actual cases according to the degree of their divergence from the ideal case is of secondary interest. What the use of the idealization is supposed to do is to permit an explanation to be advanced; the classification procedure is subordinate to this.

Precisely the opposite is true with respect to the use of extreme types: they are used to classify in the hope that an explanation of the behaviour of actual cases will be suggested by the comparison of the ideal and actual cases. The explanation can only be *suggested* because the properties of the extreme type, as the example of the folk society reveals, are not related by the hypotheses of a deductive system. What, for instance, are the logical consequences of the assertion that a society is 'traditional, spontaneous, and uncritical'? Obviously the assertion has consequences, but it is so vague that there would be considerable difficulty in working them out. It would not be impossible, however. Redfield himself provides a number of suggestions, e.g. that in a folk society there is 'no disposition to reflect upon traditional acts and consider them objectively and critically'.[2] This in itself would require much refinement, of course, but it might be transformed into a hypothesis which, in conjunction with others similarly refined, could be applied in the explanation of actual social processes. Yet unless these hypotheses formed part of a deductive system they would be of secondary importance in the use of extreme types. For they would be isolated hypotheses, and there would still remain the major work of relating the hypotheses to each other so that the presence of some explained the presence of others. We should

[1] *Ibid.*, p. 308.
[2] *Ibid.*, p. 299.

want to know, for example, why in a folk society there is 'no disposition to reflect upon traditional acts'; we should also want to ask how this generalization is related to such other generalizations as those about the isolation or the size of the folk society.

5

The problem which we have been discussing is part of the more general problem whether outside economics, deductive systems are in fact used – not merely produced – by social scientists. And this topic, like that of the explanatory power of idealizations, is one upon which we have already embarked. We exclude economics because no one doubts that in one sense of 'used' formal theories are used in it. What is often doubted is the success of their application to the world. But this is a somewhat different matter from the question with which we are faced, namely, whether other social scientists can and do employ formal theories to explain social behaviour, even when that behaviour is taken to be drastically simplified for the occasion. It may be true that economists have difficulty in applying their theories to actual situations, and in *this* sense they may not use formal theories as much as some kinds of physicists do. Nevertheless, economists constantly formulate and try to apply deductive systems. We wish to know whether in this sense of 'use' their use of formal theories differs from that of the other social scientists.

We said earlier that there are two interpretations of the phrase 'use of formal theories'. One refers to the construction of calculi which can be transformed into empirical theories. The other refers to empirical theories which are sufficiently developed to admit of formalization. The two procedures are, of course, intimately connected in practice, for calculi are usually constructed with a view to a specific kind of interpretation. At least this is the case when the authors are scientists rather than mathematicians. In the social sciences, if the development of economics can be taken as a guide, we should expect that both procedures would be tried and that the results of each procedure, with respect to a given problem, would affect the other. What has so far occurred is that the attempts to rewrite sets of empirical hypotheses in the form of deductive systems – as in the theory of group interaction put forward by Simon – have revealed the deficiencies of the original theories. In the case of the theory just referred to, these defects included the absence of a measuring procedure for the properties of interaction, friendliness, and activity. Two courses of action were then possible: a method of measurement might be found; or failing that, the original theory might be abandoned. If the latter course were chosen, anyone who was seeking a calculus suitable for interpretation as a theory of group interaction would be influenced in his search by the knowledge that one interpretation would be ruled out, namely, that in terms of the three un-measurable properties. But the relation between the two procedures is even closer than this. The way in which calculi are actually used in the production of rigorous empirical theories is not, at the present stage of social science, that of calculus seeking. Nor is it that of simply revealing the logical skeleton of informal theories. The process is perhaps best illustrated by some additional features of the example already con-sidered – that of Simon's treatment of the theory of group interaction.

Firstly, the rewriting of an informal theory is likely to display its omissions. Thus once the generalizations of Homans' theory were stated as axioms it became necessary to make some further assumptions: for example, that the amount of activity and the level of friendliness referred to in the first axiom as producing the intensity of interaction, have an almost instantaneous effect upon that intensity. Nothing was said about this in the original generalization.

Secondly, the equations serving as axioms may be generalized so as to obtain conclusions previously unobtainable. When the assumption that the variables, I, A, F and E have linear relations was removed, it became possible to derive such new results as these: when E ('amount of activity imposed on the group by the external environment') falls below a certain value, F ('the level of friendliness') will fall to zero; if E is at or below this value, then A ('amount of activity carried on by members within the group') will fall to zero. To say that F and A are at zero is to say that the group disintegrates. This point was not dealt with in the initial generalizations or in their initial rewriting.

Thirdly, the axiom-set may be further extended so as to permit a number of empirical interpretations, that is, used as the logical structure of different empirical theories. There are three equations used as axioms in the linear system. These are reduced to two in the non-linear system; and in one of them the time rate of change of A as a function of A and F, with E as an independent variable, is represented by $\frac{dA}{dt} = \psi(A,F;E)$ where ψ is a function with unspecified properties. In order to apply this equation as an axiom in another theory, a theory about clique forma-tion, Simon alters it somewhat. I, A, F, and E are defined as specifying behaviour in a group G_1. Then I_2, A_2, F_2, and E_2 are defined as specifying behaviour in Group G_2, the latter group being a sub-group of the former one. The new equation gives the time rate of change of A as a function of A_1, F_1, and A_2. An additional equation supplies the time rate of change of A_2 as a function of A_2, F_2, and A_1. In other words, the activity carried on by members within the larger group is taken to influence the activity within the clique, and vice versa. Another suggested interpreta-tion of the same variables has the four letters with subscript one referring to the intensity of a particular person's activity within a certain group, and the four letters with subscript two referring to the

186

intensity of that person's behaviour within a second group. The full set of equations then provides a theory of groups competing for the membership of a given person.

What we shall take this example to show is this: in the social sciences that we have been considering, with the possible exception of economics, there is no clear-cut difference between the application of the two procedures of calculi interpretation and theory formalization. This distinction is only useful in sciences which are mathematically more developed than the ones under discussion. When, as in most of the social sciences, the use of calculi has merely begun, no calculus can be fully interpreted in a satisfactory manner. The defects of the informal theory must first be revealed by the attempt to state it rigorously; then the effort to repair or improve the theory may suggest new sets of equations whose application to fresh topics can be investigated.

Hence, the question whether 'deductive systems are in fact used – not merely produced – by social scientists' has as its answer: 'Yes, work has begun in certain fields.' There are, for example, earlier publications like Rashevsky's book on the *Mathematical Biology of Social Behavior* in which such theories as that of imitative behaviour and of the distribution of wealth are put forward; Anderson's paper on obtaining probability distributions of changes in attitude over time;[1] and the two essays by Simon and Guetzkow concerned with group mechanism for ensuring social uniformity and for dealing with deviant members.[2] In the last few years there has been a spate of theoretical and experimental work on the topics which were released for general academic consumption by the development of servo-mechanism theory, learning theory, mathematical theories of communication, and the theory of games. But the rise to popularity of topics like those of rational choice and decision-making under uncertainty, or optimal information networks in social groups, ought not to mislead us. The extension of the mathematical methods of modern economics to the other social sciences is devoted only in small part to explanatory theories. Definition, classification, measurement, observation, testing and design, still require the major share of the scientist's attention. We can hardly expect, therefore, to identify the present mathematical revolution in the social sciences with an immediate and revolutionary increase in the number of useful theories. The lag between the rate of increase in the application of mathematical procedures to social science and the rate of increase in the production of formal theories may be considerable. In claiming that deductive systems are already being used by social scientists in much the same way as by economists, we are not claiming that the number of

---

[1] 'Probability Models for Analyzing Time Changes in Attitudes' in *Mathematical Thinking in the Social Sciences*, ed. by P. Lazarsfeld, 1954.

[2] In Simon: *Models of Man*, 1957.

these theories is large. There is every prospect, however, of the number increasing substantially, and with it – for reasons previously suggested – the number and importance of idealizations as compared to extreme types.

We have said that the complaints about the exclusive use of empirical generalizations in the social sciences are based upon a conflation of three questions. The first is whether there are idealizations in the social sciences. To this we answered 'Yes, particularly economics'. But we could also have supplied examples from such fields of interest as the theory of behaviour within small groups. The second question is that of the presence of formal theories, and with this we have just dealt. The remaining question is whether there are ultimate explanations in social science – ones that terminate a series of 'why' questions by asserting the existence of a fundamental feature of nature. It is this query which we must now take up briefly

6

What the people who ask this question have in mind is not entirely clear. They may believe that explanations in social science are reducible, in some sense of the term, to another and more fundamental kind, perhaps psychological ones. Or they may simply hold that quite independently of the problem of reducibility there is a problem concerning the types of properties – variables – which are employed in social explanations. But to say that there is such a problem can only amount to saying that we must distinguish between two sorts of social explanations: those which explain in terms of social properties, e.g. cohesiveness, free exchange, jural authority – and those which explain in terms of non-social properties like soil fertility, length of snow season, distance from the sea, and the average height of adult males in a given population. The first type of explanation provides an account of social events or situations in terms of other social events; the second type supplies an explanation in terms of non-social events. A social scientist is chiefly concerned with the first kind: with explaining, for instance, the presence of incest taboos in terms of avoidance of sexual competition within the family, and not by means of a reference to an innate disposition of people. Our efforts to discriminate between these two kinds of explanation are made more difficult by the fact that statements of social events can themselves take two forms. In one form they are statements about the properties of individuals who are members of classes or groups. In the other form they are statements about the properties of classes or groups of human beings. The difference is illustrated by the statements (*a*) 'Any person who participates in high involvement relationships will show high ability to empathize' and (*b*) 'The higher the cohesiveness of a human group, the higher will be the

188

correlation between popularity rank and perceived leadership rank.' Whereas the former refers to the properties of an individual person, the latter refers to the properties of a group of people.

Now the phrase 'fundamental feature of nature' is both pretentious and vague. Hence, when we ask whether the social sciences contain ultimate explanations – ones that assert the existence of such fundamental features – our question is the poorer for its use of this phrase. A social explanation can be ultimate in the sense that the properties or variables upon which it relies are not social ones, that is, are neither social group (and class) properties nor properties of members of these sets *qua* members. But an explanation supplied in the social sciences can also be ultimate in a different sense, in the sense that it is the terminal explanation in a series of a certain kind. This series will consist of explanations which refer only to social properties, and the last element of the series will be that explanation whose variables require explaining in terms of non-social properties. In other words, the ultimate explanation will be the final member of a series of social explanations – final because it will not itself have a *social* explanation. We might, for example, say that Ann's continued absence from meetings of her club was due to the low cohesiveness of the group, and account for the low cohesion in terms of the small satisfaction Ann and the other members received from belonging to the group; the explanation of this, in turn, might be stated by means of a reference to the needs arising from their self-images; these accounted for by referring to child-rearing practices, and the origin or persistence of the practices explained as the outcome of innate drives. Which member of the series is to be taken as ultimate, as asserting a 'fundamental feature of nature'? There is no way of telling. It is only if we know what mystifies a questioner that we can know what answer will satisfy him on this point. Is the human need for sleep a feature of this kind? If not, what is? In commencing the series which begins with 'Why do they need sleep?' we may continue until we reach either a physical explanation or a confession of ignorance, whichever occurs first.

There is, of course, another interpretation to be given to the demand for ultimate explanations. It may be interpreted simply as a confused way of claiming that statements about group properties are 'reducible' to some other sort of statement. It may be the claim that the reduction proceeds from group properties to the properties of individuals as members, or from either of these to the properties of individuals who are not members of the relevant groups or classes. Yet whatever type of reduction relation is supposed to be present, and whatever this relation is thought to hold between – concepts or statements – the search for an ultimate explanation will be a pursuit of the irreducible. It does not matter which non-social explanation is fixed upon as an irreducible one. For it will be trivially true that the social sciences do

189

not in this sense of 'ultimate' provide ultimate explanations. However, the point of our previous arguments has been to help remove any critical force to which this admission may seem to expose us.

We can add one brief remark here. It is this. No matter what kind of reduction relation may hold between the hypotheses of the social sciences and those of, e.g. psychology, it does not follow that genuinely useful laws cannot be found in the social sciences. It does not follow for this reason: social generalizations are either about group-members or about groups. The only way in which these statements can be entailed by psychological generalizations – those about individuals *not* organized into groups – is by the addition of co-ordinating laws, i.e. laws connecting the psychological properties of an individual person with his social properties, his behaviour as a member of a group. But these co-ordinating laws have as much right to be called 'social laws' as have the social generalizations which they are to be used to entail. Thus if the reduction relation does hold, some genuine social laws must be present in order to make it possible. Clearly, all that the present attack on social laws can establish is that generalizations about group-properties are not useful because they are entailed by the conjunction of psychological laws and co-ordinating laws; that is, group-traits are causally determined by other sorts of properties. Even if this were established, however, it would be no argument for excluding generalizations about group members from the social sciences. Hence, it would not show these sciences to be lacking in genuine laws.

We have argued that there are theoretical hypotheses in the social sciences and formal theories as well. But we also know that they can be present when ultimate explanations of the irreducible variety are not present. The complaint about empirical generalizations arose from the mistaken view that they do not provide satisfactory explanations because they are not assertions of the existence of fundamental properties. We have denied their unsatisfactoriness, claiming that the two favoured features – theoretical hypotheses and formal theories – whose absence from the social sciences was thought to be responsible for this condition, are in fact present in those sciences. We have gone on to say that the demand for ultimate explanations in the social sciences is by no means clear. In any case it is not important, since the lack of such explanations is not a defect having to do with a want of theoretical hypotheses and formal theories. The latter are present and the former (ultimate explanations) are not; at least they are not present if the word 'ultimate' is interpreted in certain ways. In the face of this, it is wrong to assert that the social sciences produce only empirical generalizations, and that for this reason genuine explanations, ultimate ones, are missing from these fields. There are, we have said, many genuine explanations which are not ultimate in the sense of being irreducible. Any continued pressing of the criticism that the explanations of the social sciences are unsatisfactory because they are reducible must be based on the vacuous complaint that social science is not physical science. Similarly, the case against the social sciences may be given another – but probably short – lease on life by altering the charge from that of inherent inability to that of lack of success. But this is merely to say that the social sciences are not as successful as the physical sciences, and this has never been in dispute. What has been in question is whether there are good grounds for believing that social scientists cannot do better in the future. And our answer has been 'There are no good grounds at all for this belief, only poor ones'.

7

We have still to touch upon one final question. It is whether genetic explanations may also be scientific ones. The problem, in brief, is that of the relationship between theories and historical explanations. Now a moment's thought will remind us that we have not paid attention, so far, to the problem of time lag in the causal relations among the properties (or variables) referred to by laws and formal theories. Yet it is clear that if we try to explain the presence, for example, of numerous strikes for higher wages in 1956 in terms of the strikers' beliefs about their own ability to support themselves and their employers' ability to pay, we are faced with three alternatives.

We can take our question to be that of explaining why the number of strikes in 1956 differed from that of some other year – such as 1936. In doing this we are trying to account for the dissimilarity of the two situations, that is, for the change in the direction of an increased number of strikes.

But we may also be interested in another question, the question whether the second ten years of the period show a greater increase in the number of strikes than does the first decade. We may then try to explain the difference between the two rates of increase rather than the fact of the increase. Both of these alternatives are concerned with the explanation of a change in a property, the property of frequency of strikes. One explanation deals with the direction of the change (more strikes in 1956 than in 1936). The other alternative deals with the rate of change (higher rate of striking in one decade than in the other).

A third alternative is to account for the presence of the property itself. We can ask why strikes have ever occurred at all – have ever occurred with *any* frequency. Now in the first two alternatives it is always possible, in principle at least, to have explanations in terms of properties whose instances are roughly contemporaneous with the explicandum. The increase and rate of increase in workers' strikes during the period 1936–56 can be legitimately, though perhaps not correctly, explained in terms of the strikers' beliefs and the level of

191

economic prosperity during those two decades. If we try, however, to explain why strikes have occurred at all in a particular society we must be contrasting that community with otherwise similar communities in which strikes have never occurred. We must, therefore, be concerned with the differences in the *history* of these communities, in certain of their past conditions, since what is causally responsible for the present difference is something that happened in their past. Hence our attention will be fixed upon earlier variables than the explicandum; for example, upon the social and economic conditions of the period during which the strikers' beliefs first appeared. The explanation of why strikes *ever* occur will be an historical (or dynamic) one in the sense that the explanatory properties used will belong to an earlier period of time than the properties that are being explained.

Suppose we devise a deductive theory to account for the presence of an institution in a particular society. Then what we shall find most useful is an historical explanation, historical in that it will explain both the presence of the institution and the rate and direction of its development. Only when earlier causal influences, as well as contemporary ones, are taken into account can this be done. If we assume that our theory need not provide for time lags in the causal relations amongst the relevant properties, then we are assuming that the influences produce changes instantaneously, or at least very quickly. In the case of those parts of a society which are taken to be self-persisting systems with negative feed back, it must be assumed that the equilibrium positions, old or new, are reached immediately after displacement has been concluded. Thus we should be claiming that the level of employment amongst knappers – to revert to our earlier example – would respond instantly to changes in the tariff on imported metal axes. There are so many reasons why this response might take some time that the limited usefulness of non-historical (or non-dynamic) explanation is clearly revealed.

If we regard an entire society as a social system consisting of a very large number of variables that are organized into a variety of sub-systems, sub-systems which undergo change at different rates of speed, the limitations of this kind of theory are even more apparent. Unless we are trying to explain the presence of a social feature that has no history – has only recently appeared – we may find non-historical explanations less satisfactory than historical ones even for explaining differences in the rate and direction of change. These differences are what theories of the former type can at most explain. But they need not be successful at doing even this much. The rate and direction of a particular change may have been unaffected by the operation of any variable contemporary with some later portion of the development. A set of religious practises, for instance, might be carried on by the members of a sect according to the instructions of a founder who laid down both the rate of change (add one candle at every third year, two candles at every sixth year . . .), and the direction of change (the number of candles should increase in geometric progression to infinity . . .). If the instructions were faithfully carried out we should have to say that no variable later than the inception of the practices need be used to explain their rate and direction of change. We should say this, of course, only if we believed that no later variable had in fact any influence. Yet it might be reasonable to think that no such variable had.

The relationship, in the social sciences, between a fully developed theory and an historical explanation – historical in this simple sense of either referring to initial conditions of the past or using laws of temporal succession – is very close. The attempt to treat societies as changing systems requires that the initial conditions for a given social feature be looked for in the past. And the fact that social scientists wish to account for differences in the growth and decline of these features requires that the law statements which are used be laws of temporal succession, laws that connect earlier causes with later effects. To fulfil these two requirements, however, is to incorporate one kind of historical explanation into a scientific one. It is to bring together a partial explanation which appeals 'to specific events and to particular stages of processes of the past' with a partial one which appeals 'to uniform associations between kinds of events and properties, whether these be contemporaneous or successive'. The resulting combination of initial conditions and generalizations is, we have said, the standard form taken by complete law-explanations of particular events. In this respect the social sciences do not differ from the physical and biological sciences. Nor do these various sciences differ amongst themselves in their need to discover initial conditions by inquiring into the past. For in order that a theory – a set of deductively related hypotheses – may be applied in the explanation of a particular kind of event, the theory must be combined with existence statements of an appropriate sort. To this extent, then, historical explanation is part of every scientific one, and their earlier divorce at our hands was one of convenience and not of incompatibility.[1]

---

[1] I am indebted to J. Harsanyi for a most useful discussion of this and related points in his article 'Explanation and Comparative Dynamics in Social Science', *Behavioral Science*, Vol. 5, No. 2, April 1960.

INDEX

195

INDEX

Empirical generalizations, and function-explanations, 115–6, 122–3, 128–32; as explanations, ch. X; and qualifying 'text', 147–56 passim; and holism, 167–8; and theories, ch. XI passim

Equilibrium, social, 116–9; in physics, 117–8

EVANS-PRITCHARD, E. E., 104

Existence claim, of unobservable entities, 164, 177–9, 188–90

Extreme types, and idealizations, 180–5

FANELLI, A., 3n.

Fertility rates, in occupational groups, 137–8

FESTINGER, L., 97n.

Folk society, as ideal type, 183–5

Formal theory, 168; in social science, 174–7, 185–8

FORTES, M., 113n.

FREUD, S., 28–9

FRIEDMAN, M., 139n.

Function statements, as explanations, ch. IX

Functional relations, 110

GALBRAITH, J., 51n., 52, 54

GALILEO, laws of projectile motion, 148, 163

Gambling, in Cornerville, 14; pschological description of, 16

Gay-Lussac's Law, 3

Genetic statements, as explanations, ch. V

GIBSON, Q., 2

GINSBERG, M., 2

Goal – directed behaviour, and intentional behaviour, 65; and social explanation, 72–6; and motives, 84–91; and rule conformity, 92–3

GOULDNER, A., 25n., 38

GROSS, L., 180n.

Group interaction, theory of, 175–7

GUETZKOW, H., 187

GURIN, G., 2n.

Habitual acts, explanation of, 80–3; and custom, 82

HAITZMANN, C., 28

HAMPHIRE, S., 64n.

Hano kinship system, 33

HANSEL, M., 16n.

HANSON, N., 160n.

HARSANYI, J., 193n.

HART, H., 64n.

HEMPEL, C., 2

Henry's Law, scope of, 157

Hepatoscopy, 12

History, and social description, 25–39; and genetic explanations, ch V; and uniform connections, 54; and deductive theories, 191–3

Holism, sociological, 167–8

HOLLINGSHEAD, A., 169n.

HOLTON, G., 148

HOMANS, G., 145n, 152n., 172n., 175, 186

HORTON, D., 120n.

HU, H. C., 36

Human action, and social explanation, 73; paradigm case of, 75–7

Hypotheses, universal, and function – explanations, 115–6, 122–3, 128–32; as explanations, Ch. X; and qualifying 'text', 147–56 passim; and holism, 167–8; and theories, ch. XI passim

Idealizations, and unobservables, 178–85

Ideal types, 179–83

Illegitimate births, explanation of, 9–10

India, partition of, 29, 31–2

Intention statements, as explanations, ch. VI; and function statements, 68–9; and reason statements, 101; see Goal-directed behaviour

Jamaica, changes of birth-rates, 36

Joking relationship, 115–6

Jural authority, and marriage, 151–2; explanation of, 172–3

KAUFMANN, F., 2

KEYNES, J. M., on savings and investment, 140

KLUCKHOHN, C., 120n.

INDEX